Hangin' Times
In Fort Smith

A History of Executions
in Judge Parker's Court

Hangin' Times
In Fort Smith

A History of Executions
in Judge Parker's Court

By Jerry Akins

BUTLER
CENTER
BOOKS

The Butler Center for Arkansas Studies
Central Arkansas Library System
100 Rock Street
Little Rock, Arkansas 72201
www.butlercenter.org

Paperback: ISBN   (13) 978-1-935106-34-0
                   (10) 1-935106-34-1

Project manager: Rod Lorenzen
Book and cover design: Cathy Peterson

On the front cover: John Childers was the first man hanged in Fort Smith, Arkansas, by the U.S. District Court of the Western District of Arkansas. (Image courtesy of Linda Seamans McGahan)

All photos and images, unless otherwise noted, are courtesy of the Fort Smith National Historic Site.

Library of Congress Cataloging-in-Publication Data

Akins, Jerry, 1935-
 Hangin' times in Fort Smith : a history of executions in Judge Parker's court / Jerry Akins.
    p. cm.
 Includes bibliographical references and index.
 ISBN 978-1-935106-34-0 (pbk. : alk. paper)
 1. Capital punishment--Arkansas--History. 2. Criminal justice, Administration of--Arkansas--History. 3. United States. District Court (Arkansas : Western District) 4. Parker, Isaac Charles, 1838-1896. 5. Fort Smith (Ark.) I. Title.

 KFA4165.C2A75 2012
 364.6609767'36--dc23

                        2011041125

This book is printed on archival-quality paper that meets requirements of the American National Standard for Information Sciences, Permanence of Paper, Printed Library Materials, ANSI Z39.48-1984.

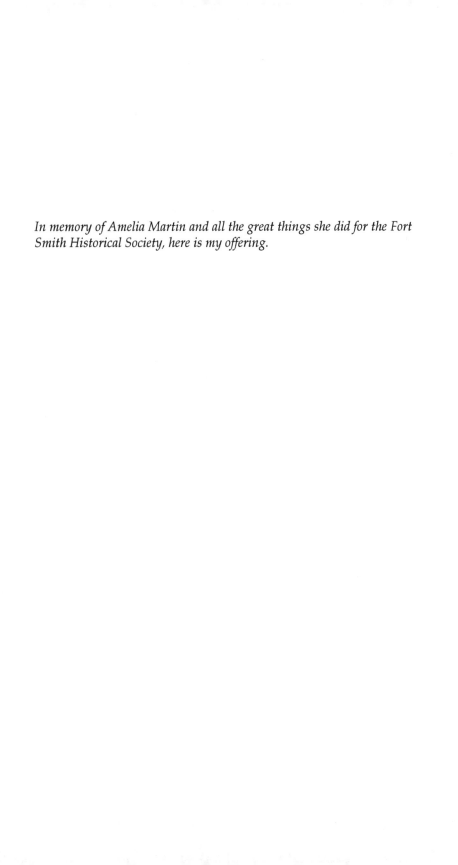

In memory of Amelia Martin and all the great things she did for the Fort Smith Historical Society, here is my offering.

CONTENTS

FOREWORD

The history of Fort Smith, Arkansas, runs as deep as the Arkansas River, but much like the river, it has taken a century for that depth to be realized. Fort Smith has always been a practical town, looking toward the future and until the last few decades, leaving the past largely unexplored. From the foundations of the first fort built along the river, frontier necessity was a reality. Fort Smith sat on what was the edge of the world for almost eighty years. Chosen specifically because of geographical location, the fort created a launching point for supplying western exploration, witnessed the forced relocation of thousands of Native Americans along the Trail of Tears, and celebrated the victory of the Mexican War as well as survived the social upheaval and destruction of the Civil War. Fort Smith became infamous in the later decades of the nineteenth century, not as an outpost for westward expansion, but for the long shadow of a gallows built to serve the judicial needs created by that expansion.

The U.S. District Court for the Western District of Arkansas relocated to Fort Smith in 1873, from across the river in Van Buren. The fort had been abandoned two years earlier as the military presence moved farther west, so the immediate needs of the expanding judicial system moved to the legal if not literal edge of the frontier. Chaos in the aftermath of the Civil War and the often-overt criminality of U.S. citizens in the Indian Territory resulted in the creation of the largest federal court district in history. The 74,000 square miles of rural and wild landscape in Indian Territory provides a backdrop for stories, many of which will be told for the first time in this book.

The Indian Territory was a complex creation of the United States Congress and numerous presidential policies, where legally sovereign but militarily subjected Native American nations from eastern state homelands were relocated to the area that eventually became modern Oklahoma. These nations held legislative and judicial power over their own citizens, but were forbidden by treaty from enforcing their laws against citizens of the United States or to punish anyone for crimes committed against citizens of the United States.

To further complicate this legal climate, these treaties also stipulated that the U.S. government would enforce laws against the importation of spirituous liquors into the Territory. The profitability of liquor prohibition, a vast rural landscape with little law-enforcement, and the criminality in war-torn areas of Arkansas and Missouri following the Civil War combined into a chaos never before or since seen in the United States. The people on both sides of the border demanded something be done. That something became the infamous gallows at Fort Smith, Arkansas.

The first two years of the court at Fort Smith were plagued with corruption until President Grant selected a Missouri congressman and former Missouri circuit judge, named Isaac Charles Parker, to re-establish the reputation of the U.S. District Court for the Western District of Arkansas. Judge Parker was chosen initially on a short-term basis to clean up the court and, it was hoped, to establish law and order in Indian Territory. Parker had shown a legislative interest in federal Indian policy, and serving on the bench in Fort Smith made him the spokesperson for much of that policy. He would serve on that bench for twenty-one years. Parker died on November 17, 1896, at his home a few blocks from the court.

Just as every rope on every gallows has a story in this volume, every story begins with a victim. That is the one lesson Judge Parker would want us to remember. It was the job of the U.S. District Court in Fort Smith, Arkansas, to determine this story and a jury to decide the fate of the accused. In an 1896 interview, near his death, Judge Parker answered his critics by saying, "They see the convict alone, perhaps chained in his cell. They forget the crime he perpetrated and the family he made husbandless and fatherless by his assassin work." Parker wanted the victims of crime to find justice in his federal court, and in the following book, the stories of the victims play a prominent role.

Jerry Akins presents for the first time in a single collection the numerous stories behind the infamous gallows at Fort Smith. The accounts of the victims and the accused bring to light an entire world of Wild West crime and those who paid the ultimate punishment. From senseless drunken acts, homicidal high drama, and Wild West law enforcement, these stories fulfill the old saying, "Truth is stranger than fiction." Much like the current depth of the Arkansas River, these stories have taken a century or more to come to light. Jerry Akins has pulled from the newspapers and the court documents of the era to tell the untold history of Fort Smith. For the first time in book form, this is the truth behind the long shadow of the gallows.

The U.S. District Court for the Western District of Arkansas between 1873 and 1896 executed eighty-six men. Under Judge Parker in twenty-one years, seventy-nine men met their fate on the gallows. One cannot overlook this large number, although this is of 160 originally sentenced to die. Capital crimes were a small part of the 13,000 total cases heard by Parker, but federal law specifically stated that a jury conviction for rape or murder would result in a sentence of death. The stories of Fort Smith in the following book show that Isaac Parker was not the "hangin' judge" that casual legend portrays. In most cases the guilt or innocence is really not in question once the story is told. These horrible crimes would almost scream out for justice from history had it not been for Parker's court.

I encourage the reader to sit back and relax with a book you may not put down for a while. These stories show the depth of human depravity, the senseless loss of life, and the difficult moral position given to those who presided over the trials. Once the reader knows the story behind the crimes, the shadow of the gallows might appear to be as practical as the men who worked to build justice on the frontier. While these are the stories of the criminals and their victims, they are also the stories of the Deputy U.S. Marshals, the Indian Lighthorse Police, the numerous posse members, jurors, and attorneys who helped to create a just court process for all. These stories also represent the tireless work left by the often-unnamed newspapermen who worked to inform the public of daily court proceedings. Jerry Akins has taken their stories and brought to life a new resource of true Wild West crime drama told in the words and deeds of the men and women in the United States Indian Territory under the U.S. District Court for the Western District of Arkansas.

Jon Derek Wright
May 15, 2010

ACKNOWLEDGEMENTS

Credit goes to Amelia Martin for starting me on this project and to Eric Leonard for getting me on the path to authenticity in researching and writing. Caryl Linton spent many hours proofreading the articles for *The Journal of the Fort Smith Historical Society*, and Clara Jane Rubarth spent a like number of hours proofing for this book. Carole Barger and Cathy Peterson spent many hours on the final proofing, editing, and formatting for submission to the publisher. Thanks to David Turk, U.S. Marshals Service historian; Aaron Holt and Laverne Owens, National Archives, Fort Worth, for their contributions. And to Devon Mihesuah, descendant of Charles Wilson, who was killed by Jackson Crow, and others who provided additional information on the Jackson Crow chapter. Thanks to all the staff at the Fort Smith National Historic Site, those who have come and gone, and those still there, for help in re-searching. And to everyone whom I have not mentioned who gave me moral support, thanks.

—Jerry Akins

This photo shows a re-enactment of a condemned man being escorted
to the gallows for an execution carried out by the U.S. District Court for
the Western District of Arkansas. Condemned men were provided with
a complete set of clothing from the skin out—underwear, shoes, socks,
suit, shirt, and tie. Participating in the re-enactment are Al Drap, left, as
spiritual adviser for the condemned man; author Jerry Akins, center, as
the condemned man; Sam Trisler, foreground, and Roger Carter, background, as guards; Susan Trisler as the grieving widow; and Harold
Trisler, rear, as chief deputy. The court building and the Hell on the
Border Jail are shown in the background.

—Photo by Glen Gilley

INTRODUCTION

This book is the result of a phone call from Amelia Martin, editor of *The Journal of the Fort Smith Historical Society* for more than a quarter of a century. Amelia called in early 2001 to ask me to do a series of articles on the hangings by the U.S. District Court for the Western District of Arkansas in the late 1800s. I like to flatter myself and believe that Amelia had great faith in my abilities, but she probably just picked my name from a list of board members. So, in memory of Amelia Martin and all the great things that she did for the Fort Smith Historical Society, here is my offering.

I thought that writing articles on the hangings would be no problem; all I would have to do would be pull one of the books on that subject from my bookshelf and go to work, but I was soon to learn this was not so. At the same time, fortunately, I met Eric Leonard, park ranger at the Fort Smith Historic Site, where all of the trials and hangings took place. Eric was working on his master's thesis on a subject parallel to what I would be writing. So, to Eric goes credit for authenticity in this tome.

The gallows at the Fort Smith National Historic Site was built in the 1980s and is an exact replica of the gallows built in 1886.
(Image courtesy of the Fort Smith National Historic Site)

This book is only about the U.S. District Court for the Western District of Arkansas and the people who were tried there and executed. It is not about the U.S. Marshals Service, and any reference to marshals and deputy marshals is only incidental to the arrests of the criminals the stories are about. The stories of all of the eighty-six men who were executed are told as well as many of the stories of the seventy-six men and four women whose sentences were commuted and the one man who was shot. With few exceptions, the information came from local newspapers, court documents, and other primary sources. There are occasions where information is cited from other reliable sources. But no information came from any of the existing books that purport to chronicle the history of the Court, Judge Isaac C. Parker, or the Marshals Service. All of the information presented here is true and verifiable, but it by no means is all of the truth. Like most history, knowing all of the truth is not possible.

Local Fort Smith newspapers are a reliable source of information on the trials and hangings. Out-of-town newspapers are the source of much of the dime novel stuff. The local papers probably could not afford to fabricate stories often, as there were too many people nearby who knew the truth. Also there were several publications in Fort Smith at any given time, and they did not hesitate to point out each others' errors and untruths. Sometimes it took a newspaper a couple of issues or more to get a story right. In the case of Elizabeth Owen, three different stories of the event were printed, the last being the correct one. There were one or two publications that sometimes had more thrilling details of an event but their story, overall, was the same as reported by other papers. Sometimes it appears that the reporters were quoting from the trial transcript, and that is not surprising. The newspaper reporters were sitting in court taking down the same information that the court clerk was taking.

The local newspapers were very defensive of the town of Fort Smith. At times they went to great lengths to point out that all of the capital crimes for which people were tried were committed in the Indian Territory. Whenever newspapers of another town published false stories implicating Fort Smith citizens, a local paper published an "I told you so" rebuttal.

Of course, the National Archives records are the best primary source, but they are not available in all cases. Trial transcripts for cases that occurred before 1888 are almost nonexistent. However, in many of the early cases, depositions from the proceedings before the commissioner, what is today called pretrial hearings, are available. That is true of the case of John Childers, the first man executed in Fort Smith. Those depositions are nearly as good a source as trial transcripts because the statements are expected to be the same as what the witnesses will utter in court.

With a very few exceptions, all of the information in these articles was taken from copies of actual court records and local newspapers. There are a few cases where other reliable sources were used and are cited, as are all the rest of the sources. No doubt, there are cases where there is more to be known. Unfortunately, as in all history, not all can be known. But I have done my best to assure that all that I have written is fact.

—Jerry Akins

CHAPTER 1

THE BEGINNING:
THE BLACK CAP

A falling trapdoor, violent winds, lightning, crashing thunder, and pouring rain. No, it's not a scene from a 1930s Vincent Price or Boris Karloff horror movie; it's the first execution in Fort Smith by the U.S. District Court for the Western District of Arkansas. The date is August 15, 1873, and John Childers has just gone to his death for the crime of murder.

THE COURT

First, an explanation of the U.S. District Court: The court was established by the Intercourse Act of 1834, "An Act to Regulate Trade and Intercourse with the Indian Tribes and Preserve Peace on the Frontiers." In 1837, Congress created the Court of the United States for the District of Arkansas, and in 1851, it divided the court into two districts. The Western District included the northwestern counties of Arkansas and what was then Indian Territory. No court ever existed with jurisdiction over so great an expanse of territory. The seat in 1851 was at Van Buren, and in 1871, the seat was moved to a building at what is now Second and A streets in Fort Smith.

The court had jurisdiction over non-Indians committing crimes in Indian Territory and over Indians of one tribe committing crimes in another tribe's territory, with capital crimes being rape and murder. For those crimes, 167 people were convicted and eighty-six actually hanged, seven during Judge William Story's administration, and seventy-nine during Judge Isaac Parker's twenty-one years. There was no right of appeal until May 1, 1889, except directly to the president of the United States. The court had no jurisdiction over local matters unless the crimes fell under federal statutes. Then, as now, local crimes were administered by state and local law. In other words, Parker did not clean up Fort Smith.

THE MAN

John Childers was born in the Cherokee Nation on May 3, 1848, and like his father and many boys his age, he fought for the Confederacy. And like Frank and Jesse James and others, he turned to outlawry after the war.

1

The front and back of a photograph of John Childers, the first man hanged in Fort Smith, Arkansas, by the U.S. District Court of the Western District of Arkansas.
(Image courtesy of Linda Seamans McGahan)

The following is a condensation of Childers's statement as taken down by Captain C. E. Berry and published in *The New Era* on August 20, 1873:

Childers returned to the Indian Nation in August 1865, and from that time until the incident for which he was arrested, he roamed through Kansas, the Nation, Texas, and Missouri. His companions "were of the worst class and character." Their purpose was "to get our own back from those that took it away from us during the war." They took horses from the Osages, their enemy, as often as possible. They did not look upon it as a crime to take anything and everything from the Osages. But, he claimed to have never taken anything from white people. They would trade and sell their plunder wherever in the states that they felt safest. There were eight in the band, three whites and five Indians; two of the white men and one Indian (himself) were living at the time of the statement.

In their travels, John said, they always paid their way honorably; their war was upon the Osages. He then claimed that he looked on their acts as wrong but was urged on by his associates. He then cited

2

his wrongs and averred to God that he wanted to repair as much as he could. He went on to say that no one in his family knew of his activities with his associates and that he was the only one to dishonor the family name.

Whenever the band was in the Nation, it was led by Childers, and when in the states, by first one then another. Murder was committed more than once, but according to John, never by him and never when he was present.

The group disbanded about four years prior to the time of his execution, and he went to Fort Gibson, Indian Territory, where he worked for about a year driving a government team. He married Miss Mary Colby, a white woman. The couple separated after about two months for which separation he took the blame.

Childers then went to Kansas with a companion to raid the Osages again and stole about thirty or forty head of cattle. At the same time, marshals were pursuing them for crimes he claimed his companion committed. He felt that they were also after him, although he did not know why. John went on to berate the other man for cowardice and to say that the man had walked the streets of Fort Smith within the last thirty days but said that he would never reveal his name.

After he returned home from the Kansas raid, he got into some "difficulty," which he does not describe, with his cousin and his wife. Whatever the difficulty was, it resulted in the separation of the cousin and wife in the spring of 1869.

Childers then hired on with Dorsey and Allison of Texas for a legitimate job of driving a herd to Aberdeen, Kansas. When they reached the edge of Kansas, they were stopped by a vigilance committee headed by one Joseph Vannoy. Vannoy stopped them from entering Kansas, and he and Dorsey had "high words." Dorsey called on his drovers and asked them if they wanted to come out and fight their way through. Childers, by his account, was the only one to come forward. He wanted to kill Vannoy then and there for his abuse of old man Dorsey, but Dorsey prevented him. The citizens of Kansas and some Osages kept them surrounded for three or four days, but they eventually made their way to Aberdeen and returned without further incident. On his way home to Broken Arrow, he came to Big Caney near the edge of Kansas and then to Little Caney (this was near the place and time where the murder was committed) where he stayed all night. He then made his way to his home about seventy-five miles from there.

That was the end of the written statement taken by Captain Berry, but Childers then made a full confession of the murder that was not written down. A similar statement was given to R. J. Topping, a guard. However, Childers publicly professed his innocence until minutes before he was executed.

3

THE CRIME

On October 24, 1870, near Caney Creek in the northern part of the Cherokee territory, John Childers murdered Reyburn Wedding. Wedding was a young white man from Dexter, Kansas, on his way to Texas in a wagon loaded with his provisions. Childers had traveled some distance with his victim that day in order to determine what valuables he possessed. The two separated, then Childers came back that night and hit Wedding in the back of the head with an axe while he sat at his campfire. The force of the blow knocked Wedding's body into the fire. He then dragged the body to a creek and dumped it and several blankets and sacks of flour into the creek.

In the proceedings before the commissioner at Fort Smith, Deputy U.S. Marshal Joseph Vannoy stated that early on the morning of October 25, 1870, he was traveling north near Double Creek when he found a wagon from which the horses had been unhitched but the harness was still attached to the wagon. He described the condition and position of the wagon and its contents, including flour, oats, sugar, two saddles, and clothing. Vannoy, as was common at the time, went to local residents, the nearest being eight miles away, and inquired about the ownership of the wagon and a gray mare that he had found nearby. Near the crossing of the Big Caney, he was told by local resident John Lewis that the mare belonged to a man who had crossed there the evening before, presumably Reyburn Wedding.

Vannoy returned to the area where he had found the wagon and mare, and about two o'clock in the afternoon, after following the wagon track, he found the body of Reyburn Wedding in the creek. The beginning of Vannoy's deposition reads as follows (spelling, grammar, and punctuation are directly from the document):

> Joseph W. Vannoy sworn says have seen Riburn Wedding—saw his body floating in Double Creek in Cherokee Nation on the 25th day of October ad 1870 it was about 50 yards from the road and 8 miles from any house—he was a white man. I examined the body the skull was crushed in as though with an axe, it was the back part of the head that was crushed—I found a little fire within 8 feet of the creek—also a hat was by it, a coffee pot was in the creek. I saw some brains near the fire—a wagon track went from the main road to the camp fire and back into the road thus; (a drawing of the creek, road and track followed and a description of the items found in the creek) It was a dark plush hat on

4

the bank. There was a dent in it on the side and inside there were brains over the dent. The body had on a dark brown coat and dark brown corded pants. It had on a common vest and dark woolen shirt. — I found a pocketbook lying on the bank opposite the flour on the south side of the stream it had come to pieces there was nothing in it — the pants were tucked in the boots. — the fire was still smoking — the track was a fresh one — the blood was apparently fresh — I found the body about 2 PM it looked as though it had not lain long when I turned it over it bled freely.

On December 26, 1870, Vannoy found and captured John Childers at Childers Ferry near present-day Bixby, Oklahoma. Childers, who was still in possession of Wedding's other horse, stated, according to Vannoy's deposition, that "he could have been a thousand miles away but did not expect anyone to come from that side of the river to arrest him. Said I had got the drop on him or I would not have got him — this statement was made voluntarily there was no inducement or threats." Childers further stated that he had crossed Big Caney with Wedding about October 24.

The lawmen started toward Kansas with their prisoner, but due to his past experiences with Vannoy and the citizens of Kansas and fearing that he would not be taken to Van Buren, Childers escaped after they had traveled about ten miles.

Again quoting from Vannoy's deposition:

About 26th of January [1871] I arrested him the 2d time near Judge Perryman's between Ft. Gibson & the ferry. Witness Eckert was with me. — about the 3d of February he made voluntary statements while we were traveling north and a few miles from Kansas line. He told me he crossed the Big Cana with the young man — that there was a gray & black horse in the team. This was after I told him about the young man being killed — then said I know you have got the Dead Wood on me — also said his friend had a plenty of money — spoke of Pole [Napoleon Bonaparte] Childers getting about $12,000 from the Government for damages. Told me to keep it low and I would get well paid for it. That I might bring him to Van Buren and put him in jail and for me to say nothing about it and I could have all the money I wanted which would be placed in my hand before he was released. He offered me his pony then

5

also his saddle and bridle. He made a statement which he asked me to reduce to writing which I did. This was read to him before two witnesses — he signed it by making his mark in the presence of these witnesses.

More from the proceedings before the commissioner (depositions) states:

> David Ugulant duly sworn told me he got the horse near Aberdeen after he was arrested — since then he said he got him near Big Caney. He asked me if I thought $1000 would take these chains off his legs. Ask if I thought he could buy of from Vannoy. This was when he was coming this way from Baxter [Baxter Springs, Kansas] He said he had made an acknowledgement to Vannoy in writing.

Childers was taken to Van Buren, where the Western District Court then was held. He was brought before U.S. Court Commissioner Colonel Churchill and remanded to stand trial at the next session of the court. On May 3, 1871, his birthday, Childers again escaped and remained free until September, when deputies Vannoy and Peavey again captured him. He was brought to Fort Smith, where the Western District Court now resided, and released on bond. He reported to the court for the May 1872 session but was jailed and the trial continued for want of witnesses. At the November 1872 term of the court, Childers was convicted of murder, and on Monday, April 19, 1873, he was sentenced to hang on August 15, 1873.

After the sentence was pronounced, the prisoner had one request — that he be permitted to wear his long hair and not have it cut off. At that time, it was the ruling of the jailer that all prisoners were required to have their hair "shingled." Judge Story stated that he had no control over that matter but hoped that the request would be granted. Captain Berry, the jailer, assured him that his wish would be granted and "the prisoner seemed much pleased."

The evidence presented at the trial had all been circumstantial since there were no witnesses. However, because Childers was found in possession of Wedding's horse and given his reputation and association with outlaws and the introduction of his signed statements, he was convicted. Apparently, judging from the opinions expressed in the newspapers, a contingent of Kansas citizens at the trial did not want Childers to return to their area. *The Weekly Herald* stated that he would probably have been acquitted due to lack of witnesses had it not been for Vannoy and the Kansas people. The same paper was also convinced that Childers was guilty and received his just reward.

INTERVIEW

Both local newspapers of the day, *The Weekly Herald* and *The New Era*, interviewed the condemned man and gave reports of his appearance and demeanor. *The New Era* visited the prisoner about eleven o'clock on Thursday, the day before the execution, and reported that, "We found him in good spirits, apparently showing neither bravado nor fear. He was cool, courteous and collected throughout." John S. Childers was described as being about five feet, eleven inches tall, well built with clustering, dark hair and heavy mustache and lively gray eyes, "his whole appearance, however, somewhat sinister and reckless." *The Weekly Herald* reported, "Up to 11½ o'clock a.m., an hour and a half previous to his execution, when we last interviewed him, he positively refused to confess his guilt...."

To *The New Era*, Childers gave most of the biographical information that is contained in the first part of this article. He also spoke of the kindnesses received, while a prisoner, from Captain Berry and his wife and his spiritual adviser, Reverend J. M. Harrell.

Shortly before his execution date, Childers had been removed from the jail with the other prisoners and housed in the fort guardhouse near Washington Street (now Second Street). His old cellmates had sent him a letter, which he allowed the reporters to read. In the letter, they let him know that they were thinking about him and admonished him that it was not too late to seek salvation. It was signed, "To Mr. John Childers, from his Old Associates in the Garrison Jail."

THE EXECUTION

At one o'clock, August 15, 1873, John Childers exited the guardhouse opposite Washington Street escorted by six guards, U.S. Marshal Colonel Sarber, Colonel Main, Captain Berry, and attended by Reverend J. M. Harrell and Dr. C. W. Pierce. The prisoner had been given the customary "hearty breakfast" and cigar. He smoked his cigar and his demeanor was of "cool indifference and courage" as if the event concerned someone else as the group walked the 200 yards to the south end of the fort to the gallows.

The gallows was enclosed by a board fence, and on the front of the platform, a screen was hung so that the victim was not seen after the drop fell. Outside the scaffold and fence, a large area was enclosed by a stout rope. Two fire companies, Alert and Excelsior, guarded the roped-off area. Outside the roped area, the crowd was estimated to be about 2,000.

The prisoner, Captain Berry, Deputy Messler, and Reverend Harrell mounted the scaffold, and Captain Berry read the sentence, after which the condemned man made a statement. He rambled on for sixteen minutes, during which time he denied any guilt and occasionally turned to Berry and Messler to ask about the pain the act of hanging would cause. "But he did not at any time show any fear or trepidation." Finally, at the end of his monologue, he did admit that he had killed Reyburn Wedding for his money and because he was a Kansas man.

Following Childers's speech, Reverend Harrell made a statement of hope for the condition of the condemned man's soul followed by a prayer. Childers shook hands with everyone on the scaffold and was visited by Mrs. Emma Foreman, "a comely looking Cherokee woman" who was jailed for selling whiskey. The black cap was placed over his face, and Deputy Messler released the drop. At this point there are two slight conflicts in the reports of the two newspapers; one states that the drop fell at 1:40 p.m. and the body hung for eighteen minutes, the other says "at 2 o'clock precisely" and that "he lived and breathed for 14½ minutes." However, both agree that all went smoothly and, other than a few slight initial twitches, the body never moved. The body was cut down and put in a coffin that had been placed at the scaffold for that purpose and taken to the city cemetery.

In the time leading up to the falling of the drop, the skies had been darkening and the wind rising to a gale, evidence that a storm was at hand. Immediately after the drop fell, the sky unleashed a furious rainstorm and scattered the multitude of spectators.

The last paragraph of the report by *The New Era* expresses that, "His death doubtless freed the region of one of the most dangerous characters, and the only regret of peaceable, law-abiding people is, that a hundred or two of characters like him who now infest the Indian Territory and adjoining border states are not served like Childers."

CHAPTER 2

"TWO MEN HUNG

Both Cherokees, for Murder
Young Wolf and Tu-na-yee
1500 People Present"

On Friday at 1 o'clock P.M., the two prisoners were led from the old guardhouse, halting at the old jail to bid farewell to their old chums; to the gallows, under a strong guard.

So read the headline and first paragraph in *The Weekly Herald* in Fort Smith on October 11, 1873. The column describes the second hanging in Fort Smith by the Court for the Western District on Friday, October 10, 1873.

Because there are variations of both men's names in available documents, I am going to list the various names and then the names most commonly used on government documents. The one called Tu-na-yee in *The Herald* article will be found as Tu-na-gee, Tu-na-ha, Tu-na-hi, and Tuni. In court files he is identified as Tuni. In his confession, he said, "My name is George Tuni." *The Cherokee Advocate*, which was printed in both the Cherokee language and alphabet and English, spelled his name Tu-ni-ah. Young Wolf's Indian name was Wha-na-nee-tah; his English name, George Young Wolf Sixkiller. The variety of names is probably what led at least one author to say that three people were hanged on October 10, 1873. Records of court proceedings in *The Weekly Herald* and records at the National Archives in Fort Worth, Texas, identify them as Tuni and Young Wolf.

These two Cherokee men were in their late thirties and, like John Childers, were veterans of the Civil War. Unlike Childers, they had fought with the Loyal Cherokee for the Union. Both lived near Horse Creek in the Cherokee Nation. Neither could understand English. Tuni believed that he was thirty-eight years old, although he was not sure, and Young Wolf thought that he was thirty-six. Tuni had a wife and no children, but the couple had a boy who had been given to them to raise. Young Wolf had a wife and one child about a year old.

The confessions of the two men were taken down word for word by jailer Captain Charles E. Berry as translated by "an intelligent old Negro interpreter, Edmond Ross." The full text was printed in *The New Era* on September 3, 1873. The following information is from that publication.

9

At the time of publication both men professed Christianity, having been baptized on the previous Thursday, August 28, 1873, by a Cherokee minister of the Methodist faith. But they denied that they made a fuss because they were not allowed to be hanged with John Childers "as a paper in this town stated at the time, with more regard for the sensational than the truth" (*The New Era*, September 3, 1873).

George Tuni said he lived at the mouth of Horse Creek in the Nation and that he did not understand English. He immediately stated that he was charged, tried, and convicted of the murder of two white men and that he was guilty. He desired to confess to all and make his peace with God and began to tell in detail of the murders.

In the winter of 1873, Wha-na-nee-tah came to his house and told him of two white men with a lot of traps camped on the Grand River and said they should go and kill them. He had seen the men himself and some women had told him about them. Tuni agreed, and after considerable discussion about how they should kill the men, the two set off, both armed with government muskets. They started between daylight and moonlight, and when they reached the camp, they could still see "tolerably well—some thirty yards." They found their victims asleep on some coffee sacks about fifty or sixty feet from the river. Young Wolf shot first the man on the right, who rose up on his hands and knees and uttered, "Oh, Lord." Young Wolf then told Tuni twice to shoot before he shot the man on the left, who died instantly. Young Wolf then beat his victim with his musket, killing him and breaking the gun in the process.

They then collected their loot, which consisted of fifty cents, thirteen steel traps, two pairs of boots, a pistol that was no good, a shotgun, two axes, cooking utensils, and two canoes, one of which was "of no account." The bodies were taken to a deep spot in the river and disposed of, then the murderers took the traps to Tuni's house and hid them. The women, Tuni's wife and Lydia Martin, who would later be a witness, were in bed. The next morning, they went back to the site of the murders and moved the traps, which they never used, to a new hiding place.

The murderers had never seen the men before, and it appears that no one ever knew their names. One body was found farther down the river the following spring, and the other was never found.

Young Wolf then told of another time that he had killed a man accidentally, a friend who served in the Union Army with him. He had started to clean his gun, which was loaded with buckshot, when it discharged and hit his friend in the leg. The friend died the next day. His penalty was to do the duty of the man whom he had killed.

The two confessions are almost identical or at least in total agreement on the basis of facts. Both men showed remorse and recognized that theirs was a senseless act. From their words it appears that their deed started to weigh upon their minds immediately. Tuni stated that he thought that every white man that he saw was a lawman coming for him, and Young Wolf said that when the marshal came for him, he gave up and never tried to get away. They both asked God to forgive them and said that they were ready to die for their crime.

I found no mention of the capture of Tuni and Wha-na-nee-tah in the papers of the time, but that was not unusual. When the deputies brought in prisoners, the deputies' names and sometimes the number of prisoners were mentioned. However, prisoners' names seemed to be mentioned only if they and their crimes were particularly noteworthy.

The first mention on Tuni and Young Wolf is in the listing of court proceedings of the spring session of the federal court. On June 20, 1873, there is a listing of U.S. v. Tuni and Young Wolf, murder — pending; on June 21 is a listing for U.S. v. Tuni and Young Wolf, jury trial, pending; and on June 23, U.S. v. Tuni and Young Wolf, murder — jury trial, verdict guilty.

The New Era, June 28, 1873: "Young Wolf and Tuni, the two Cherokees who so cruelly murdered, last spring, two white men on the Neosho River were found guilty last Monday in the U.S. court, the jury not being out over five minutes. Sentence has not been pronounced." Actually, according to their confessions, the crime took place on the Grand River.

The New Era, August 6, 1873: "To Be Hung. — Tu-nee-ha and Young Wolf, two Cherokees, convicted at the present session of the U.S. District Court of the murder of two white men near the Neosho River last Spring, were sentenced on Monday by Judge Story to suffer death by hanging on October 10th next."

In its October 10, 1873, edition, *The New Era* announced "Tu-ni-ha" and Young Wolf would be hanged on Friday, October 10, and that a large crowd was expected when people learned that the execution would be public.

In the October 8 edition, *The New Era* made an announcement that Young Wolf had been baptized on the previous Sunday by a Cherokee minister. He must have been making double sure since the same paper said on September 3, 1873, that both men had been baptized on the previous Thursday, August 28, 1873, by a Cherokee minister of the Methodist faith.

The Saturday, October 11, 1873, *The Weekly Herald*, after describing the prisoners' stop at the old jail on the way to the gallows, went on to say that they "manifested neither fear, care, nor concern; and ascended the steps with as much nonchalance as if going to a ball-play."

Their escort included two preachers, Young Pig and Walking Stick, Marshals Messler, Sheldon, and Maledon. Jailer Berry read the sentence, and Jackson King was the interpreter.

The men gave long talks in Cherokee, the text of which was to be published only in *The Cherokee Advocate*. On October 18, 1873, *The Cherokee Advocate* published an account of the execution that was essentially the same as the accounts of the Fort Smith papers plus Tuni and Young Wolf's address to their people. The following is as translated by *The Advocate* translator:

> We think it our duty to make this our confession to our people hoping they will thereby learn the truth more perfectly, that crime sooner or later will surely be punished and "murder will out." The crime for which we must suffer was hidden in darkness a long while, and it seemed for a time that it was to be one of the numerous crimes that escape detection, but—the wages of sin is death, and the reward will come sooner or later. Most persons who do evil deeds, regard legal penalties only as far as to seek to evade the consequences of their acts. Our views of that have changed decidedly since we have been confined. We do not wish to avoid the legal consequences of what we have done. All our desire now is to seek forgiveness for our crime we have committed against Heaven, and to prepare ourselves to go where temptations are unknown, and our awful crimes will not be remembered against us.
>
> Now we wish to say something to those we leave behind. We leave this world willingly, and would not if we could, have our sentences set aside or commuted. In the ardent wish that our victims could be restored to life so that they could be better prepared for death, we forget ourselves.
>
> We give our warning. We are well aware that many of our young people are growing up in crime. Indulgence in the commission of crime makes each offence easier to be committed. Each successive crime is darker than the preceding one, until, if not stopped, murder is apt to end the list, with all its terrible consequences. It is true, all criminals do not suffer in this world, but no punishment is more dreaded than a successful life of crime with the penalty to suffer afterwards.

One of us leaves an orphan—a little one. It is yet too young to have been soiled by criminal associations. We bespeak for it the charity of those we leave behind, and hope it will lead a life different from its parent. Do not visit upon it the sins of its father, but let it have a fair chance to be an honor to the country and a true Christian.

We are not alone here. Crime has its representatives here from all Nations, charged with all crimes known to law. That, however, does not excuse us in the least. The fact is a warning to all.

Let not our people think ignorance justifies crime in us or any one. Neither does blood or race. Ignorance is a justification of crime in no one of any Nation or Race.

Following their joint address was a half column titled, "REMARKS FROM TU-NI-AH," in which he exhorted his people to follow the Christian way of life.

All preparations had been made and actions carried out and the execution went in a quiet and orderly manner. At about two thirty that afternoon, the black caps were drawn, the ropes were adjusted, and "two more souls were launched into eternity."

Interestingly, during the time that Tuni and Young Wolf were being tried and about the time that they were sentenced, Judge William Story was being investigated for taking bribes. Specifically Story and Attorney J. H. Huckleberry, at that time judge of the 3rd Judicial District of the state, were accused of taking heavy bribes from one Frank J. Nash, a merchant at Fort Gibson, Indian Territory. Nash was charged with introducing and selling liquor in Indian country. It was charges such as this and outrageous spending and little results from the court that led to Story's resignation in 1874 to avoid impeachment. In March 1875, he was replaced by Isaac C. Parker.

CHAPTER 3

"THE AWFUL DOOM"
(*The New Era*, April 8, 1874)

The "Three Human Beings In a Moment Launched Into Eternity!" on April 3, 1874, were, although all Indian, a diverse group. Two were Choctaw, one Seminole; but one of the Choctaw lived in the Creek Nation. The men ranged in age from sixteen to fifty-five. They varied from ordinary Indian citizen to "too indolent and too worthless to work for a living" to one of the most "dreaded through the Territory."

The following is from an interview granted *The New Era* on April 1, 1874:

The reporter had gone to the U.S. Marshal's office and made the request to see the condemned men. Then, the reporter was taken, along with two interpreters, "a Choctaw, nearly white, and a Seminole Negro," to the guardhouse where condemned men were kept until their execution. On the way, the group stopped at the general prison. They found the men securely ironed and guarded sitting by a fire in a little room to the left of the entrance, a favor granted them by Marshal Sarber. At night they were locked in their cells.

JOHN POINTER

In the District Court of the United States of America for the Western District of Arkansas November Term A. D. 1872.

The grand jurors of the United States of America duly selected empanelled sworn and charged to enquire in and for the Western District of Arkansas aforesaid upon the oath do present One Pointer late of the Indian Country in the Western District of Arkansas aforesaid not having the fear of God before his eyes but being moved and seduced by the instigation of the Devil on the 10th day of September A. D. 1872 with force and arms in the Indian Country aforesaid in the Western District of Arkansas aforesaid in and upon One Blue not an Indian by birth marriage or adoption.

These are the words of the true bill that goes on for six pages of repetitive and convoluted words to say that Pointer "did kill and murder" a man named Blue.

John Pointer, Seminole, was eighteen years old, "of middle size and good countenance." He very possibly was innocent of the physical act of killing the white man for whose murder he was executed. However, he was present at the killing and, if not guilty of the act, did share in the proceeds, his share being some of the effects of the victim and eleven dollars and fifty cents.

Pointer's story was that he was with his brother and one Sam McGee in the Choctaw Nation near the Canadian River when McGee "declared that he was bound to kill somebody." Upon meeting a drover, McGee declared he would kill him while Pointer and his brother tried to discourage him. When the drover was killed, the Pointer brothers ran away. Pointer protested with great emotion, both at the interview and on the gallows, that he was innocent. He said that McGee had money to buy witnesses, while he, Pointer, was poor, and because he was poor and unable to speak English, his defense, through an interpreter, had been grossly neglected. But now he was resigned to die for something of which he was innocent. From Pointer's demeanor, the reporter was inclined to believe that he was telling the truth.

The existing documents seem to bear out Pointer's assertion about witnesses. In his petition for witnesses, he named several people who he said could be found in the Creek Nation and Cheyenne Agency. However, the subpoenas show the deputies searched in the Cherokee Nation. Pointer's attorney pointed this out in his request for a retrial and also stated that one woman, Jenny McGee, was found more than 150 miles from where she was supposed to have lived and that he doubted it was the same person. Other irregularities were pointed out in the retrial request, and the documentation supports some of them.

ISAAC FILMORE

Isaac Filmore, a full-blood Choctaw, sixteen years old, with a wife and one child and a countenance "dull and apathetic, yet cunning," spoke English. Filmore seemed utterly unconcerned about his fate and laughed and joked as though he were a free man "among boon companions." He seemed to the reporter to be low on the scale of humanity and hardly conscious of any distinction between right and wrong.

The previous June, Filmore had gone out to kill and rob someone when he met a traveler who had come all the way from California on foot. After passing the man, he had turned back and passed him again by a few steps and wheeled and shot him. His entire take was a dollar and a half and a pair of shoes. When asked if he knew the name of the man he had killed, he scowled and replied, "Doggone if I know." He would not confess to the murder and was not disposed to be interrogated by the reporter.

That was the profile of Filmore and his crime as rendered by the reporter for *The New Era* in the April 1, 1874, edition of that paper. The court documents, however, tell a more detailed story of someone who appeared, at least until the time of his sentencing, not "utterly unconcerned about his fate." Filmore's lawyers filed, in his behalf, an application for witnesses citing what information those witnesses would provide and how their testimony would prove his innocence.

On August 1, 1873, a warrant was issued stating, "Isaac Filmore and Black Bill did, in the Indian Country, Western District of Arkansas, on or about the 15th day of July, 1873, feloniously, willfully and of their malice and aforethought kill and murder—a German—a white man and not an Indian, whose name is unknown, against the peace and dignity of the United States...." Both men were arrested on August 6, 1873, but after examination before the U.S. commissioner, Black Bill (a.k.a. Grayson) was discharged and Filmore committed to trial.

In the proceedings before the commissioner, Hickory Rogers described in his deposition how he and others had found the body and the condition of the surrounding area. Among the things they found was a small roll of paper, about the length of a match, which turned out to be money—a dollar and a half. They also found a wooden ramrod of a gun with blood on it. Both of those items would lead to Filmore's conviction when he acknowledged association with both.

Witness Rogers stated that Filmore had been at Rogers's house the day before the murder and was carrying the shotgun presumed to have been used in the killing. He further stated that Filmore made a statement in the presence of other witnesses and that "no threats or inducements were held out." That statement, as recited by Rogers for the commissioner, reads verbatim:

> On Saturday morning as he was going South down on the R. R. he met defendant Grayson he asked him (Filmore) where he was going. He (Filmore) told him he was going South of the Canadian to hunt for work. Grayson said he was going to Mr. Thornberry's to get work. He (Filmore) then said I will go back with you & go home. He said that after passing up the road they came to two paths one going to his mother's and the other to Thornberry's at this point they had considerably talk together, that they saw this man who was killed passing along the Emigrant road. Deft. Grayson told him you go over and kill him and I will come to your house and divide with you this evening, that they then separated, that he (Filmore) overhauled the man and shot him. He said he walked along in the grass out

16

of the road until he got past the man, and then turned
and shot him.

Here, the statement of the defendant ends, and the witness continues with a description of the crime scene. Toward the end of his deposition, Rogers returned to statements of the defendant saying, "Afterward he told my brother in my presence that he started out with the intention of killing the first man he came to because he was in destitute circumstances — was barefooted and without anything to eat at the house." [All spelling, punctuation, grammar, and spacing as in original.]

Further testimony by witnesses reveals that Filmore tried to make excuses about the bloody ramrod, but they just mired him deeper into his tangled story. Filmore's gun had no ramrod when he was arrested. He asked the arresting officers if they found a ramrod at the scene, then claimed that the blood was there because he had had a nosebleed. In another version, he traded ramrods with someone he met. He admitted seeing the roll of paper but said he thought it was a bundle of matches. He did, indeed, weave a tangled web.

Apparently, the reporter for *The New Era* misunderstood the information he was given. The dollar and a half that Filmore supposedly got was lying with the body, as were the shoes of the deceased. The victim was carrying his shoes and had a large bandage on his toe, according to other witnesses. Also, by his own statement, he did not pass the victim then turn and pass him again. However, considering that the prisoner "was not disposed to be interrogated," the reporter got the story reasonably straight, no gross errors or misrepresentations.

JOHN BILLY

John Billy, alias Chuffer Tubbe, was a full-blood Choctaw, fifty-five years old with a "cunning and forbidding countenance." At the time of the interview, Billy still wore a bandage on his head from a wound he had received when he had tried to escape the arresting deputies. Billy denied his guilt and refused to make any confession and did not care to be interviewed. After a "lively jabber" with the interpreter, he said that he would make some statements on the gallows but not before.

From other articles in *The New Era*, it appears that Billy had a long history as a bad character in his area. He had originally been arrested and was being brought in for assault with intent to kill a black man named William Mason. A request for writ, a warrant, and two true bills were issued for that crime between March 6, 1872, and December 6, 1873, with one bill stating that the assault took place on December 18, 1871, and the other saying December 26, 1871. However, those documents became immaterial. On the way to Fort Smith after his arrest for that crime, he committed the crime for which he was executed.

On the night of November 2, 1873, U.S. Marshals Willard Ayers, Perry Duval, J. C. Wilkinson, and Ed Grayson were bringing in four prisoners—John Billy, Peter and Dave Eufowler, and Jim Blacksmith. They had stopped to sleep at the home of a Mr. Douglas at the Creek Agency. Ayers was chained to three prisoners, and Duval was sleeping at his side. During the night, Billy slipped his handcuffs, reached over Ayers, took Duval's gun from his belt, and shot Duval in the head, killing him instantly. He then shot Ayers through the left hand and breast, cutting off his left nipple. Jumping to his feet, he then shot Wilkinson, who was at the opposite end of the room, the bullet passing through the kidneys. Ayers, being only wounded, had risen and grabbed Billy's weapon when Ed Grayson raised and attempted to shoot. Grayson's weapon failed to fire, and he grabbed another and fired twice, one ball striking Billy in the waist and the other entering above his left eye and exiting through the top of his head. Billy fired three more shots after being shot in the waist. His wounds were first thought to be fatal; however, as you see, it would take more to put him away.

Ayers had suspected that there would be trouble that night from expressions made by Billy before retiring. He had said that he did not want to go to Fort Smith because they hanged Choctaws there and begged the deputies to kill him. Because of that, Billy had been handcuffed and chained differently from the rest of the prisoners. But, obviously, he overcame that and, in so doing, sealed his fate.

The court proceedings of John Pointer and Isaac Filmore appear to have taken some time, according to the court proceedings published in the newspapers. On June 26, 1872, there appears U.S. v. One Pointer, murder motion for continuance overruled; application for witnesses for defense at U.S. expense granted. Similar notices appear on December 6, 1872, and Tuesday, November 18, 1873. But then, on Wednesday, November 19, 1873, came the notice, "U.S. v. One Pointer, murder, jury trial, verdict guilty." The following week on Tuesday, November 25, 1873, Isaac Filmore applied for witnesses and it was granted, and on December 17, 1873, Filmore was found guilty.

John Billy appears to have taken less time than the others. Only two notices appeared with his name—on December 18, 1873, U.S. v. John Billy—murder, jury trial, pending, and on December 19, 1873, U.S. v. John Billy—murder, jury trial, guilty.

An article from January 7, 1874, in *The New Era* mentions all three names in saying that they had been sentenced by Judge Story to be hanged April 3, 1874.

On Friday, April 3, 1874, the condemned men were allowed to visit the general prison where they were hugged and cried over by their former jail mates, so much so that John Pointer "became quite un-manned." The men were then taken back to their cells at the guard-house where they were attended by Reverends McManus of the Epis-copal Church, J. W. Bushong of the M. E. Church, J. L. Hobbs, M. D. and D. D. missionary and prison physician, Ab. Mansfield and F. A. Foster of the Colored Baptist Church. At eleven o'clock that morning, the condemned took their last meal, which they seemed to relish.

At one o'clock the three men were led from the guardhouse with the ministers in the lead singing hymns. Members of the press and of the medical fraternity and other privileged people followed. The whole procession was surrounded by an armed guard who had difficulty keeping back the immense crowd, which pressed in from all sides as they crossed the parade ground.

At the scaffold, thousands of spectators were kept back by a stout rope and deputy U.S. marshals. After the prisoners, guards, officers, and clergymen had taken their positions on the gallows, Mr. Alnut, a clerk in the U.S. Marshal's Office, read the death warrant of each of the condemned. George Munday translated in Seminole for John Pointer, and Turner Graham in Choctaw for John Billy. Isaac Filmore under-stood English.

After the readings of the sentences, Marshal Sarber told the men that they could make any remarks they desired. At that time Pointer, through the interpreter, again declared his innocence and stated that his defense had been neglected by his counsel and by his interpreter and that McGee had money and was able to buy off witnesses against him (McGee).

Next, Filmore declared in English his innocence, but in his case, it was reported that the proof was overwhelming and he had confessed the murder to Commissioner Churchill. The only redeeming feature in his case was his age, about sixteen or seventeen.

Last to speak was John Billy. He calmly confessed that he was guilty of murder and that he deserved to die. He said that his sentence was just and that he had been a very bad man. He hoped for for-giveness, though unworthy of it.

Dr. Hobbs then read in English the portion of the scriptures giving the narrative of the penitent thief on the cross. He read the same in Choctaw and then led in singing a hymn, joined by the condemned men who held hymnbooks in their hands. After the singing, Reverend I. A. Foster offered a prayer for the souls of the deceased, followed by Reverend Gilbert Hampson, a Choctaw, who at the request of John Bil-ly offered a prayer in Choctaw.

After the prayers the condemned men took leave of their friends, ministers, and guards. Pointer and Filmore were greatly affected but Billy remained unmoved and showed no signs of weakness, only once

19

grinning "horribly" at the dangling rope. The officers then quickly pinioned the arms and legs of the men and pulled on the black caps. The three men stood in a row on one trap, and at a signal, the rope was cut, the trap fell with a thud, and all was over.

Pointer died without a struggle, and the limbs of the other two showed some slight contraction but only for a few minutes. Billy's heart stopped beating in thirteen minutes, Filmore's in fourteen, and Pointer's in sixteen. The bodies were taken down, placed in coffins, and taken to the city cemetery, and there buried.

CHAPTER 4

"MY FATHER...BROUGHT ME TO THE SCAFFOLD"

McClish Impson

January 15, 1875

My name is McClish Impson. I am 19 years of age. As I am about to meet my Maker I am desirous of making the following statement:

The crime for which I have been tried, convicted and sentenced to be hanged today, viz: the murder of a white man, name unknown, in the Indian country during February 1873. I am guilty. I have made my peace with God and look to him alone for mercy.

My father, who is now dead, has brought me to the scaffold; it was through his teachings that I am now compelled to die. May God bless him and I humbly ask forgiveness of everyone in the world

his

Attest: McClish X Impson

mark

J. A. Graham, interpreter, Witness

The preceding paragraphs are the confession given by McClish Impson on January 15, 1875, to Major Pierce, deputy U.S. marshal, through interpreter J. A. Graham in the presence of the reporter for *The New Era* about one hour before his execution.

Impson's mother had died when he was an infant and he had been adopted by a Christian Indian family, given an English name and given a Christian education. When he was about fourteen years old, his adopted father died, and his biological father took him and introduced him to his drinking, gambling, horse-stealing, murderous, vagabond way of life. The two had been part of a deadly band of horse thieves. The father had been killed in an encounter with the Choctaw Lighthorse about two years before McClish's murder conviction.

McClish Impson had committed a murder when he was but seventeen years of age. In the vicinity of Boggy Depot, he had killed a white man with whom he had been riding and whose name he did not know and whose name was never determined. His entire gain in the murder/robbery had been the man's horse and twenty-two dollars and fifty cents.

Impson had bragged of his deed to some friends in whom he thought he could confide since he knew that they had killed a woman. However, they reported the crime, and he was captured. According to *The New Era*, he was captured almost immediately after boasting to his comrades of his deed. But following the information of the same paper, several months passed between commission and capture. In his confession, Impson said that the murder was in February 1873. The notice of his capture, which appeared in the October 1, 1873, issue of that paper, says that he had been brought in the previous Tuesday, which would have been September 30, 1873. So, it appears that he must have evaded the law for some length of time.

Impson's first appearance in court was on November 17, 1873, when it was noted: U.S. v. McClish Impson, murder, application for witnesses granted. He was convicted and sentenced to hang in November 1874 by Judge Caldwell.

On January 15, 1875, the reporter was admitted to Impson's cell in the old guardhouse as noted before. There he heard the prisoner's confession and observed him take his last meal. Immediately after the confession, the head guard, Charles Burns, removed the prisoner's shackles. In the tedious operation of removing the shackles, Impson assisted "with great readiness, as though he was again to be permitted to walk forth a free man." The attendant then brought the last meal, which consisted of broiled quail, biscuit, and good, strong coffee. Impson ate his meal and, as soon as he was finished, reached for his Chickasaw hymnbook, read a hymn, and sang it "in a pleasant and steady voice." He then kneeled and offered a prayer "in a clear, steady and fervent voice."

The Reverend Dr. Hobbs, Choctaw missionary, who had been working with the prisoner preparing him for eternity, came in after the meal and prayer, and the condemned's eyes lighted with pleasure, and the two greeted each other with a smile and warm handshake. The next half hour was spent in religious exercises, and then the final moment had come. Major Banks then entered, and the prisoner removed his coat and put on the black robe.

At twelve thirty, McClish Impson exited his cell accompanied by Deputy Marshals Lauderback, Cox, Twyman, and Somerhill as advance guard, followed by Deputy Alnut and Reverend Dr. Hobbs. Next was the prisoner with Major Ed Blanks and Major George S. Pierce as his supporters, followed by the rear guard, Deputies Rector, Oppenhiemer, Winters, and Wallace. The group proceeded to the scaffold, where Impson ascended the steps without hesitation and "stood there with that cool, calm indifference as to his fate, that none but a brave Indian could assume."

The death warrant was read by Major Blanks, prayers, and singing in Choctaw by Reverend Hobbs and singing of the farewell by the condemned. At about one o'clock the drop fell, and McClish Impson was dead almost instantly of a broken neck. He was officially pronounced dead in sixteen minutes by Doctors Main, Johnson, and Chaney and was cut down after twenty minutes. The body was placed in a coffin and "conveyed to the Cemetery and decently interred."

McClish Impson was the last man executed by the court that was originally presided over by Judge Story. Impson made his first court appearance before Story on November 17, 1873, but he was convicted by Judge Caldwell in November 1874 because Story had resigned in June 1874 to avoid impeachment.

The Western District Court in general, and Judge Story in particular, had been under scrutiny almost since the court was moved to Fort Smith. There seemed to always be a shortage of funds, that owing to insufficient funding by the federal government and, some said, a mishandling of money by Story and the court. Before the November 1873 session of the court, there was speculation as to whether there would be a fall session due to lack of money.

An article in *The New Era* on April 6, 1873, describes charges of accepting bribes against Judge William Story and ex-District Attorney J. H. Huckleberry. They were alleged to have accepted bribes from Frank J. Nash, a merchant in Fort Gibson, Indian Territory, who had been charged with illegal sale of alcohol.

Charges and accusations such as those just described persisted until early 1874, when a formal investigation took place. There was no May or spring session of the Western District Court due to the fact that Story and the court records were in Washington, D.C., where the judge was defending himself.

All during the tenure of the court and its investigation, there were numerous and long articles in the newspapers of the day regarding the goings on, but on June 17, 1874, *The New Era* ran one line: "It is reported that Judge Story of the U.S. District Court has resigned."

On May 8, 1875, *The Weekly Herald* announced, "Judge I. C. Parker, the newly appointed judge for the Western District of Arkansas, arrived here on Tuesday; and will enter upon his duties on the 10th inst." On May 10, 1875, Parker presided over the court for the first time and made his famous charge to the grand jury.

CHAPTER 5

"EIGHT MURDERERS TRIED AND CONVICTED IN A U.S. COURT"

(The New Era, June 30, 1875)

The sonorous, solemn voice of Judge Isaac C. Parker called up the first of the men to be sentenced. William J. Whittington stepped forward, standing very erect and keeping his eyes fixed on the judge during the long and impressive address of the latter.

Isaac C. Parker
Judge of the U.S. District Court of the Western District of Arkansas, at about age 36, when he first came to Fort Smith

John Whittington; you have been indicted by the Grand Jury of this district for the murder of John J. Turner in the Indian country. You have had a fair and impartial trial in which you have been aided by faithful and intelligent counsel who have done all for you during the progress of the trial that would or could have been done under the terrible state of facts which surrounded your case.

After a patient and deliberate investigation of your case by the petit jury which tried you, they have been constrained by their consciences and oaths as honest men and good citizens to pronounce you guilty of a most foul and aggravated murder.

Have you anything to say why sentence of the law should not now be pronounced against you? The feelings and emotions with which I now enter upon the discharge of the solemn and important duty which devolves upon the court and which I am now about to perform are too painful to be expressed.

To pronounce the dreadful sentence of the law which, is to cut a fellow being off from Society, to deprive him of existence and send him to the bar of his

Creator and his God where his destiny must be fixed for eternity, is at all times and under any circumstances a most painful duty to the court.

But to be compelled, in discharge of my duty, to consign to the gallows a young man who, but for his crime, might have been a useful member of society, who has but just entered upon a vigorous manhood, standing as you do to others in the delicate relation of husband and father, presses upon my feelings with a weight which I can neither resist nor express. If in the discharge of this most painful duty I should, in portraying some of the horrid circumstances of this case, make use of strong language to express the enormity of your guilt and deep depravity which it indicates, I desire you to rest assured it is not with any intention of wounding your feelings nor for the purpose of adding one pang to your afflictions which the righteous hand of an offended God is pressing so heavily upon you.

It is to endeavor, if possible, to soften your heart and produce a reformation in your feelings, that by contrition and repentance you may be enabled to shun a punishment infinitely more dreadful than any that can be inflicted upon you by human laws — the eternal and irretrievable ruin of your soul. From the testimony which was given on the trial in your case there is no room for doubt the certainty of your guilt or the aggravated circumstances attending the commission of the bloody deed.

The man you murdered was your friend, you had spent most of the Sabbath day upon which you killed him in his company. In an unsuspecting hour, when he no doubt was treating you as a trusted friend, you stole upon him unperceived, you aimed the deadly weapon at his head and with the fatal knife you literally hacked his throat to pieces and with these fatal instruments of death you mangled, you murdered your victim.

But your guilt and your depravity did not stop here. Scarcely had you committed the bloody deed before you entered upon the commission of another crime, you converted to your possession, as spoils of the murder, your victim's money.

To the crime of murder you added that of larceny or, at common law, robbery.

The punishment of death has been pronounced against the crime of murder, not only by the laws of civilized nations, but also by that law which was written by the pen of inspiration, under the dedication of the Most High. And as God himself has prescribed the righteous penalty for this offense, so there is strong reason to believe that very few murders are committed which are not ultimately discovered and the wickedest perpetrators finally, if not by the law, by some other agency, brought to merited punishment. I must say to you, debased and unfortunate man! In vain was this most foul and horrible deed perpetrated where no human eye saw it. In vain did you try to get away from the mangled body of your victim without being discovered.

You forgot that the eye of your God was fixed upon you, the eye of that God who suffers not the sparrow to fall without His notice.

You forgot that you were in the presence of Him to whom the light of day and the darkness of night [are] all the same, that He witnessed all your movements, that by His inscrutable will it is that this dark and bloody deed has been portrayed to the minds of men. His vengeance has at last overtaken you. The sword of human justice trembles over you and is about to fall upon your guilty head.

It will not be long until you will be compelled to take your final leave of this world and enter upon the untried retributions of a never ending eternity.

And I beg of you not to delude yourself with the vain hope of pardon or escape from the sentence of the law.

In my judgment your destiny in this world is fixed and your fate is inevitable.

Let me therefore entreat you by every motive, temporal and eternal, to reflect upon your present condition and the certain death that awaits you.

There is but One who can pardon your offenses, there is one Savior whose blood is sufficient to wash from your soul the guilty stain even of a thousand murders.

Let me therefore beg of you to fly to Him for that mercy and pardon which you cannot expect of mortals.

When you return to the solitude of your prison let me entreat you by all that is still dear to you in time, by all that is dreadful in the retribution of eternity, that you seriously reflect upon the conduct of your past life. Bring to your mind all the aggravated horrors of that dreadful hour when the soul of the murdered Turner was sent, unprepared, into the presence of its God where you must shortly meet it as an accusing spirit against you. Bring to your recollection the mortal struggles and dying groans of your murdered victim.

Recollect the horror that seized you after you had committed the deed and were getting away from the place where it was committed, when you beheld the son of that victim.

Remember the terrible agony of your soul when, with the dead father in sight, you met the son with a falsehood upon your lips.

Think of the dreadful agony of the unnatural widow-hood to which you have reduced the unfortunate partner of your bed and bosom. Think upon your poor orphan child which is now to be left fatherless in the mercy of the world.

And when, by such reflections as these, your heart shall become softened, let me again beseech you before your blood stained hands are raised in supplication before the judgment seat of Christ, that you fly for mercy to the arms of the Savior and endeavor to seize upon the salvation of His cross.

Listen now to the dreadful sentence of the law and then farewell forever until the court and you and all here today shall meet together in the general resurrection.

Thus was Parker's address on Saturday, June 26, 1875, to the first man he sentenced to hang. Similarly he would address many more unfortunates over his twenty-one years with the Western District Court. The text is verbatim—except for added commas, a spelling correction, and a word insertion—from the June 30, 1875, edition of *The New Era*.

WILLIAM J. WHITTINGTON

William J. Whittington was one of eight men convicted of murder in the spring session of the Western District Court. Of the convicted, one would be shot attempting to escape and one would have his sentence commuted to life in the federal prison at Joliet, Illinois. The remaining six were executed on September 3, 1875, in the largest mass hanging Fort Smith had seen.

Whittington was a white man about thirty years old, "of dark and sinister aspect," a resident of Pickens County in the Chickasaw Nation near the Red River. He had a wife and two children.

On Sunday, February 7, 1875, Whittington had gone with his neighbor, J. J. Turner, to a "dram shop" or Texas "whiskey ranch" and spent the day drinking. Turner had received one hundred dollars while at the tavern, and the two men had started home, both inebriated. As they neared their homes, Whittington knocked Turner from his horse, cut his throat, and took his money.

Turner's son had ridden out to meet his father and, near a crossing of the Red River, saw Whittington standing near two horses. When Whittington saw young Turner approaching, he mounted and fled. The younger Turner pursued and almost succeeded in capturing his father's killer, but Whittington escaped into Texas, where he was soon captured.

Two newspaper articles give different accounts of the evidence, one saying that Whittington's bloody knife was found on him, the other that the knife was found near where the body lay. Nevertheless, it was found with blood on it and a hundred-dollar and a five-dollar bill were found in his possession and identified as belonging to Turner.

Reportedly, the jury spent little time on June 16, 1875, in finding John Whittington guilty of murder.

After Judge Parker had given the prisoner his long and fervent address, he pronounced sentence in a similar way ending with the words, "And may that God, whose laws you have broken and before whose dread tribunal you must then appear, have mercy on you."

DANIEL EVANS

The next man to appear that Saturday afternoon was Tennessee native Daniel Evans, twenty years old. He had been convicted of killing William R. Seabolt near Eufaula, Choctaw Nation.

Evans and Seabolt had been riding together from Dennison, Texas, and were seen together just before Seabolt's disappearance. Shortly after the murder, Evans was seen riding Seabolt's horse and leading his own. The horse, which he later gave to his counsel as a fee, would become part of the evidence against him. Seabolt's body was found a week after the murder and identified by a patch that he wore over one eye and by a memorandum book that listed his name and all of his family.

Evans wore his victim's boots even after his arrest, and those boots were among the deciding factors in evidence. Seabolt's father testified that before his son had left Texas, they had bought identical pairs of boots, even to the size. The son's boot heel had come off, and he had gone to a blacksmith and had it nailed on with horseshoe nails. The description matched the boots Evans had, and those, along with the horse and other items of Seabolt's, were enough to convict him.

Judge Parker addressed Evans briefly and with feeling told him to prepare for death. He then pronounced the sentence of death by hanging on September 3, 1875. Evans bowed and said flippantly, "Thankye," turned and began laughing and joking.

The court that day was "a most impressive scene." The deputies brought the prisoners in two by two, surrounded by a strong guard with pistols drawn. Those precautions had been taken because a few days before, Frank Butler, a convicted murderer, had been killed while running from a guard. The prisoners were seated within the railing and were free from shackles. The courtroom was packed with spectators in anticipation of the event and "an impressive and ominous silence prevailed."

Both Evans and Whittington were taken back to the prison, and two more prisoners were brought in.

EDMUND CAMPBELL

The next man to face Judge Parker was Edmund Campbell, a black man, twenty years old, born and raised near Scullyville in the Choctaw Nation. He and his fourteen-year-old brother, Sam, and half brother, Frank Butler, had gone to the home of Lawson Ross in the Cherokee Nation on February 18, 1875. Their purpose had been to avenge some wrong supposedly done their father and mother by Ross. There they killed both Ross and a young girl.

Campbell and Butler were both convicted of murder but Butler was killed a few days before the sentencing while attempting to escape. When asked by Parker why the sentence of death should not be pronounced upon him, Campbell replied that he did not think that it was worthwhile to say anything but blamed the killing on Butler. The judge then sentenced the prisoner to hang on the same day as the rest, September 3, 1875.

JAMES MOORE

James Moore, a native of Johnson County, Missouri, twenty-eight years old and more than six feet tall, was next to come before the bench. Moore had sold some cattle in Washington County, Arkansas, about a year before, but before he left, he, along with a man named Hunton, stole horses from an old, crippled man named Cox. The neighbors of Cox gave chase and followed the thieves 200 miles through Indian Territory.

In the Territory, the pursuers were joined by Captain Irwin, a former deputy U.S. marshal, and John T. Spivey. The posse came upon the thieves at a little creek near the Red River where the latter opened fire. Spivey was killed instantly, and Moore badly wounded Irwin. Hunton and Moore were captured and put in jail at Fort Smith in October 1874. Hunton later escaped, only to be killed in a quarrel with a like character in the Territory.

Moore had a wife and two children who had moved from Texas and were living near Fort Smith. His mother, seventy-nine years old, was still living in Texas and a few days earlier had come to visit her son, who was the youngest of a large family. His grandmother, 105 years old, was still living in Kentucky. Also, several brothers and sisters were living respectable lives in northern Texas. Since boyhood, Moore had led a rough life as a cattle herder, had been in many fights with Indians, and associated generally with "a hard set of fellows" until he ended up in his final situation.

Judge Parker, "after a very pathetic [emotional] address" sentenced Moore, as he had those before him, to hang on September 3, 1875. Moore and Campbell were then removed back to the prison.

SMOKER MANKILLER

Next to come before the judge was a man who lived up to his name: Smoker Mankiller. Mankiller was Cherokee, about nineteen years old, married and had one child. He was "medium sized, full faced, thick lipped, the coarse hair of intense dull blackness, face pock marked and yellowish tinted, dark eyes and countenance apathetic and apparently listless." He stood before the bench with eyes downcast, pivoting first one foot then the other on the heel.

Mankiller had been convicted of killing a white man named William Short on September 1, 1874, in the Flint District about forty miles north of Fort Smith. He had also killed another Cherokee but was tried and acquitted by the Cherokee court, it being a crime by a Cherokee against a Cherokee in their own nation. According to *The New Era*, "There never is anyone convicted in the nation for such a trifle as killing anybody...." Mankiller believed that his present conviction was the result of prejudice.

William Short had been out hunting, and as he rode by Mankiller's home, Mankiller and his brother spotted him. Mankiller stopped Short and asked to see his gun. When handed the gun, he backed up a few steps and shot Short with his own gun. Short was not killed by the shot and tried to escape, but Mankiller chased him down and stabbed him. Others witnessed the whole affair, and Mankiller bragged afterward of his deed. He was promptly arrested by deputy U.S. marshals, and on June 2, 1875, he was convicted of murder.

On June 26, 1875, Judge Parker handed down to Mankiller the sentence of hanging, to be carried out on September 3, 1875. The whole address and sentencing was interpreted, sentence by sentence, by Jackson King. When told, as the other condemned were, to prepare for death and to select a minister to prepare him for his fate, Mankiller declared emphatically that he wanted no minister to come near him.

OSCAR SNOW

One more man, Oscar Snow, received the death sentence on that day, June 26, 1875, but because his story has a different ending, it will be reserved until later.

SAMUEL FOOY

On Monday, June 28, 1875, Judge Parker returned to the bench, and on that day sentenced Samuel Fooy to hang on September 3, 1875.

John Emmett Naff of Leavenworth, Kansas, known as "the barefoot school teacher," taught school near Tahlequah in Indian Territory from February to July 1872. On July 16, he was paid $200 and started toward the Salt Works on the Illinois River. He spent the night of July 17 at the home of Captain C. R. Stevenson, deputy U.S. marshal. On leaving the next morning, Naff presented a five-dollar bill to pay for his lodging, but Mrs. Stevenson had no change. Naff promised to leave the amount due, fifty cents, at the store at the Salt Works and left carrying a small satchel in the company of Samuel Fooy. Naff was never seen again.

Some weeks later, Fooy confided to family members that he had killed the schoolteacher. Still later, Fooy let his secret slip, this time to "a woman of easy virtue." But for the time being, everyone kept his secret.

About a year after the schoolteacher disappeared, a man named Roach found a skeleton under a high bluff near the Illinois River. The victim had been shot from behind, and the bullet was retrieved from the bone near the nose. Roach reported his find, and conjecture began as to whose skeleton it might be. The chain of evidence began to point to Fooy and his victim.

In the spring of 1874, a young Indian boy out hunting approached the spot where the skeleton had lain. Looking down from the bluff, he saw something protruding from under a rock. On investigation, he

31

found a partly burned page of a book. Under the rock he found the rest of the book with the name "John Emmett Naff, Leavenworth, Kansas," in elaborate German script. Also written in the book was a quotation in Latin from the poet Horace apropos of Naff's fate: *"Pallida mors aequo pede pauperum taberuas Regumque turres,"* which translates as, "Pale death, with impartial tread, beats at the poor man's cottage or at the palaces of kings." Other papers and articles further confirmed that the skeleton found was that of Naff. Fooy denied his guilt during the trial, but his previous confessions and the circumstantial evidence were enough to convict him.

Judge Parker addressed Fooy in the same manner that he had the other condemned and sentenced him to die on the same day as the others. Fooy took his sentence calmly and was returned to the prison where he "was received uproariously by the other six condemned."

Samuel Fooy was born in Fort Smith during his parents' temporary residence in the city. His father was white and his mother part Cherokee. In 1860, his sister, Alice Fooy, had attended the school established by Valentine Dell, editor of *The New Era*, the first co-ed school in Fort Smith.

Fooy was the last of seven men sentenced to hang by Judge Parker in his first judicial session. There had been eight men convicted of murder and eligible for the death sentence, but only six would hang. Frank Butler and Oscar Snow, although by very different means, avoided the rope.

FRANK BUTLER

Frank Butler, half brother of Edmund Campbell, had been convicted of murder along with Campbell and, but for his premature death, would have been hanged with the others. *The Weekly New Era* on Wednesday, June 16, 1875, published this article:

ESCAPED THE GALLOWS

Last Monday night, about nine o'clock, as Frank Butler, a colored man from the Choctaw Nation, recently convicted of murder in the U.S. Court but not yet sentenced, was being taken from the prison to the courtroom above to testify in the case of another colored man on trial for assault with intent to kill, he broke away from the guard on the steps just outside the courtroom and ran toward the north gate, to the right of which was a pile of rocks by means of which the man evidently intended to scale the wall, the gate being locked and the steps to the left of the gate occupied by more than a dozen people. Captain Kidder Kidd and Maj. Cavanaugh, who had charge of the prisoner, immediately opened fire on him and when within a few steps of the pile of rocks a bullet struck him in the back of the head and crashed through his brain, dropping him dead. Butler was a bad African and would undoubtedly have stretched hemp, having been convicted, with another man, of cold blooded murder of a man and his wife in the Choctaw Nation. His death is a good riddance.

History has given credit to George Maledon for the killing of Butler. However, in the numerous times that the three newspapers of the day mentioned the incident, never once did they mention Maledon's name. Also, there was never any mention of Butler's parents waiting outside the wall for him and taking away the body as history has reported. All of those things might have happened, but the contemporary newspapers never reported a word of it. What the newspapers did report, though, was the list of grand and petit jurors. Maledon's name appears in the list of petit jurors for that term of court.

OSCAR SNOW

Oscar Snow was the last of the men sentenced Saturday, June 26, 1875, to hang and the only one to escape the gallows by commutation of sentence. It has been said that Snow was commuted because of his age, and that was probably a factor; however, several people his age and younger (John Pointer, eighteen, Isaac Filmore, sixteen) were hanged. Also a factor, he and his witnesses testified that although Snow was a conspirator, Henry Lewis actually did the deed for which Snow was convicted.

Oscar Snow, eighteen years old, blue eyes, brown hair, fair face, tall and slender, lived in the Choctaw Nation, where he and Henry Lewis had "become pretty intimate" with George Beauchamp's wife and another girl living with the Beauchamps. The four had, on a Monday in the early spring of 1874, conspired to kill George Beauchamp. And on the following Friday, Snow and Lewis carried out their plan.

Snow and Lewis went to the field where Beauchamp was planting, and Lewis shot him while Snow stood by. The murderers then went back to the house and "to the wicked women." They later returned to the field, dragged the body to a furrow, and left it for twenty-four hours, as "the faithless wife" testified. Lewis, the real murderer, escaped and at the time of the sentencing had not been seen. Snow was arrested on November 9, 1874, and convicted on Monday, June 7, 1875.

At the sentencing Snow tried to appear unconcerned. While Judge Parker spoke, Snow's mother stood outside on the porch listening to her son being sentenced to be "hanged by the neck until dead." At that moment there was "a piercing shriek from without." The two prisoners were returned to the jail, and as soon as the iron door was locked, the mother thrust her arms through the bars and, sobbing, pressed her face to her son's through the opening. She then threw herself on the breast of Marshal Fagan and implored him to save her son.

From the time of conviction on, there was a movement to get Snow either a pardon or commutation of sentence. The efforts were eventually successful, and Snow's sentence was commuted to life in prison. On September 1, 1875, *The New Era* announced that Oscar Snow would shortly be taken to the federal prison at Joliet, Illinois. And on September 8, 1875, the same publication announced, "Capt. James McIntosh left last Friday with Oscar Snow in his charge for Joliet, Illinois."

CHAPTER 6

"THE BLACK CAP

The Black Gown
Six Men Atone For Crime
5,000 People Present
The Crime Committed in the Indian Country
ARKANSAS NOT RESPONSIBLE
Bad Men will be Punished, Good Men will Punish them.
Justice is Slow, Justice is Sure!
The Eye of Man may be closed. The Eye Of God is always open.
LET JUSTICE BE DONE!"
(*The Weekly Herald*, Fort Smith, September 4, 1875)

The first six men to hang during Judge Isaac C. Parker's tenure as judge for the Western District of Arkansas: William J. Whittington, Smoker Mankiller, Edmund Campbell, Samuel Fooy, James Moore, and Daniel Evans.

As shown by these headlines and subheads, Fort Smith proclaimed loudly that the crimes were committed elsewhere and that while Arkansans might "have to bear the name and the blame" they would show "that the people of Arkansas will hold up to the penalty of the law, all offenders against it."

At nine thirty the morning of Friday, September 3, 1875, the six condemned men emerged from the guardhouse two by two. But a crowd had been gathering on the grounds since before seven thirty and was estimated to total more than 5,000. The fire department was there to keep order, and Marshal Fagan allowed no armed person inside the walls. "The strictest order and decorum was observed."

The press was well represented with reporters from the *Kansas City Times*, *The St. Louis Times*, the *Missouri Republican*, *The Globe Democrat*,

35

The Booneville Enterprise, The Fort Smith Independent, The New Era, The Weekly Herald, and from Muskogee in Indian Territory, The Associated Press.

Early that morning, the prisoners had had their shackles cut off, been bathed and dressed, and had a hearty breakfast. About that time the ropes were being put in place on the gallows and some doubts were expressed as to their "efficiency." The ropes were thoroughly tested (the testing procedure was not explained) and found to be sufficient for the occasion, and all was declared in readiness.

The prisoners, under the supervision of Marshal Fagan, exited the prison in pairs and, with guards on both sides and the ministers leading the way, started their procession across the grounds to the gallows about 150 yards away. On arriving at the gallows, they went quickly up the steps without manifesting fear or emotion. The condemned men were then seated on a bench at the rear of the platform, and the death warrants were read for each man. Majors Blanks and Pierce, U.S. jailers, read the warrants with Jackson King, Cherokee, interpreting for Smoker Mankiller. After the warrants were read, the prisoners were asked if they had anything to say.

These are the statements of the men in the order that they stood on the gallows:

James Moore said, "I have lived like a man and I will die like a man. I am prepared." He went on to thank the people of the town for their kindness to him and to wish the Heavenly Father to bless them.

Samuel Fooy said, "I am as anxious to get out of this world as the people who have sent me here today are to see me. I will not delay you."

Daniel Evans stated that he had participated in other robberies and killings but made no confession to Seabolt's murder.

Edmund Campbell protested his innocence and said, "I did not shoot anyone. I am innocent and ready to die."

William J. Whittington said nothing on the gallows but had previously admitted his guilt and had written a letter, which he asked to be read by Reverend Grenade. The letter was long and expressed how his father had taught him to be honest and avoid the sins of the world. But, he did not teach him to be a Christian. Furthermore, he had set the example for him of drunkenness. Whittington said that when he was drunk he knew not what he was doing and would have killed his own brother. He lamented then the fate of his wife and children and admonished all to "leave off drinking" and parents to "train up your children in the way they should go."

Smoker Mankiller stated that he had little to say and that he was ready to die. He still denied his guilt and blamed his conviction on prejudice and false testimony.

After the prisoners' remarks, religious services were performed by Father Lawrence Smythe of the Catholic Church for Moore and Evans, and for the remaining four, Reverends Sample, Babcock and Grenade. At the request of the condemned men, the following hymns were sung: "Jesus Lover of My Soul," "Come Let Us Join our Friends Above," and "Nearer My God to Thee." Then came a benediction by Reverend Grenade.

The prisoners then rose, shook hands with all who were on the scaffold, expressed their wishes to meet them in a better world, and reaffirmed their willingness to die.

The handcuffs were removed from one hand of each prisoner and the black robes drawn over their bodies. The manacles were again replaced on both hands and their arms pinioned back with strong cords. In that condition they moved forward onto the trap. The nooses were slipped over their heads and the black caps placed on. "Lord Jesus receive me," was uttered by one of the men, the lever was moved, and the trap fell.

Fooy, Mankiller, Moore, and Evans died almost instantly. The bodies hung for about twenty minutes when they were all pronounced dead by Doctors Bailey, Bennett, DuVal, Maine, Boothe, Eberle, Price, and West. They were then cut down and delivered to their friends. By eleven that morning, it was over.

These were the first hangings under Judge Parker's administration and would be the last until April 21, 1876, about seven and a half months later.

CHAPTER 7

"DOOMED

Six Men Condemned To
Die At One Time

Four Indians, One Negro
And One Paleface"
(*The Fort Smith New Era*, February 9, 1876)

On Saturday, February 5, 1876, six men faced Judge Isaac C. Parker to hear themselves condemned to die on April 21, 1876. The six men were: Aaron Wilson, black; Isham Seeley, Chickasaw; Gibson Ishtonubbee, Chickasaw; Orpheus McGee, Choctaw; Osey Sanders, Cherokee; and William Leach, white.

Judge Parker addressed the first man in the same tone and with many of the same sentences as he had John Whittington on Saturday, June 26, 1875.

Virginia native Aaron Wilson, "a full blooded negro" of "Herculean strength," stood immobile before the bench, betraying no emotion while he listened to the judge's address. When asked if he had anything to say before the court pronounced sentence on him, he said he had applied for witnesses who did not appear and on whose testimony he had relied and that he was not guilty of the charges against him. After Wilson's remarks, the court resumed with Judge Parker describing Wilson's crime in picturesque language and admonishing him to seek redemption, as he had others before him.

The subpoenas for witnesses in this case are interesting. One was issued October 9, 1875, for "Four persons whose names are unknown...in a certain cause pending, and then and there to be tried, between the United States of America and One Wilson." Another, issued December 15, 1875, lists eight people and "2 persons whose names are unknown." Its reverse side has a note that says, "Not served."

Wilson had served five years in the U.S. Army, having been discharged about a year previously in Indian Territory. He was convicted of the murders of James Harris and John Franklin Harris, father and son, near the Wichita Agency in Indian Territory. The Harrises were traveling to Texas through Indian Territory on their wagon loaded with goods. Wilson followed them for some distance and then at night killed the father, John, while he slept. The son, James Franklin Harris, about twelve years old, awakened to the killing of his father and tried to escape. According to the reports, Wilson overtook him after a chase of about 175 yards. While the young boy pleaded for his life, Wilson shot him. One report said the boy was "literally riddled with buckshot."

The New Era reporter may have taken some journalistic liberty in his detailed description of the killing. The only living witness would have been Wilson, and he denied any involvement in the incident. The grand jury's true bill says only that he shot both victims and cut the throat of James Harris.

After the murders, Wilson took the horses from the wagon, hid the wagon and dressed himself in clothes that he took from the wagon. He gathered some other loot and went to the Wichita Agency, where he told the Indians that he had taken the things from two white men he had killed. Based on his assessment of Indian character, he had the mistaken belief his acts would recommend him to them. The Indians, however, were repulsed by his deeds and reported him to their agent.

Wilson later denied all knowledge of the killings, but the circumstantial evidence was enough to remove all doubt of his guilt. A brother of the murdered Harris identified the stolen property. And then there was the dog. Harris's dog had followed his owner's horses and belongings after his master had been murdered. The dog was introduced as evidence and identified by Harris's brother.

After Judge Parker's address and the sentencing, Wilson was escorted back to the prison under a "very strong force of Deputy Marshals." He had expressed that he would risk death by being shot attempting to escape rather than by hanging.

THREE INDIANS

Next to enter the courtroom were Isham Seeley, Gibson Ishtonubbee, and Orpheus McGee. The New Era was most unkind in its description of these men:

> The appearance of these three children of Lo would sadly disappoint those whose knowledge of the noble red man is derived solely from Cooper's stories or similar creations of fiction. In fact they were a shabby set; two of them under-sized, the third large and burly; all of an indefinable dirty color, with a very small amount of intelligence discernible in their physiognomies. It was plain that the brute predominated in their organizations fitting them for the heinous deeds they will have to suffer death for.

Another description is more benign, simply saying that Seeley and Ishtonubbee could be mistaken for brothers, being about the same age and height, about five feet, eight inches, "not remarkable for blood-thirsty or ferocious countenance." Both Seeley and Ishtonubbee were about the same age, about twenty-five.

In a letter written on March 10, 1875, to the U.S. commissioner, the local law officer at Stonewall, Chickasaw Nation, was no more complimentary of Seeley and Ishtonubbee. In it, T. J. Phillips says:

Sir,
 The parties the Dept. wrote about are here and don't think there is any dout [sic] but what they did the killing. They are bad men and don't due [sic] anything but steal. I would like to have them taken to Ft. Smith. I think the evidence is Sufficient to convict them.

Respectfully,
T. J. Phillips

SEELEY AND ISHTONUBBEE

Isham Seeley and George Ishtonubbee were tried for the same crime, the murder of an Indian doctor named Funny and his cook, a black woman named Mason. Had it not been for the murder of the woman, a U.S. citizen, their trial would not have been in the federal court because the tribal court tried crimes by an Indian against an Indian in their own tribal area.

Nearly four years before the sentencing, the two men had gone to the home of Funny, near Stonewall in the Chickasaw Nation. Reportedly, they had threatened Funny's life sometime in the past. Nevertheless, they had gone to the old man's home to stay all night and had been accepted. During the night, Ishtonubbee split the doctor's head with an axe, and Seeley beat the woman to death with a gun barrel that was used to prop the door shut. A nephew of Funny, Chiwaha, found the bodies of the victims the next day. He and Baptiste Williams, a grandson of Funny, were chief witnesses.

Seeley and Ishtonubbee's loot consisted of a few articles of clothing, boots, a dress, and a pair of pants. Next morning after the killings, the murderers told other Indians near their home that the items belonged to Funny and that they had killed him. They later burned the items, and their neighbors kept their secret. The criminals might have gone free if Ishtonubbee had not told Kitsie Cobb, a woman with whom he lived, of the incident. The two later had a disagreement, and Cobb turned the murderers in.

Both Kitsie Cobb and Batiste Williams gave depositions before the U.S. commissioner that agree in every way with the newspaper reports of the events.

When the murderers were asked if they had anything to say as to why sentence should not be pronounced on them, Ishtonubbee said that he had been convicted by malicious testimony and that he never killed anyone. Seeley said that he could say nothing that would do him any good. Neither showed any emotion when sentence was pronounced. The entire proceeding was carried out with Major John Page, a Choctaw, acting as interpreter.

ORPHEUS MCGEE

Orpheus McGee, Choctaw, about twenty-three years old, was next to stand for sentencing. Judge Parker announced that a motion in his behalf for a new trial had been overturned and that the address that he had made to the other two Indians was intended for him as well.

McGee and his brothers, David and Charles, lived near the mouth of Boggy Creek on the Red River in Choctaw Nation. The three, along with their brother-in-law, Moses Homer, were "known throughout the country as a wild and reckless set of men." Also in that area lived the Alexander brothers, Robert and W. V., white men, who often aided the authorities against the McGees and other lawless types.

About April 20 or 22, 1875, the three McGees and Moses Homer murdered and robbed Robert Alexander within a mile and a half of his house. One report says Alexander left the home of a Mr. Miller a little before dark to shoot wild turkeys that he had heard. A short time later, Miller heard a gunshot. He waited supper on Alexander until after dark. The next morning, Miller and W. V. Alexander found Robert's body where he had been shot, apparently by someone on horseback.

The McGee brothers bragged to friends of their deeds, and a few months later Orpheus was arrested. Some of the dead man's belongings, his guns, were found in the possession of Orpheus McGee. Moses Homer was killed in the attempt to capture him. David McGee was brought in during November 1875, just after Orpheus had been shot four times while trying to escape from the federal jail. David McGee was tried and cleared of the murder charge. Charles McGee was killed by law officers who were trying to arrest him for another offense.

OSEY SANDERS

Osey Sanders was the next to face Judge Parker that Saturday in February 1876. His crime was detailed in *The New Era* in a Victorian verbiage and style that modern language cannot compare to. So the details of his crime will be related verbatim, misspellings, punctuations and all, as it appeared on February 9, 1876.

Osea Sanders, a full blood young Cherokee, middle size, light complexioned, stood up, considerably agitated. His case is a very bad one, he being convicted of a most

HORRIBLE, REVOLTING
AND FIENDISH MURDER.

On August 6th, 1875, he in company of one Wm. Matier, also Cherokee, approached the house of an old neighbor, Thos. H. Carlisle, a white man, but married to a Cherokee woman.

Carlisle was an intelligent, industrious farmer in very good circumstances, living about 50 miles north of this place, near the State line in Cherokee nation. He was sitting on the porch of his house, after the day's labor, in the cool of the evening, in company with his wife, who was in very delicate health, and several children. He directed a little son to step down and open the gate for the young men, who were well known to all the family, the latter rising from their seats and offering them to their visitors.

But, oh, horrible to relate, the pen almost refuses to record the hellish deed, which immediately thereafter took place and changed a scene of domestic peace and happiness into one of blood, crime, and despair. For on reaching the porch the two fiends, who had kept their weapons in readiness, with the utmost premeditation deliberately, shot down their unsuspecting host before the eyes of his

HORROR STRUCK FAMILY.

A more treacherous savage deed was rarely ever perpetrated.

The poor wife and children fled in despair to the fields. Late in the night they got some neighbors to return with them to their dwelling and found their husband and father cold in death at the foot of the porch. The fiends had also taken off with them about fifteen hundred dollars in national Cherokee scrip, and among some other articles, the shoes off the feet of the murdered man, and which were found two days afterwards on the feet of Sanders.

The Weekly Herald tells essentially the same story with only slight variations, such as naming a daughter who opened the gate and stating that Mrs. Carlisle returned with her children instead of going to and returning with neighbors.

Cherokee authorities captured Sanders on August 8, two days after the murder, and turned him over to U.S. authorities. "Sanders was identified by Mrs. Carlisle, who, to add to the terrors of that fearful night, was delivered of a child." The Carlisle children also identified Sanders. Sanders's accomplice, Matier, was killed in the attempt to capture him.

When asked if he had anything to say before sentence was pronounced upon him, Sanders professed ignorance of the crime and said he was convicted by false testimony, that he felt he was innocent, and that his mind was perfectly easy as to the future.

The court then addressed him "very earnestly" and sentenced him to hang on the same day, April 21, as the others.

Between February and April 21, Cherokee authorities made "strenuous efforts" to get Sanders taken from U.S. Court jurisdiction and tried by a Cherokee Court. Their argument was that the victim was an adopted citizen of the Nation and, therefore, the tribe had jurisdiction. *The New Era* on May 3, 1876, expressed this opinion; "Should this ruse be successful, Sanders will very probably not only go free, but it will establish the fact, that other Indians hung for murdering white men, adopted citizens, in the Territory, suffered death unlawfully and every white man in the Territory is at the mercy of an Indian assassin."

WILLIAM LEACH

Last to face the judge that day was a white man, about thirty-five, native of Georgia, "whose intelligent countenance strikingly contrasted with the stolid, apathetic or brutal features of his fellow prisoners. He served in Fort Pillow Forrest's command during the rebellion and his cold, steel gray eye denotes him to be a resolute, dangerous man" (*The New Era*, February 9, 1876).

William Leach showed some emotion and nervousness on entering the courtroom and glanced around the densely packed room. As those condemned before him had, he professed innocence and blamed his conviction on false and malicious testimony. His motion for a new trial had been overruled.

Leach had lived in the Cherokee Nation for several years, about twenty-five miles from Fayetteville, near the state line. He had moved his family there from Georgia after he had traveled through the Indian Territory and Colorado.

He had served the Thirty-ninth Georgia Infantry and was wounded three times at Jonesboro, Georgia. He was transferred to the First Georgia, where he stayed until the surrender. He went back to farming, but was captured by some men dressed as Federals, but claiming to be Rebels, who robbed him. He followed them to Chattanooga, Tennessee, where they were arrested and his property restored.

After that, he was charged with the murder of his wife's brother and a man named Quarels, but was acquitted. He claimed that if he had ever killed anyone, it had been in battle. He also said that he had lived peaceably in the Territory and had no trouble with the law. However, in the proceedings of the U.S. Court, as reported in *The Weekly Herald* on June 28, 1873, "June 19, U.S. v. Wm. Leach, retail liquor dealer and selling liquor to Indians, jury verdict, guilty." And on July 28, 1873, "July 11, U.S. v. Wm. Leach, selling liquor to Indians and retail liquor dealer not paying tax—sentenced six months in penitentiary at Little Rock and fined $1000 and costs." So, his veracity is questionable at the least.

On March 8, 1875, in the Cherokee Nation, Leach murdered a white man named H. Watkins, a wagon maker and resident of Washington County, Arkansas. The two had started from Cincinnati, Arkansas, together, Leach on foot and Watkins riding. They had stopped at Freeman's blacksmith shop west of Cincinnati, where it was noted by two people that Leach wore shoes and Watkins, boots. Watkins had been in possession of a violin and a small four-barrel pistol and Leach, a gun.

About eight miles west of Cincinnati, Leach shot Watkins from behind, dragged the body to a large log, piled brush on it, and set it afire. The body was not found until April 9, 1875. The fire had not consumed all of the articles. Identification was made by scraps of clothing, like what Watkins was known to have been wearing—part of a violin bow, screwdriver, pistol, and boots. It required the testimony of seventeen witnesses to make the chain of evidence complete.

William Leach was convicted December 14, 1875. The following is the description of that scene as reported by *The Weekly Herald* on December 25, 1875:

> Convicted. On Monday morning the jury in the case of U.S. vs. Leach, murder, came into court with a verdict of guilty.
>
> The wife of the convicted man was in court when the verdict was read, and to describe her feelings, and manifestation of distress and agony, when she heard it, is beyond our ability just now.
>
> If guilty, the anguish of that loving wife and her boy must be more than death to the husband and fa-

ther; if innocent, he can only feel that in his conviction, she has been robbed of him, who would protect and comfort her.

The scene in court on that occasion will not soon be forgotten by those there, and they will tell it to others, until it may reach many now steeped in crime, to whom it may serve as a warning, that if not for ourselves, for those we love, and who love us; we should shun evil company.

Mrs. Leach, for days before the execution, begged the marshal to allow her to spend a night in the prison. That request he refused for, among other reasons, there had been threats of rescuing the prisoners.

Leach himself, however, received his sentence without evidence of emotion and was returned to the prison below the courtroom where he and the other condemned were soon observed "enjoying their dinner with evident relish."

THE GIBBET
A LIFE FOR A LIFE

So announced *The Weekly Herald*, April 22, 1876, with the headline and fifteen subheads telling the history of hangings by the court and proclaiming, emphatically again, Fort Smith's innocence in the events. The fourteenth subhead announced:

The Sentence of Osey Sanders
Suspended by the President at the Eleventh Hour

On April 19, 1876, two days before Osey Sanders was to hang, this telegraphed message arrived:

> Washington D. C.
> April 19, 1876
>
> J. F. Fagan:
> I have this day granted reprieve to Osey Sanders, sentenced to be hanged on the 21st inst. Suspend the execution and acknowledge receipt.
> U.S. Grant

"So," as *The Weekly Herald* put it, "the sentence was suspended and the man was not." The sentence was remitted to June 2, 1876, then remitted again. However, they were only postponing the inevitable.

By dawn of April 21, 1876, all of the approaches to Fort Smith were crowded with people coming to witness the execution. They represented all ethnic groups from the surrounding area and the Territory and were estimated to number from 3,000 to 5,000. U.S. District Marshal J. F. Fagan made sufficient preparations to deal with such a crowd and prevent escape or rescue. Deputy Marshal W. S. Whittington, in charge of a force of volunteers attached to the Marshals office, had things in such good order that the event passed off in orderly fashion.

The scaffold was enclosed around the area in which the court officers, guards, and others were permitted. On the scaffold preparations were made for the accommodation of clergy and press.

The press was represented by the three local papers, *The Gazette* of Little Rock, two papers from St. Louis, and *The Chicago Times.*

At eleven o'clock that morning, the signal was given and the prison doors opened. The five doomed men, in irons, started their walk to the gallows. They were escorted by a strong guard composed of Deputies Stirman, Wilkinson, Topping, Sharp, Rutherford, Twyman, Cox, Tinker, Neis, and Donnelly. The marshal was in front of the procession and in command, and the ministers preceded the prisoners. When the prisoners arrived at the scaffold, they ascended without showing fear or emotion and took their places with Wilson on the right and McGee on the left, the others in between, facing the crowd.

The sentence and death warrant was read to each man in order. William Leach's was read to him by G. W. Pierce, jailer; the sentence and warrant of the Indians, McGee, Seeley, and Ishtonubbee, was read by Ed Krebs, Chickasaw and Choctaw interpreter. Deputy Wilkinson read the sentence and warrant to Aaron Wilson, who could read and understand the English language. Only Leach showed any emotion.

From the scaffold the condemned men spoke to the crowd, Leach first. He admonished all not to do as he had and put off repentance too long. He forgave all and felt that he was forgiven.

McGee spoke next, expressing the same thoughts, that he was ready and willing to go and sure of salvation.

Ishtonubbee said that he did not fear anything ahead, he was prepared to exchange this world for the one to come, and his was the gain; he would lose his life but save his soul.

Seeley said that he had led a very bad life and, too late, was sorry. But, he had found mercy in coming to Christ for it. He warned parents to bring up their children right.

Aaron Wilson said he was not afraid to die and proclaimed his faith in the Catholic Church. He thanked all the officers for the way they had treated him. He forgave all and hoped to be forgiven.

At "11½ o'clock the formalities were over and the friends of the condemned shook hands all around and bid them a long last farewell.

The hoods, gowns and ropes were then put in place and at 11:53 o'clock the drop fell. Shortly thereafter the crowd began to disperse. The bodies hung for 16 minutes and then were examined by the physicians present: Dr. Worth Bailey, surgeon in charge, and seventeen assisting physicians."

It would be four and a half months before there was another hanging; Osey Sanders would be among them.

Note: Judge Parker had arrived in town on the day that the fall term of the court began. He had gone to St. Louis, Missouri, to visit his family. He had intended to bring his family along, "but for the arrival, not entirely unforeseen either, of a little stranger in his family who decided to remain for the present in loco. This happened last Friday week" (*The New Era*, September 29, 1875, birth occurred September 16, 1875).

CHAPTER 8

FOUR MORE EXECUTIONS

"Murder Cries Aloud for Vengeance"
(*The Weekly Herald*, September 9, 1876)

On Friday, September 8, 1876, for the second time that year, a procession of condemned men marched to the gallows. As *The New Era* stated under its headline, "Four Indians Stretch Hemp for the Murder of Four Whites in Oklahoma," only one of the four, John Valley, confessed and said he was worthy of his fate. The others claimed to be innocent victims and martyrs of the white man's cruel law. Only one, Osey Sanders, committed his crime for any significant monetary gain.

Osey Sanders had, by order of President Ulysses S. Grant, evaded the gallows April 21, 1876, and again on June 2. His argument and that of the Cherokee Nation court was that his victim was a Cherokee by adoption and marriage and the case was therefore subject to tribal law, not the U.S. District Court. His lawyers petitioned for a writ of habeas corpus on that premise on November 16, 1875, and were denied.

Failing in his argument of jurisdiction, Sanders went back to his original claim of ignorance. He said that he knew nothing of the crime until the day of his arrest, August 9, 1875, adding that he had been at home sick on the day of the murder. On November 17, 1875, Sanders petitioned for witnesses, and that request was granted. Among the witnesses he requested was Sallie Eagle. Eagle had already testified at the proceedings before the commissioner in August 1875 that she had been at Sanders's house on the day and evening Thomas Carlisle had been murdered. She said that Sanders had been sick in bed with a fever and that he had left only long enough to go to a neighbor's house for medicine. However, three of the witnesses who had testified at those proceedings earlier were recalled. They all said that Eagle was "a woman of bad character" and was known for "not being an honest woman." "Her general character for truth and honesty is very bad."

Sanders's lawyers did all that could be done for him but to no avail. His last petition for pardon was denied by the president. He was accordingly sentenced to hang on September 8, 1876.

On September 7, 1876, Sanders made a statement to the authorities detailing his version of his activities on the day of the crime and on the day of his arrest. On the day of his execution, about an hour before the prisoners were led to the gallows, he made an additional statement and requested that it be published in the newspapers. The statements were published the following week.

In his first statement, Sanders credited his attorneys, Duval and Cravens, for faithfully defending him and thanked jailer Major Pierce for his "uniform goodness" to him. He said he had no unkind feelings toward anyone and asked his friends not to "entertain any ill" toward those who had caused his death. All through his statement he expressed faith that he would see Jesus and said he had no fear of death.

> I am prepared to meet death. I am tired and want to sleep. Soon my troubles will be over and I will be where the wicked cease from troubling and the weary are at rest.

On September 8, 1876, Sanders declared he did not know "the least particle" about and was innocent of, the murder of Thomas Carlisle. He said that he first heard about the murder the day after it happened from a boy named Young Pig. He had just gotten up from bed, he and his children having been sick that day and the day before. He claimed that he and one of his children had a very high fever. Between the time he was informed of the murder and his arrest, he had gone to a neighbor's home for medicine but otherwise had been home.

While at the Carlisle home after his arrest, Sanders was sick and vomited. Sheriff Ross kept him there all night because he was too sick to travel. On arriving at Tahlequah in Indian Territory the next day, the sheriff got medicine for him, and they stayed there for two days. On the way to Fayetteville, Arkansas, Sanders was still sick.

He went on to say that Almighty God knew that his words were true and that if he had a confession to make, he would make it now and not wait until he got on the gallows. He later wrote to his friends, saying that if the real murderer were ever found that they "ought to let him alone—as I will pay for it with my death."

The fact, as the jury saw it, is that Sanders and his accomplice, Matier, killed Carlisle in the presence of his family for about $1,500 in cash and Cherokee scrip. Matier was killed while resisting capture but confessed before he died. Sanders, while on the way to Fort Smith, wanted to confess if he would be used as a witness and not be prosecuted.

Sanders was said to be a man of considerable influence in his tribe, and there were rumors that there were fears among some that on execution, he might make some confessions that would implicate others in "some deeds of darkness." However, he made no such confessions.

JOHN VALLEY

John Valley, a Peoria Indian about twenty-seven years old and married, was convicted of the murder of Eli Hacket, a white man, in the winter of 1873. Hacket, a few days before his murder, had a quarrel with a brother of Valley about an annuity due Hacket's daughter. Hacket's daughter by his Indian wife had been living with Valley's brother, and both men claimed the money. The Indian agent, on learning that the girl was Hacket's daughter, gave the money to Hacket. That disagreement apparently was the cause of the killing.

Hacket was visiting at the house of a man named John Beavers when John Valley went to the house. Valley, Hacket, Beavers, and his wife were seated around the fire engaged in conversation when Valley, without warning, shot Hacket. Valley fired twice, and at the first shot, Hacket jumped up and grabbed his breast and ran out. Valley then sat down and remained there for a few minutes.

Hacket made it to the gate of the home of Frank Boyer where he fell. "The inmates of the house, hearing some groaning, made a search and found him lying at the gate almost unconscious." They took him into the house and applied hot irons to his feet (a practice at that time to revive an unconscious person). Hacket had been at the Boyer house a short time when Valley came to the house. There he made attempts to shoot Hacket again but was thwarted by the people living at the house. Valley left the house, boasting to people he met along the way that he had shot Eli Hacket and that he "would learn him how to cheat his brother anymore." Hacket died about midnight of the next day.

All of the aforementioned incidents occurred in the winter of 1873, but Valley was not indicted until May 9, 1876. He was convicted on May 20, 1876, and sentenced on June 21, 1876, to hang on September 8, 1876.

SAMUEL PETERS

In October 1875, Sam Peters, a Choctaw, twenty-eight years old, went to the home of Frank Page and tried to trade for a pistol. He failed to make the trade and rode off in the direction of the home of a family named Hanson.

Peters and James Hanson had had a disagreement before, and Hanson had accused Peters of stealing. Peters went to the home while Hanson was away and murdered Charity Hanson, the wife, a white woman, while she held her four-month-old baby in her arms. She was found the next morning, still holding the crying baby. The condition of the crime scene showed that there had been a terrific struggle.

James Hanson described in his deposition the conditions he found when he returned home after receiving news of his wife's death. "I went home and found her dead, there was one big knife wound in her side, several wounds in her back, one in her arm and several small wounds in other parts of her body." Further on he says, "Blood was

50

scattered all around the room, there were evidences of having been a big struggle, my wife's elbows and knees had been skinned." Concerning the child, he said, "My child was four months old. When I came home it was in the cradle, its clothes were bloody."

Peters used every legal avenue to try to escape his conviction. As many defendants did, he petitioned for witnesses who would verify his alibi that he could not have been at Hanson's at the time of the murder. But his main defense was that he did not speak or understand the English language. In a long petition for retrial, he detailed how he was disadvantaged, by both being in jail and not speaking the language. However, some members of the arresting posse stated that he spoke English well enough when arrested. One posseman did state, though, that Peters told him through signs, which the posseman demonstrated during his deposition, that three others were involved in the crime. In all of his communications with the posse and his protestations to the court he, through his denials and accusations of other people, demonstrated knowledge of the crime he could not have had without being there.

All of the men involved in the arrest of Peters testified that he appeared to have blood on his pants. T. A. Summerhill, who appears to have been the arresting officer and the one who brought Peters to Fort Smith, stated, "When I arrested him he had a right smart of blood on his pants, and as we came along he stopped several times to urinate, in doing so he wet his pants and would rub the spots of blood." The pants were displayed at the time of Summerhill's testimony.

The evidence against Peters was circumstantial but it was enough to convince a jury to deliver a guilty verdict.

SINKER WILSON

Sinker Wilson, alias Flyer Wilson alias Acorn, a Cherokee, was described as appearing to be at least thirty years old but claimed to be twenty-two. That claim was made in an attempt to deny that he was the person who murdered Datus Cowan, a white boy, in 1867.

Wilson had been convicted of the murder of Cowan at the November 1867 term of court while it was known as the District Court of Arkansas. At that time, the court was located in Van Buren, Arkansas, and presided over by Judge Caldwell.

Wilson applied for four witnesses who he claimed could support his alibi. But if those witnesses appeared, they were insufficient to save him. Wilson was sentenced to hang on February 7, 1868, but escaped from the Van Buren jail. After his escape, he returned to his home in the Saline district, married, and continued his old habits. He lived free until April 1876, nearly nine years. Had it not been for the fact that he committed other offenses after his escape, he might have remained at large. He was suspected of burning a neighbor's house, and that neighbor informed on him.

Wilson was arrested and brought to Fort Smith for trial. This trial was on the question of identity. Wilson claimed to be only twenty-two years old, and therefore, being only twelve or thirteen years old at the time of the murder, he could not be the murderer. However, his appearance, the fact that he had married within a year of his escape, and other evidence convinced the jury that he was the same man convicted. He was found guilty on June 2, 1876, and the sentence of death was revived and imposed on June 21, 1876, to be carried out September 8, 1876.

*****

At eleven o'clock on the morning of Friday, September 8, 1876, the signal was given, the prison doors opened, and the condemned and their entourage started the walk across the garrison grounds to the scaffold in front of the old powder magazine. The doomed were preceded by their clergy and guarded by G. S. Pierce, U.S. jailer, and Deputies R. Topping, J. R. Rutherford, J. C. Wilkinson, and John Porter in advance with Deputy Fowler and a bodyguard on each side. They mounted the scaffold "with firm and fearless tread, manifesting comparatively no emotion."

On the scaffold was Reverend Father Lawrence Smyth for John Valley, Reverend W. A. Sample, Presbyterian, for Sanders and Wilson, Reverend Waldrop for Peters, and Reverend Greathouse. After the proper officers read the sentences, Sanders, Wilson, and Peters addressed the crowd briefly through interpreters. Singing and prayers followed, joined in by the three men just mentioned. The four men were then arranged on the trap; the ministers shook hands with them and retired. The arms and feet of the condemned were pinioned, the ropes placed around their necks, and the black caps placed over their heads. At noon the drop fell. In eleven to thirteen minutes, all four were pronounced dead by Doctors Dunlap, Duval, Price, Pierce, Davenport, Main, Massey, and Evans.

The crowd was much smaller, estimated at fewer than 1,000 at this hanging, and the newspapers gave less detail of the procedures preceding these hangings. In the past, the papers had published details of the trials and sentencing as well as the hangings. There had been three multiple hangings in the span of a year. Between September 3, 1875, and September 8, 1876, fifteen men had met their doom on the gallows at the old garrison site. Of those fifteen, nine were hanged in less than five months (five on April 21, 1876, and four on September 8, 1876). The people and the newsmen may have become sated with the sight. However, there were no more hangings for the rest of 1876, none at all in 1877, and none for most of 1878. They would have two years and three

52

months plus a few days to recover their morbid interest. There would be no more hangings until December 20, 1878, when two men would hang. From then on, the executions would be more of an annual event rather than weekly or monthly, as misguided imaginations would lead us to believe.

But the District Court for the Western District of Arkansas would not be idle. The court would be busy processing some of the more than 13,000 cases that were adjudicated before Judge Isaac C. Parker in his twenty-one years on the bench.

CHAPTER 9

THE GALLOWS GETS A TWO-YEAR HIATUS

The gallows did indeed get a vacation, but Judge Parker and the Court for the Western District of Arkansas did not. Three weeks after the hangings on September 8, 1876, Judge Parker and William Henry Harrison Clayton, prosecutor for the Western District Court, left for Helena, Arkansas, to conduct court there. On their return to Fort Smith, they opened the fall court session on the first Monday in November 1876. And in the next two years, they prosecuted and convicted criminals for every crime within the jurisdiction of that court.

The court proceedings were published weekly in all of the local newspapers of the time, and the reports show a very busy schedule. There were large numbers of larcenies, probably the predominate crime, followed by assaults, and next liquor and related tax violations. There were also manslaughter cases, and in some cases, a jury returned a verdict of manslaughter when a man had been charged with murder.

The court convened in November, and by December 13, 1876, it had tried two Arapahos, Black Crow and Creeping Bear, for murder. They were accused of riding up to the house of a Dr. Holiday near Fort Sill in Indian Territory two years earlier and shooting his young son through the window just for fun. Black Crow was convicted, but his brother, Creeping Bear, was acquitted. The two were riding on one horse, but Black Crow was the only one who could be identified because when he fired, he threw the blanket off his face.

On December 16, 1876, Irving Perkins (spelled "Irwin" in the news report) was convicted of murder. Quoting *The New Era* from December 20, 1876:

> The fellow, Irwin, was living in the Creek Nation, a couple of hundred miles west of here and deliberately killed his own child, a babe two weeks old, by his wife's daughter. The case is too disgusting to particularize.
>
> So is a rape case, committed in the Territory. It was nolle prosequi (case abandoned by the prosecution) because the main witnesses, wife and daughters, when they found out that it was a hanging affair, refused to make the same statement previously made at U.S. Commissioner's preliminary examination.

Court records for January 15 and 16, 1877, show the cases of U.S. v. Houston Brown, murder; U.S. v. Al Newberry, et al, murder; and U.S. v. Litaka, Joseph Riley, et al., were continued to the next term. However, the next term would be further off than anyone expected. More on that subject a little later.

On Monday, February 26, 1877, Judge Parker pronounced sentence on three men to hang on April 27, 1877, for murder. The first was Irving Perkins, whose crime has already been described. When asked why sentence should not be pronounced on him, he gave a long speech of denial. That was followed by Judge Parker's usual sentencing and remonstrative speech.

The next man to stand before the judge would create a scene described by one newspaper as a "THRILLING INCIDENT!" and "A LEAP FOR LIBERTY OR DEATH." Charles Thomas, "a colored man from the Indian country, about 27 years old, well formed, tall, lithe, intelligent looking," was convicted of having killed another man. The trouble originated about the deceased's wife. Thomas, after killing the man, gave himself up, claiming self-defense.

When told to stand and say why sentence should not be pronounced on him, he said that he thought that nothing he could say would do him any good. He had killed the man in self-defense and that if he had not expected to be cleared, he would not have surrendered voluntarily. After Thomas finished, Judge Parker began reading the sentence when all at once the prisoner, who was entirely unshackled, gathered himself and made a "spring like a panther" directly at the judge. His goal was a window directly behind the judge, the Poteau River about 400 yards away, and Oklahoma beyond. However, he had overlooked a railing behind the judge, which he struck violently, and in the next instant, Judge Parker had him by his shirt collar. He offered no resistance to the judge, but when a half-dozen deputy marshals took him, he struggled to be free. Even after he was brought back before the bench he continued to struggle. Someone suggested that he be thrown down and tied hand and foot, but Parker ordered that he remain unshackled while the sentence was being read. Meanwhile Thomas struggled and stated that he would rather be shot than treated like a dog, that he had acted like a man in giving himself up, having killed a man in self-defense, and that it was a shame to be treated like this.

The third prisoner was an Arapaho, Black Crow, whose crime has also been described. When asked through his interpreter why he should not have sentence imposed, he claimed innocence and blamed his arrest on the work of hostile Cheyennes. When told to prepare to meet his fate, Black Crow laughed aloud and told the interpreter that he did not believe it. He said that if he had to die, he would die, but he did not want to be hanged. Black Crow showed no emotion except once or twice when he laughed aloud.

However, none of those sentences would be carried out. On April 14, 1877, *The Weekly Herald* announced that Black Crow's sentence had been commuted to life in prison at Moundsville, West Virginia. The editor went on to express the opinion that the sentence was worse than death to an Indian. The article also said that the two black men, Thomas and Perkins, would probably hang, but by the appointed day, April 27, President Rutherford B. Hayes commuted all to life at Moundsville.

On Wednesday, May 2, 1877, the week after the executions were to have taken place, *The New Era* ran two one-paragraph articles pertaining to the men and the event. The first noted that Black Crow, Perkins, and Thomas had left that morning in the charge of personnel from the Marshals Office for the prison at Moundsville. The second article, titled "Disappointed," said that at least 1,000 people had come to town to witness the hangings. When they learned of the commutations by the president, "many were intensely disgusted." Later, none could be found who had come to see the hangings; all had some particular business in town.

Two weeks previous to those events and in the week previous to the scheduled hangings, this notice ran in *The New Era* and was repeated the next week in *The Weekly Herald*:

Office U.S. Marshal
West. Dist. Ark.
Ft. Smith, Ark., April 12, 1877.
There will be no May term of the United States Court at Fort Smith. Witnesses and others will not be required to attend until the first Monday in August next.

The cause of the postponement was that Congress had not appropriated funds to administer the court. Not only that, there were no funds for the Marshals Office either. And that second item was addressed in another article in another column of the same issue.

Valentine Dell, editor of *The New Era*, had begun calling the Indian Territory "Pandemonium." Quoting his article from April 18, 1877:

Pandemonium is Happy.—The appropriation having run out and no money in the office, the U.S. Marshal of the Western District of Arkansas can't send deputies and must let things, therefore, take their own course in the Indian Territory, swarming with outlaws and malefactors of every description. Perhaps this is all the better, for it will then give expression perhaps to the desire of the better portion of the people there to have the land divided up and be admitted as a U.S. Territory.

Again on May 23, 1877, Valentine Dell published an article under the title "Pandemonium." This one seemed incredible, until an attorney who worked in the current Cherokee Court and studied the history of that 1800s period gave an opinion that, at that time, it was probably true.

The story involved a murder in Crawford County, Arkansas. A man named Harvey murdered another named Stultz, who was plowing in his field in Crawford County near the state line between Arkansas and the Indian Territory. Harvey then crossed into the Indian Territory and was safe, because there was no law by which he could be lawfully arrested. Any warrant issued for him would be a Crawford County warrant or a state of Arkansas warrant. Arkansas law authorities had no jurisdiction in Indian Territory, and the U.S. Marshals Office had jurisdiction only on U.S. warrants, not local warrants.

Dell pointed out that the man could have been extradited from almost any country in the world, but the one place where he was safe was right in the middle of the United States. Dell went on to point out that if John Wilkes Booth and others had known that fact, they might have pointed their steps toward the Territory and remained free. He went on, "Yes, let it be known to all murderers and outlaws in the Union, yea, and from the lands beyond, that the Indian Territory, alias Oklahoma, alias Pandemonium, is the place for them."

During that same period the deputy marshals who were still working were regularly bringing prisoners, and all of the newspapers of the time were running articles such as one on July 18, 1877, in *The New Era*: "Deputy marshals are constantly arriving with batches of prisoners and report the Indian country completely overrun and terrorized by every species of lawless characters. During the present month thirty prisoners have arrived and the number is rapidly increasing by large accessions."

In the spring and summer of 1877, *The Cherokee Advocate* of Tahlequah, Indian Territory, and *The Weekly Herald* ran a verbal sparring match about the virtues and vices of having the U.S. Court in the Territory versus Fort Smith.

This is from *The Advocate* as quoted in *The Herald* on June 23, 1877:

The cry throughout the country has been and still is for a United States Court in the Territory. The most violent opposition to this measure has come from Fort Smith and the Court there, and yet a Court here would be much more inexpensive, convenient and effectual for the prevention of crime in the Territory, and take away much of the reason *The Fort Smith Era* has for calling the Territory Pandemonium. But there is bread and butter somewhere in the business, and that consideration never does fail to modify one's views.

The last sentence of that paragraph was the telling one. Everyone wanted some of the "bread and butter." The fact was, there were no jurors in the Territory qualified to sit on a jury in a U.S. court. Jurors would have had to be imported from Arkansas.

There was no May term of the court in 1877, and the hope was that Congress, in an extra session, would appropriate money for a term to begin on the first Monday in August. However, there was no extra session of Congress, and it was wondered if there would be another postponement until after Congress met in October. But, somehow the money must have appeared, for on July 28, 1877, *The Herald* began a long article by stating that the Court for the Western District would commence on "Monday, the sixth day of next month."

On August 6, 1877, the court convened with a large backlog of cases that had accumulated through the spring and summer, plus some that had been continued from the previous term. Not only those cases, but also the deputies were continually bringing in more prisoners.

By Wednesday, August 29, *The New Era* reported that a special U.S. grand jury would be empanelled to investigate about twenty cases that "have accumulated since last Wednesday." Just below that article, it stated that of forty criminal cases disposed of since August 6, there had been only six acquittals. In that same column are three articles listing a total of ten prisoners brought in that week. Farther over on the same page is an entire column listing, in the briefest of words and abbreviations, the actions of the court from August 21 to August 28, 1877.

All of the murder cases in August 1877 were either reduced to manslaughter by the jury or acquitted. But in September, one case evoked enough interest to warrant its own column in one newspaper. That was the case of J. S. Williams for the murder of his brother-in-law, Pierson. All were from the Red River country of Indian Territory near Paris, Texas, and all reported to be wealthy, which added to the interest of the trial. In addition, both sides had brought their ladies with them; hence, the courtroom was filled with local ladies.

The trial lasted four days and was prosecuted by U.S. Attorney William H. H. Clayton. For the defense were DuVal and Cravens of Fort Smith, senior counsel Thomas H. Barnes, and W. B. Wright of Paris, Texas. All of the attorneys were reported to have given admirable and persuasive arguments. When the case was closed and the court charged the jury, the details of law bearing on the case were "quite minute." The jury was out less than one hour and returned with a verdict of not guilty. That ended a case that had attracted more attention than any case had in a long time, and J. S. Williams was discharged by the court "to go hence without [delay]."

For all of September 1877, seven people were tried for murder, and all but two, T. J. Robinson and W. J. Meadows, were found not guilty or, in the case of William Mead, *nolle prosequi*. One interesting note in the listing of cases in *The Herald* on September 28, 1877: "U.S. vs. Wm. J. Meadows—murder by wrecking train on M.K. & T.R.R. Jury trial; not guilty on second count." However, he was convicted of murder.

All during the court term, the newspapers were noting the number of new prisoners brought in by the marshals and the number of convicted prisoners being taken to Little Rock to serve the shorter terms or to Detroit, Michigan, for the longer sentences.

On October 3, 1877, *The New Era* ran under the headline, "Convicted of Rape and Doomed for the Gallows," the story of Joshua Wade, whom it described as big, burly, and brutal. He was convicted of "committing rape on an aged and respectable Indian woman of the Choctaw Nation." The evidence in the case was said to have conclusively established the guilt of Wade but was "too disgusting for publication." The difficulty of securing a conviction in such a case was enhanced by the fact that all of the witnesses were Indian and an interpreter had to be employed for all testimony. In spite of the difficulties, the case was ably prosecuted and the jury lost no time in rendering a guilty verdict.

> The penalty is death, and Joshua very appropriately completes the trio of victims for the gallows, furnished by the present term of the court.
> — *The New Era*, October 3, 1877

It appears that the specially scheduled August 1877 term of the court ran into the regularly scheduled November term without letup. Occasionally there were special grand juries empanelled to handle the accumulation of cases and they were dismissed when their work was completed. But, no new petit jury list was published in the papers.

For November 1877, there were the usual lists of larcenies and similar crimes, but only two murder trials were published. In the case of John Procter, the jury's verdict was, "We, the jury find that this court has not jurisdiction in this case." The case of U.S. v. Tezekiah Harjo and Joseph Riley—murder, jury trial, was listed as pending. The Harjo and Riley case must have led to something other than a death sentence, for they were not among those sentenced to be executed later. However, another case came up in December that occupied the newsmen more than Harjo and Riley.

In the third week of December 1877, the Fort Smith newspapers reported on an unusual trial that had lasted, including jury deliberation, nine days. On trial were nine citizens of the Creek Nation, and there was at least one remarkable witness.

The defendants were Carolina Grayson, Peter Grayson, Man Lewis, Robert Love, Barney Lucky, Anderson Davis, John Lucky, James Wells, and Jacob Bruner, "all stalwart young negro men and citizens of the Creek Nation" (*The New Era*, December 19, 1877). They were accused of the murder of Henry Ross, "a negro, a non-citizen of the Nation." On May 15, 1877, the defendants had gone to the home of Ross and accused him of stealing hogs. Ross denied their accusations and volunteered to stand trial on the charge and invited them to search his property. He produced a pot of cooking pork and said that the man who made the search and failed to find any more meat should die in the door.

Carolina Grayson, the leader of the group, entered Ross's home and had a social smoke with him. Afterward all parties must have exited the house for there was an altercation between Ross and Peter Grayson in the yard. Carolina took up the quarrel and shot Ross in the back of his head with a musket as he entered his house. Ross lived for about two hours, attended only by Anderson Davis, who alone remained after the rest of the conspirators had gone.

On the way to Ross's house, Carolina Grayson had told several people that he was going there to see the boys kill Ross. The listeners had tried to dissuade him from going, but he replied that it was no harm to kill a hog thief. That, according to one newspaper, was one of the principal points of evidence.

There were seventeen witnesses in the case, "and as a whole, probably the most grossly ignorant specimens of humanity that ever testified in a court [of] justice" (*The New Era*, December 19, 1877). Hardly any of them knew their own ages, and the brother of the victim had difficulty designating the months, did not know if Christmas came once or twice a year, and his knowledge of the Civil War was based on a rumor of a "big battle across the ocean." And so it was with the others, "*ad infinitum et ad nauseum.*" One old man with a wooden leg "was a perfect hurricane." He stormed at the attorneys for "flattering" him and had to pause to let his emotion cool.

The trial lasted six days, and Judge Parker's charge to the jury lasted one hour and forty-five minutes. The jury was out for three days and finally returned a verdict of guilty for Carolina Grayson, Peter Grayson, Man Lewis, and Robert Love. Those four would not be sentenced until the following February. The rest of the conspirators were acquitted.

During December 1877, Judge Parker rendered a very controversial decision in a murder case. On the surface it appeared to go against the decision that had been given in the case of Osey Sanders, in which Sanders and the Cherokee Court tried to get the trial removed to the Cherokee jurisdiction. Their argument was that the victim was married to a member of the Cherokee tribe and was an adopted citizen. Judge Parker ruled that in the case of a Major Reynolds, the same arguments did not hold and the application for writ of habeas corpus was granted.

Major Reynolds and the victim, Pruyear, were both domiciled in the Choctaw Nation, married to Choctaw women and, therefore, members of the Choctaw Nation within the true intent of Article 38 of the U.S.-Choctaw treaty of 1806. The wording of the pertinent paragraphs and the explanation of the decision were published in detail in *The Weekly Herald* on December 24, 1877.

So 1877 ended with no executions. The January 9, 1878, edition of *The New Era* noted that the petit jury was discharged and that twenty-three more prisoners had been brought in, "a motley mixture of white men, Indians and negroes." And that the three prisoners, Robinson, Meadows, and Wade, sentenced in August to hang January 18, 1878, had been commuted to life in prison by President Rutherford B. Hayes. By the following Saturday, January 12, 1878, new grand and petit juries had been selected and the cycle started again.

By the time the February 1878 term of the U.S. Court began, the sentences of all of the people who had been convicted of capital crimes in the previous terms had been commuted to life in prison. Cases awaiting trial in that term were: murder, seven; rape, one; assault to kill, nine; and larceny, twenty-two. Of those thirty-nine, five were women, and of the women, two were charged with murder.

The two women murderers were white women, Elizabeth Owen and her daughter, Dorcas, from the Choctaw Territory. The daughter had her child of three years with her. The women were accused of holding Ezekial Hurd while the husband of the older one killed him.

Some of Hurd's horses had gotten into the Owens' fields, and Mrs. Owen had "treated her neighbor's stock rather roughly." "Hurd had sent her a rather rough message such as is customary among people living without the civilizing influences of public schools and churches." Sometime later, Elizabeth Owen confronted Hurd with a shotgun as he was riding by and demanded that he "give an account of himself" about that threatening message. Hurd, in explicit language, told her where to go and rode on. On his return, Elizabeth Owen stood in the road and forced Hurd to dismount. After dismounting, Hurd grabbed the gun and a struggle ensued. Dorcas ran from the house and joined in the struggle. All this time Mr. Owen had been nearby at the house skinning a coon. Hearing and seeing the struggle, he ran to the road and, with the knife that he had been using to skin the coon, stabbed Hurd. Mr. Owen immediately fled and at the time of the trial had not been seen. Hurd died about three weeks later.

On Tuesday, February 19, 1878, the jury acquitted Elizabeth and Dorcas Owen of the charge. Some felt that if they had been men, the verdict would have been different, as it was in the case of Carolina Grayson and friends in which one person had committed the actual murder but all who were armed were convicted. An extenuating circumstance in the Owen case was that Mrs. Owen had nine living children, the oldest seventeen, and all, large and small, were in the courtroom. It was believed that the presence of the children surely weighed on the jury's decision.

The New Era noted in the last issue of February 1878 that Judge Parker in his "expeditious manner" had disposed of forty-one sentences in one day. There were thirty-one yet to be tried, but they would have to wait until the next term. This term had been abbreviated because of lack of funds.

Among the prisoners sentenced that February were the four convicted of the murder of Henry Ross. On February 25, 1878, Carolina Grayson, Peter Grayson, Man Lewis, and Robert Love were sentenced to hang on Friday, June 21, 1878. But on Friday, June 14, U.S. District Marshal D. P. Upham received a telegram from President Hayes commuting the sentences of Man Lewis, Robert Love, and Peter Grayson. Only Carolina Grayson, the actual shooter, was not granted commutation.

As of June 19, 1878, the plan to hang Grayson on June 21 was proceeding, and he was resigned to his fate. This hanging, unlike the ones preceding it, was to be a private affair. The platform was to be lowered four feet, and it was to be surrounded by a sixteen-foot plank fence. The only witnesses were to be the guards, doctors, members of the press, and family. "We think this arrangement will meet the approval of all enlightened people" (*The New Era*, June 19, 1878).

At five forty-five the morning of June 21, 1878, this telegram was sent from Washington, D.C., to Marshal Upham:

> Suspend execution of Carolina Grayson until further notice. Acknowledge receipt by telegraph. Charles Devans, Attorney General

Grayson had requested to set his execution for nine o'clock in the morning. However, that being such an early hour for a hanging, it was set for later. Had it not been for the delay, Grayson would have been well into the preparation for his execution when he received the news. Grayson's sentence would eventually be commuted to life in prison at Detroit, Michigan.

It was speculated by *The Weekly Herald* that someone named Tilghman Knox "threw the weight of his influence at Washington in the breech" and saved Grayson's life.

So ended the proceedings of the first session of the Western District Court for 1878, and on the first Monday in July 1878, what would have been the May session began. That session would run almost continuously through the fall and produce slightly different results.

CHAPTER 10

"A VICTIM FOR THE GALLOWS
HANGING TOO GOOD FOR HIM"
(The New Era, August 21, 1878)

A White Man and his Wife Fiendishly
Murdered — Their Remains Devoured
By Hogs and Their Little Child
Abandoned to Starvation
— *The Weekly Herald*, August 26, 1878

The acts of John Postoak and their results outraged the editors of the Fort Smith newspapers, and they described, in gory detail, the crime scene. During the July term of the Western District Court, only the case of Joseph Bonheur, charged with the serial raping of a seven-year-old girl, had elicited the indignation that Postoak's case did. Bonheur, however, would be acquitted in the same month that Postoak was convicted, cause for more indignation.

The July 1878 term had begun with cases to be tried as follows:

Murder	8
Assault with intent to kill	5
Larceny	31
Robbing U.S. Mail	2
Rape	1
Violating Int. Rev. Law	4
Bigamy	1
Total	52

Of the murder cases, only Postoak and one other were convicted, and the other man would not stand trial until November 1878.

John Postoak, a Creek Indian about twenty-five years old, went to the home of John Ingley near Eufaula in Indian Territory in October 1877 to ask Ingley's wife to "back or direct" two letters for him that he expected to send to Okmulgee by Ingley. Ingley, who had been outside, came in and informed Postoak that he was not going to Okmulgee and that he did not want him around his house anyway. Postoak then asked Ingley for tobacco. Ingley replied that he had no tobacco to give away and that Postoak was no better than a dog. Postoak, angered, went to the home of a neighbor and borrowed a gun, supposedly to kill a hog for said neighbor. He returned to the Ingley home where Ingley

64

was feeding his son of about eighteen months. Postoak asked him if he was a man, and when Ingley answered that he was, Postoak reached up, took the victim's gun, and threw it on the floor saying, "If you are a man, be a man." When Ingley reached down for the gun, Postoak shot him. Ingley reached his gun and fired a shot that hit the doorframe. Postoak shot him again, and Ingley fell out of the door, dead. Postoak took the empty gun and crushed the head of his victim and then broke the gun over a log. He then returned to the house and accused Mrs. Ingley of trying to help her husband, to which she replied that she loved her husband and had tried to help him. Postoak then pressed the revolver against her and fired, killing her and setting her clothes on fire. He then left the house, which was situated far from any other habitation and rarely visited.

About twelve days later, Postoak met some people he knew who were on their way to the Ingley home. Knowing that the deed would be discovered, he made the foregoing confession and threatened to "overtake" them if they ever told on him.

The next day after Postoak's confession and warning, another party found the gruesome scene. The body of the man was lying outside the door in the yard and the woman in the door. Both bodies had been eaten by animals, both wild and domestic. The head of the man was disconnected from the body, and one arm of the woman was gone. There was hardly more than bones for interment.

Miraculously, the small child was found in a corner of the room, still alive, though emaciated. The newspaper accounts disagree on the fate of the child. One paper said he was cared for and "recovered from the shock and regained his wanton vigor" (*The New Era*, August 21, 1878). The other paper said that he "died in the course of a few weeks" (*The Weekly Herald*, August 26, 1878). It appears, though, that he may have survived. *The New Era* on November 16, 1878, said, "But it lived to be a witness, though a silent one, against the slayer of its parents."

The trial lasted five days, ending on Friday, August 16, 1878, when it was given to the jury. The jury, after only a short deliberation, returned a verdict of guilty.

The announcement of the verdict and anticipation of the sentencing caused *The New Era* to express the words, "hang by the neck until he is dead, dead, dead." That paper stated, "He is now in jail awaiting sentence, and when the Judge shall pronounce the words that he shall 'hang by the neck until he is dead, dead, DEAD.'" There is no indication up to and including this case that Judge Parker ever spoke to a prisoner in that manner. When it came to the sentencing on October 14, 1878, the same newspaper quoted Judge Parker's entire address to the prisoner as he delivered it, almost verbatim, to every condemned person. It was the same compassionate speech that had been quoted on

A former U.S. Army enlisted men's barracks, the U.S. Courthouse in Fort Smith, Arkansas, is shown between 1878 and 1887. The portico was later removed, leaving only a porch and steps.

previous occasions with only the description of the crimes changed to fit the various cases. In it, Parker sentenced Postoak to "be hanged by the neck until you are dead" on December 20, 1878. "And may that God, whose laws you have broken and before whose dread tribunal you must now appear, have mercy on your soul."

The July term of the court, which should have been the May term, continued through October 1878 and paused only to replace the grand and petit jury pools and to name new court officers before going into the November term. All during the July term, the deputies had been bringing more prisoners and the grand jury had been turning out indictments so that there had been more than the fifty-two cases that they had started with. There were a surprising number of counterfeiters, and several women were indicted for liquor and revenue violations. Also during that term, the court tried two deputy marshals, Twyman and Scoville, for malfeasance, embezzlement, and bribery. The U.S. government sued former U.S. District Marshal J. N. Sarber to retrieve money claimed by the government.

The U.S. District Court for the Western District of Arkansas met for its first full session on Monday, November 4, 1878, and produced a murder conviction by Friday of the same week and sentencing the next day, Saturday, November 9.

The U.S. Courthouse and jail, at back, are shown in 1898 as the fort walls were being torn down.

In the summer of 1873, J. C. Gould had hired James Diggs near the northern boundary of Indian Territory to help move a herd of cattle that he was bringing from Texas. Gould also had in his employ Hiram Mann of Port Huron, Michigan.

Gould had sold a cow to Robert C. Cary, who lived near Coffeyville, Kansas, for the sum of twenty-seven dollars and was paid with five five-dollar bills and a two-dollar bill. A day or two later, Diggs went to Cary in a state of excitement and told him that during the night, two men from Texas had ridden up to the cabin where he, Gould, and Mann were sleeping and killed Mann and Gould. Diggs claimed that the killers chased him into the woods where he hid under a crooked log. A large crowd soon gathered at the news, and Diggs's story was, at first, believed. But on looking for and finding no tracks of the purported killers, suspicion was raised among the crowd, which by then had grown considerably.

In his testimony before U.S. Commissioner Stephen Wheeler, Eugene A. Osborne described how Diggs was made to show where he had hidden from the alleged murderers, and a group of five accompanied him to the spot. When the place was pointed out, it was found to be a small hollow overgrown by sprouts and covered with spider webs and appeared to have never been disturbed. Diggs was made to lie down in the hollow with the result that he demolished twigs, sprouts, and cobwebs. On the way out of the timber, the group came to an open area. At that point, Osborne told Diggs to remove his shoes, then he inspected them for blood. Another member of the party told Diggs to remove his coat and pants. Nothing was found in the pockets of either the coat or pants. But on further inspection of the lining of the coat, the group found tightly rolled bills in the identical amount and denominations that Cary had paid Gould for the cow. At that discovery, Diggs became very agitated and sweated profusely.

The committee of five, instead of taking him back to the murder scene, knowing the fate that would befall him should the crowd learn the facts, took him to Coffeyville, Kansas. Diggs was then taken to Independence, Kansas, thence to Fort Smith and the U.S. jail.

In March 1874, Diggs and thirteen others escaped from the U.S. jail but were recaptured the next day. At the November 1874 term of the court, he was set free by Judge Caldwell after being in prison for more than a year. There was nothing against him, the Kansas authorities having failed to transmit any document on the case.

The murderer, thinking that the case was closed "and justice asleep," returned to the Territory. He was mistaken not only in that belief, but also in thinking that both of the "murdered" men were indeed dead. Diggs had hit each man in the head with an axe more than once. He did not realize that Mann had recovered and that there were good witnesses against him. So, on June 24, 1878, Deputy U.S. Marshal J. C. Wilkinson arrested Diggs at the home of Louis Keys in the Osage Nation.

Mann's recovery, miracle that it was, had taken three years. He had been struck across the left temple and back of his right eye, that blow leaving a permanent deep hollow, and he had a horrible gash on his neck. His left jawbone was broken and protruded just below the eye. For a month he had lain comatose, and his first exclamation after regaining consciousness was, "Well, Diggs liked to have got away with me."

At the trial there were, besides Mann, seven witnesses, including a deputy U.S. marshal. Diggs was astounded when Mann appeared, the former assuming the latter to be dead. The trial began on Thursday, closed on Friday with the jury's verdict, and on the next day, Judge Parker pronounced sentence to be carried out December 20, 1878.

Both John Postoak and James Diggs not only were the perpetrators of heinous crimes, but also had the distinction of being the first people executed by the U.S. District Court for the Western District of Arkansas to have their pictures published in a local newspaper. Their surprisingly good-quality photographs appeared in the December 23, 1878, issue of *The Weekly Herald*.

The execution of Diggs and Postoak was not a public hanging. As was planned with the expected Carolina Grayson execution, the plank fence had been raised to sixteen feet. In addition, Marshal Upham allowed no one inside the old garrison walls except those with passes, consisting principally of reporters, doctors, lawmen, and clergymen.

At about one o'clock that afternoon, Marshal Upham and Chief Deputy Barnes entered the prison and read the death warrants to the condemned men. They were then led out, preceded by their spiritual advisers, Reverend V. V. Harlan of the M. E. Church for Postoak and Reverend C. G. Smith of the Colored Baptist Church for Diggs.

The entourage proceeded to the scaffold, accompanied by the necessary guard. The procession mounted the platform, the prisoners showing very little emotion. Religious services were then held, in which both prisoners earnestly participated. Diggs advised everyone to beware of whiskey and cards, and Postoak, having nothing to say in regard to his case, prayed at length in his native language. The prisoners shook hands all around, then their arms and legs were secured, the black caps were drawn over their faces, and the ropes were adjusted. A brief pause, a last farewell, and the trap was sprung.

Postoak's neck was broken by the fall, and he was dead in eleven minutes. Diggs's neck was not broken, and he convulsed, and his labored breathing could be heard. He expired in about seven minutes after the drop fell.

The two-year, three-month hiatus for the gallows had ended, and it would be another eight months before it served in another execution.

CHAPTER 11

"THE LAW VINDICATED

Hanging of Henri Stewart
and William Elliott Wiley"

(The Fort Smith Elevator, September 5, 1879)

Dr. Henri Stewart stopped to examine the casket that his half brother had bought for him, made some remark about the kindness shown by the one who purchased it and proceeded "with firm and fearless mien" to the gallows. On that sunny Friday afternoon, August 29, 1879, he and William Elliott Wiley were to hang at the Fort Smith garrison for their separate crimes of murder.

Henri Stewart was a native of the Choctaw Nation, born there in 1848. His father was white and his mother part Indian. His mother had lived in a New England state (*The Elevator* reports Connecticut) since 1855, and Henri went there at an early age. It appears that the reporters may have enhanced his deeds and travels. Two of the newspapers have him educated at Yale and one at both Yale and Harvard. Whichever is true, it is a fact that he was a physician. The various reports have him being a ship physician and traveling to Cuba, the coast of South America, West Indies, Europe, and California. He married a woman with two children in Kansas and had lived in the Choctaw Nation since 1874. For some reason Stewart gave up the life of a doctor and turned to a life of crime. *The Elevator* even reported that it was said that he traveled with Sam Bass and his train robbers in Texas.

Whatever the reports of his life of crime, it is true that he and his cousin, Wiley Stewart, were arrested in mid-1878 on a charge of introducing whiskey into the Indian Territory. They applied to Dr. Jones of Caddo, Choctaw Nation, to go their bond, and when he refused, they threatened revenge. A short time later, while they were drinking, they rode into Caddo and confronted Jones at the railroad depot. While they quarreled with Jones, Henri shot a finger on Jones's left hand with his revolver. Wiley Stewart then shot the doctor with his shotgun. *The Weekly Independent* reported, "The shot was fired at such short range that the wound inflicted was only about the size of a silver dollar, and some of the shot passed entirely through the body."

In the same paragraph that described the shooting, *The Independent* described an exciting tale of escape that no other newspaper mentioned and that paper did not mention in any other edition, and is probably the product of a reporter's overactive imagination. After the shooting, "They rode off, made a circuit of the town, returned and defied the

70

crowds assembled at the scene of the tragedy. The Chickasaw sheriff and posse pursued and overtook them on the open prairie, when a bloody fight ensued. The murderers severely wounded a number of the pursuing party and killed two of their horses and escaped. Henri was finally arrested in Missouri, but his companion in crime is still at large."

WILLIAM ELLIOTT WILEY

Born in Ohio in 1847, William Elliott Wiley, alias Colorado Bill, served two years in the Union Army from 1863 until the end of the Civil War. He then followed in the footsteps of many former soldiers and led a wild life on the western frontier. His escapades sound much like those described in the dime novels popular at the time. After roaming for a while, he took up residence in Muskogee, Indian Territory, at "Ruth Sheppard's house of ill fame."

The essential description of Wiley's crime is nearly the same in all three newspapers of the day, but the dates vary. *The Independent* is specific in saying that it happened on "the night of Sunday, July 2" but *The New Era* said, "last February," which would have been February 1879. *The Elevator* said that the event took place on February 28, 1879, which, in that year, was a Sunday. The July 2 date is probably in error because Wiley was tried and convicted in May 1879, so the date given would had to have been in 1878, in which case, he would have been tried in the fall term of court in 1878, not May 1879.

On the night of the crime, two men, David Brown and Ross Cunningham, went to Ruth Sheppard's house and played cards and "drank freely." Brown lay down and went to sleep, and Cunningham continued to carouse. About three o'clock, Cunningham tried to wake Brown and get him home. Finally Wiley ordered Brown to leave the house. Brown appeared to obey but then grabbed Cunningham's pistol. Wiley immediately commenced firing, striking Cunningham once in the leg and Brown three times in the breast and head. The last time Wiley fired, he placed the gun near the victim's head and put a bullet through his brain. He then rubbed his weapon over the face of his victim and boasted that he had killed many a better man. Giving Cunningham's pistol to his mistress, he ordered her to shoot the first man who "darkened the door." He permitted no one to leave the house except John Woods, whom he sent for a horse. Failing to get a horse, Wiley started away on foot and was arrested the same day while asleep in the woods. At his trial, the jury delivered a verdict of guilty after only a few moments of deliberation.

The information in the preceding paragraph was taken from *The Fort Smith Independent*, which appears to be given to more flamboyant

71

detail than the other papers of the time. *The Elevator* and *The New Era* reported only the basics of the events with no reference to intimate details.

All of the newspapers commented on the coolness and apparent courage of Stewart and Wiley. They reportedly showed no emotion during their trials or when their verdicts were read. It was only after his conviction that Wiley revealed that his full name was not William Elliott but William Elliott Wiley. He said that he had not used his full name to spare his family the embarrassment of his deeds.

On the morning of August 29, 1879, the condemned men spent their time meeting with their spiritual advisers, writing letters, and wrapping up their earthly affairs. Stewart conversed through the prison bars with his half brother. At two o'clock, the condemned men were led from the prison and, with their spiritual advisers, were conducted under guard to the gallows. The execution was a private affair. No one was allowed inside the garrison compound except officers of the court, clergy, medical professionals, reporters, and a few invited citizens.

The prisoners, without apparent fear, mounted the steps to the gallows accompanied by Reverend Sample, their spiritual adviser, who made some remarks about his relations with the condemned men and their spiritual condition. He then offered a prayer in which he was joined by the prisoners. On being asked if he had anything to say, Wiley declared that he had killed Brown in self-defense and that if he had not, then he would have been killed. He acknowledged that although it was wicked for him to have been in such a place, he did not do the killing on account of a woman. He said that he forgave everybody and had made his peace with God. He then shook hands all around. As the black cap was placed over his head, he said, "Be sure to break our necks boys, and don't punish us."

Henri Stewart said that he had not intended to speak on the scaffold but would say a few words. Instead of regretting his situation, he considered it a blessed privilege and said that he had found grace and was confident that he would soon be in a better world. He referred to the thief on the cross who found forgiveness at the last moment. He bade all farewell, and jerking the rope, he said, "Thank God for giving us such a speedy means of passing from this life to eternity."

At two thirty that afternoon, Marshal C. M. Barnes signaled the jailer by a move of his hand, and the drop fell. Wiley's neck was broken by the fall, and he died without a struggle. Stewart's neck was not broken, and his limbs twitched convulsively for about five minutes, and his heartbeat ceased in nine minutes. The bodies were cut down after twenty minutes. Wiley's body was placed in a coffin and buried on the military reservation. Stewart's body was taken charge of by his half brother, Arthur T. Stewart, and placed in a fine casket that he had provided and interred at the city cemetery.

Arthur Stewart complained to reporters the night after the execution about his treatment by U.S. officials in the preceding days. He had traveled from Atchison, Kansas, and arrived on Wednesday before the Friday execution. He asked to be allowed inside the jail to spend Thursday with his brother but was refused. He was allowed to talk with him through the bars at times during the day but was ordered out of the garrison enclosure several times. On Friday, shortly before his brother was led to the gallows, he was allowed inside the jail for thirty minutes for a final farewell. He then requested (and his brother also desired) that he be allowed to walk with Henri to the gallows and was refused. He was also denied entrance to the enclosure around the gallows. He had bought a fine casket in which Henri was placed and had ordered a hearse to convey the body to the cemetery. However, the officer in charge said that he had orders from the Marshals Office to deliver the remains outside the walls and ordered the driver to take the hearse out, which he did. In order not to have the coffins tumbled together in the wagon, the brother enlisted some citizens to carry the casket outside the garrison wall, a distance of about 250 yards, to the hearse. Arthur Stewart also complained that the officer in charge refused to give him a letter that Henri had written to a friend shortly before his execution. He expressed his appreciation for the kindness and sympathy that the people of Fort Smith had shown him during his stay here.

Following is the last message from Henri Stewart to Arthur concerning an inscription for his headstone:

> How sweet it is to sleep in Jesus.
> That is the best that suggests itself to my mind at
> present. If you can improve on it please do so brother.

Apparently he never received a stone, for none exists at his grave today. The gallows again rested for just more than two years.

CHAPTER 12

"FIVE TRAPDOOR ANGELS
Sent to that Bourne
FROM WHENCE NO TRAVELER RETURNS"
(*The New Era*, September 14, 1881)

Just before ten o'clock on September 9, 1881, five men, dressed neatly in new suits, emerged from the U.S. jail, each handcuffed and guarded on each side by a deputy U.S. marshal. At the gates and on the walls of the garrison was a detachment of the Frontier Guard, a company of state troops, under the command of Captain P. T. Devany. Since July 1878, when the fence around the gallows was raised to sixteen feet, the public had not been allowed inside the garrison walls to attend a hanging, and newly appointed U.S. District Marshal Valentine Dell was not going to allow anyone except authorized people inside that day.

The five neatly dressed men were the condemned, George Padgett, William Brown, Patrick McGowen, all white men, and brothers Amos and Abler Manley, Creek Indians, all five convicted of murder.

The gallows had stood without duties for one year and one week and in the last four years had had only two "trapdoor angels." The hiatuses were not for the lack of candidates though. The U.S. Marshals Office and the grand juries had nominated many, and the petit juries had even elected some for the honor. But President Hayes and then President Garfield had commuted all except these five and the two hanged December 20, 1878, to life in prison at Moundsville, West Virginia.

George W. Padgett, twenty-four years old and first of the five to be convicted, had expected no more than a manslaughter verdict. However, it was reported that on Thursday, February 17, 1881, he had received the guilty-of-murder verdict without showing any emotion.

Padgett was charged with the murder of his employer, a Mr. Stevens, on July 26, 1880. The story, as reported in *The Weekly Independent*, was that Stevens was in the Indian Territory en route to Kansas with 2,200 head of cattle belonging to someone in Texas. Near the Comanche Agency, he met and hired Padgett for the rest of the drive. Padgett, at that time, used the alias Charley Wilson.

Among the cattle were four or five head of strays with the mark of a man named Waggoner, for whom Padgett claimed to have worked in Texas. Padgett claimed the right of taking charge of those cattle and accounting to Waggoner for them. Stevens refused and that appears to have been the beginning of the trouble. Padgett took a great dislike to Stevens and was heard, according to testimony, to have made violent threats against him. Near the Kansas line, as the herders were cutting out the cattle to be sold, Padgett approached Stevens and demanded to know what he was going to do about the Waggoner cattle. Using very abusive language, he said that no man should cut them out. Padgett had in his hand a cocked revolver. The two men had "hot words," during which time Stevens, who was unarmed, asked a bystander for a gun and, failing to get one, turned on his horse and rode off. Padgett aimed his pistol and was quoted as saying, "Damn you, I'll shoot you anyhow," and fired. The bullet struck Stevens in the side just behind the right arm and caused almost instant death.

Padgett, in his application for witnesses, requested the presence of Stephen Graham, Adolphus Lewis, and William Tuggle. Quoting from the application:

> By witnesses Graham and Lewis defendant can prove that the said cattle about which the difficulty occurred, which resulted in the killing, were the property of Wm. Waggoner of Texas. That at the time of the killing the deceased was attempting to take out the cattle by force and that defendant was resisting him. That deceased struck the defendant with the butt end of a heavy "quirt" or riding whip. And that defendant then shot him and that he did not draw his gun until after deceased struck him.
>
> By witness Tuggle who came from Texas with deceased and defendant he can prove that the cattle about which the difficulty occurred were stolen from the range in Texas by the deceased on his orders. That defendant all along the trail told him the cattle belonged to Wm. Waggoner. And that deceased was very boisterous and overbearing in his conduct toward defendant and that he was a dangerous and violent man. Said witness will testify that Wm. Waggoner gave defendant authority to take possession of said cattle and either hold them until his herd came along or sell them and get the proceeds. That this defendant and Wm. Waggoner corresponded with one another on the subject of the cattle. That he was present at the killing and will testify to the same facts as the above witnesses.

Padgett had attempted to escape but was captured about six miles from the scene of the murder. His first comment on being captured was reported to have been, "Well, I'm sorry I done it, but this is the seventh man I have killed." He later claimed that the statement was meant only as a joke.

The defense argued that Stevens was holding a drover's whip in a threatening manner and used aggravating language toward Padgett. Whether the witnesses appeared and testified as Padgett hoped they would is not recorded. Whatever the defense was able to present, the jury did not credit the argument. After twenty-four hours, it returned a verdict of guilty of murder.

Immediately after George Padgett's trial there occurred the trial of Arena Howe. Her trial would not have been noteworthy except that she was one of several women indicted for murder during Isaac Parker's tenure as judge of the Court for the Western District of Arkansas and because of the biological differences between men and women.

Arena Howe was a white woman who by her own confession and "abundant evidence" killed a white man, Albert Church, in the Indian Territory about 150 miles west of Fort Smith on August 21, 1880. She said she killed "in defense of her virtue." "From peculiar circumstances" the case "excited considerable attention." Howe was "near her confinement" (term of gestation). Also, as she sat in court she held on her knee "a fine looking boy of about four years." The scene attracted much sympathy. The jury could not reach agreement, being ten for and two against conviction and so was discharged, the case carried over until the next term of court. In the meantime, Howe would be "confined," and with no suitable accommodations at the courthouse, the U.S. marshal obtained special appropriation for the purpose. She gave birth just after her trial. Howe, in the next court term, pleaded guilty to manslaughter and was sentenced to ten years at Detroit.

In a letter dated May 13, 1881, addressed to Honorable Wayne MacVeagh, attorney general, Washington, D.C., District Marshal Valentine Dell wrote:

> Sir:
>
> Mrs. Arena Howe, a white woman, tried last term of this court for murder in the Indian Country, and who would have been found guilty then, but for her delicate condition, being shortly afterwards confined of child, plead guilty to manslaughter last week and will be sentenced to Detroit for ten years. I permitted to be with her another child, a boy about six years of age, ever since she was brought here in August last.
>
> There is positively no way to provide for the children, except to let them go with their mother, as she

has no claim upon this state, and no one in the Territory to take care of them.

Under these circumstances I would respectfully request, that the prison Authorities at Detroit be notified of the case so that I may be permitted to leave the children there with their mother.

Very respectfully
V. Dell
U.S. Marshal

Within a week after Arena Howe's first trial, the court had disposed of twenty additional cases, including the murder conviction of William T. Brown. Brown, more justifiably than Padgett, had hoped for a manslaughter conviction, but the jury did not see it that way. On the night of Thursday, March 3, 1881, the jury, after about an hour of deliberation, returned a verdict of guilty.

There were two versions of the killing reported in the local papers, but they all agreed on the circumstances leading up to the event. William Brown, twenty-seven, and his partner, Ralph C. Tate, seventeen, a man named Moore, and others were employed by a hay contractor at Fort Sill in Indian Territory. In August 1880, an argument occurred between Brown and Moore over a foot race in which Brown had outrun Moore, who was reputed to be a violent man. The result was a fistfight, and Brown was badly beaten.

The Herald describes a scene in which Moore "jumped upon him and knocked him down. He cried, 'nough' and was released." Brown then went to his room and got a pistol, returned, and fired at the first man he saw. He had shot and killed his friend, Tate.

The New Era and *The Independent* have a different story than *The Herald* but are in near agreement with each other. After the fight, Brown got a gun and, at night, waited for Moore beside a path. When a man appeared, he fired, only to realize too late that it was his friend and not Moore. Brown immediately fled, and when G. W. Tate, father of the slain man, heard the news, he went in pursuit of his son's killer. Again there are differences in the telling of Brown's capture, with *The Independent*, as usual, having the more detailed and exciting version. Its telling has G. W. Tate pursuing Brown 600 miles through Indian Territory into Texas, "and after 28 days hard travel, captured his man, and led him by a trace chain padlocked around his neck all the way to Fort Smith, 300 miles, and turned him over to the U.S. jailor." The other papers reported only that Mr. Tate pursued and located Brown, procured his arrest, and return to Fort Smith. Brown, on his arrest, admitted the killing and related all of the details leading up to the deed.

The court barely slowed its pace long enough to select new grand and petit jury pools and went from the February term to the May term of court. The court started with 111 prisoners in the jail, eleven for murder, and the marshals were bringing in more prisoners regularly. By May 17 the court had completed, along with dozens of larceny, liquor, and other cases, the murder trial of Patrick M. McGowen.

McGowen, aged thirty-five, was charged with the murder of Sam Latta in the Chickasaw Nation in the fall of 1880. Only *The New Era* gave a full account of the crime, labeling it, "for cool, calculating, premeditated and fiendish execution is almost without a parallel in the history of crime" — a considerable exaggeration.

Patrick McGowen and Sam Latta had owned more than 300 acres together, but after a disagreement, Latta bought McGowen's share. Hard feelings persisted, ending with the murder of Latta by McGowen.

Indicted jointly with McGowen was William Hunter, a man of sixty years whom the evidence revealed was the instigator of the crime. However, since the United States had no law at that time to punish an accessory before the fact, the case against Hunter was *nolle prosequi* (prosecutor elects not to proceed). McGowen took the opportunity afforded by that situation to have Hunter called as a witness for the defense. He must have placed great hope on Hunter's testimony, but his hopes were undone by the prosecutor, U.S. Attorney Clayton. Hunter broke down under Clayton's cross-examination. No trial transcript exists, so it is unknown what Hunter said under cross-examination. No proceedings before the commissioner are available either.

The testimony revealed that hard feelings existed between McGowen and Latta and that those feelings were shared by Hunter. Further, the feeling had been aggravated by some slight that Hunter had received at the home of Latta the night before the murder. Hunter, seeking revenge that he did not have the courage to carry out, went to McGowen's home the next morning, arriving about ten o'clock. Hunter found McGowen plowing in his field. After a long conversation, the plow was left in the furrow, the plow horse saddled, and after the noon meal, the two rode off in the direction of Latta's home. On the way they stopped to inquire for ammunition, claiming to be hunting. Yet when a wild turkey flew up within shooting range, McGowen refused to shoot, saying, "I don't want to waste my ammunition on a turkey."

Two miles from Sam Latta's house the two men separated, and McGowen rode to the back of Latta's field and tied his horse. He slipped through the corn until he came to a bee-gum (beehive) under a peach tree. By that time it was evening, and Latta stepped out of his house preparatory to retiring. He walked through the orchard, picked some peaches, and started back toward the house. As he came near a long outhouse, McGowen shot him down. Latta's sister "rushed from the house only to pillow in her lap the head of her dying brother and hear the murderer launch his curses upon his bleeding victim."

In McGowen's application for witnesses, he described what those witnesses would attest to. It was a very different story from what was reported from the trial. McGowen cited several occasions when Latta had threatened his life in front of witnesses and the profanities he had supposedly used. One account states that Latta told Henry Bone that he would kill McGowen, marry Mat Parker (Martha Parker), get possession of the farm where McGowen lived (which was leased for five years from Mat Parker), sell it, and move to another part of the country.

In the same document, McGowen described the incident in the orchard. According to him, it was he, not Latta, who was picking peaches. McGowen had crossed the fence, laid down his gun, and had several peaches in his pockets when Latta came out toward the tree. When Latta saw McGowen, he said, "God-damn you I've got you now." McGowen grabbed his gun, raised it, and told Latta to come no farther. "At that time Latta reached...." There the testimony ends, for the remaining pages no longer exist. However, one can probably assume what might have followed from the foregoing.

The case went to the jury at ten thirty Tuesday morning, May 17, and at eleven thirty, the jury brought in a verdict of guilty.

Amos and Abler Manley, Creek Indians, had been tried before Patrick McGowen, but the jury had deadlocked, one of the jurors refusing to agree to a guilty verdict, being opposed to capital punishment. Their crime was the murder of Eli McVay near Eufaula, Indian Territory, in December 1880. They were retried the first week of June 1881.

In their application for witnesses filed February 9, 1881, Amos and Abler requested the presence of Harley, Parnoska, Shawny, Parney, Luther, Sam, and Pedy. All of the said witnesses would attest that they and the defendants were together at Harley's house "upon the night when the murder was committed, if any there was." Apparently the testimony of the widow McVay prevailed.

The following is condensed from Mrs. McVay's testimony, as printed in *The Wheeler's Independent* on June 8, 1881: "They came to my house by themselves; I had gone to bed; they wanted to come in and warm; my husband asked them where they were going; they said, 'to Mrs. Sweet's to pick cotton,' and spoke in English." Eli McVay then made a fire in the fireplace, lighted a lamp, and made them a bed where they lay down before the fire. One of the McVays' small twins was sick, and the father sat with it by the lamp. Bill Barnett, McVay's hired man, slept in another bed in the same room.

[T]hey got up from the pallet and stood by the fire
for about two hours and were laughing and talking in

the Creek language; we did not understand what they were saying; I was in bed and Barnett in his; one of the Indians went out of doors and came back and asked my husband for tobacco; he gave him some and he took his pipe off the mantel and smoked; they both smoked some time before the fire when they turned around and fired on my husband, one with a six shooter and the other with a pocket pistol; my husband had no pistol; when they shot him he sprang up and fell on his face and threw the child on one side; then Bill Barnett jumped out of bed and they shot him; then I jumped out of bed and they shot at me; they missed me but a ball grazed Barnett on the shoulder; then the biggest man ran out of doors and while he was out Barnett was scuffling with the other man trying to get the pistol from him; then the big man came in with an axe and struck Barnett on the head with the axe, using both hands; Barnett fell to the floor; the big man struck him again on the head and cut at him with the axe, cutting off Barnett's left hand.

The big man then struck at Mrs. McVay three times but missed. McVay's dog then ran in and started barking at the outside. The attackers, thinking that someone was coming, left. Mrs. McVay, holding her children, ran to Dr. Tennent's house a quarter mile away. Surprisingly, soon after Mrs. McVay arrived at the doctor's house, Barnett arrived, hand missing, head and thigh cut to the bone.

The Manley brothers escaped conviction the first time because of one man's opposition to capital punishment. They were not so lucky the second time.

The Wednesday, June 22, 1881, edition of *The New Era* read:

Doomed Five Murderers Sentenced to be Hung

On Thursday morning, June 16th, there were sentenced in the United States District Court for the Western District of Arkansas by Judge I. C. Parker, three white men and two Indians to be hung on September 9th, 1881, for the crime of murder in the Indian Territory....

All took their doom without the betrayal of any emotions....

Regardless of their calm demeanor on June 16, all of the men entertained hopes for some kind of reprieve until September 5, 1881. On that day, District Attorney W. H. H. Clayton received a dispatch from Attorney General McVeagh, declining to interfere in any of their cases.

At ten o'clock Tuesday morning, September 6, and on Wednesday and Thursday at the same time, the Methodist Church held prayer meetings for the benefit of the five condemned men.

Just before ten o'clock Friday morning, September 9, 1881, the five men in their new suits — probably the first and certainly the last that any of them ever owned — started their walk to the gallows. Just outside the jail, William Brown fainted and was revived with water applied to his face. He said he was not accustomed to the hot sun. The procession continued on and mounted the scaffold without incident.

"The Instrument of Death" as described by *The Elevator*, September 9, 1881:

> The scaffold has been erected in the southwest corner of the walls surrounding the garrison. The place is very small and will not admit of more that fifty witnesses, hardly that many in addition to the guards and attendants. The surroundings are anything but inviting. The scaffold stands eight feet above the ground. A stairway of 12 steps, 3 feet 6 inches in width, leads up to the platform which is 14 x 15. The trap twelve feet long by three wide and is so arranged as to give way in the center when sprung, each half being on hinges. The cross beam above the platform is seven feet two inches above platform and is of heavy timber. The ropes are so arranged so as to give about six feet drop. A deep trench has been dug directly under the trap, so as to prevent the feet of the condemned men from striking the ground.

The Herald the day after the execution headlined the event in a less Shakespearean manner than *The New Era*. With a headline of at least twenty-four-point type and subheads of diminishing sizes, it proclaimed:

Fatal Drop!
Five Brave Men Gone
Down to Their Doom!
M'gowan's Eloquent Speech!
Confessions of Killing but not of Murder!
Unparalleled Fortitude!
On Their Way Upward!

All newspapers, however, gave essentially the same account of the hanging and the events leading up to it.

On the scaffold, the prisoners—in their suits, white shirts, and black neckties—were seated on a long bench in the following order: Padgett, McGowen, Brown, and Amos and Abler Manley. Chief Deputy Marshal Huffington read each man's death sentence, then Reverend Mr. Jeffett, spiritual adviser to all but McGowen, offered a prayer. Reverend Father Lawrence Smythe, who had administered the sacrament to McGowen the day before, had a short conversation with him. Handshaking all around with attorneys, marshals, guards, and others then followed. The doomed men moved to the front of the platform, stood upon the trap, and spoke their last words.

Padgett claimed self-defense and said, "They brought false witnesses to swear against me."

McGowen spoke eloquently. He also complained of false witnesses and asserted that he had killed in self-defense. He said the man he killed was an outlaw, and if he had had his just deserts, the man he killed would be standing in his place that day. McGowen also spoke of his wife and children, whom he was leaving "to the mercy of the four winds." At that point, tears filled his eyes and his voice trembled as he finished with, "I die claiming to be an innocent man, and bid you all a long farewell."

Padgett and McGowen had taken it "very hard and bitter in their anguish at not getting a stay until the President" recovered sufficiently to review their cases. President Garfield had been shot July 2, 1881. He died shortly after the executions, never having recovered from his wounds.

Brown was calmer and clearer in his speech. He said, "I realize that I am standing on the scaffold of death, feeling that my sins are forgiven, and I forgive all mankind." He acknowledged killing his friend by mistake and stated that he would rather have died himself. "I feel as if I am going off in a sweet sleep, and will meet you all in glory. I am ready and willing to go." He then spoke to Mr. Tom Barnes, who was standing in the crowd below, wishing him every success.

The Manley brothers, through an interpreter, spoke next, first Amos then Abler. They admitted they had done the killing but said that their lives had been threatened by McVay, which was in contradiction to the statement that they signed in their cell the night before.

The statement as printed in *The Fort Smith Herald* on September 10, 1881:

> Fort Smith, Ark. Sept. 8, 1881.
> This is my last night that I shall spend on this earth, for tomorrow I will be in eternity. I am innocent

of the crime that I am to be hung for. I am telling the truth as a lie could not do me any good, the good God in heaven knows that I did not know anything about it. Hans Posley and the woman swore lies on me. I will be punished for something I did not do.

Able Manley
Amos Manley

When all had finished speaking, the black caps were put in place, ropes adjusted, and "at 10:10 o'clock they were suspended between heaven and earth." When "life was extinct," their bodies were placed in coffins and taken away. The body of Padgett was taken charge of by his stepfather, McGowen's was taken to the Catholic cemetery, and the three others were buried on the reservation to be taken away by relatives when the weather was cooler.

All was over by eleven o'clock and with so little excitement and éclat, that the whole dreadful affair did not cause as much of a ripple outside the walls as an ordinary street fight.

— *The New Era*, September 14, 1881

Note: Valentine Dell, editor of *The New Era*, was appointed U.S. district marshal in July 1880. He continued as editor of his newspaper. In June 1881, Marshal Dell ordered uniforms for his officers, guards, and bailiffs. The uniforms were of a military style and of dark blue cloth with light blue cord and with gilt buttons.

CHAPTER 13

EDWARD FULSOM, HIRED GUN OR ACCIDENTAL ACCOMPLICE?

On Wednesday, August 17, 1881, *The New Era* published this account of a double murder in Arkansas on the border of Indian Territory. The same article was repeated in the Saturday, August 20, edition of *The Weekly Herald* without the headline and subhead.

DOUBLE MURDER
Wm. Massingill and George Stewart
Assassinated in the Choctaw Nation
Waldron, Scott Co. Ark.
August 15, 1881
Hon. V. Dell, U.S. Marshall West. Dist. Ark.
Dear Sir: Last Friday morning William Massingill, who has worked for me three years past, left my house and went into the edge of Choctaw Nation, west of Waldron, and stopped to stay all night at the house of John Stewart, who lives just inside the Nation. About nine o'clock in the evening James Hobbs, a white man, and Ed Fulsom, a Choctaw, came to said Stewart's house and shot Stewart seven times, killing him dead. Massingill started to run and one or the other of the assassins shot him in the back of the head, killing him instantly, and then beat him on the head till it was crushed to pieces and mutilated horribly. Massingill was an entire stranger to the murderers, and was a quiet, honest, peaceable man, and none were better thought of in this community than him.

It is hoped for and desired that you will secure the arrest of the assassins and bring them to a speedy trial in the U.S. Court at Fort Smith for this most diabolical double murder.

Yours very respectfully,
T.

Edward Fulsom was captured and tried for the murders, but his partner in crime, James Hobbs, escaped. The session of court that would try Fulsom convened on the first Monday of February 1882 with Judge Parker giving one of his famous charges to the grand jury. *The*

Wheeler's Independent printed an excerpt of that address that expressed the essence of all of the judge's charges to juries. The following is verbatim from that article:

On Monday last U.S. Court convened. The Hon. Isaac Parker delivered one of his forcible charges to the grand jury, which was listened to with deep interest by a large attendance. (The court is always crowded when Old Ironsides charges his sitting juries). We do not give the charge at length to our readers as we would wish, for they are extempore and general to the interests of the community in a legal sense, but we jotted down the following remarks, which allude to the careless and frequent abuse of the pardoning power:

"This power under [our] own system of Government is properly placed in the hands of executive officers to be exercised only when injustice has been done the party convicted. When exercised without understanding the facts of the case, it becomes an instrument of great wrong and grievous outrage upon the people who look to the vigorous enforcement of the law for their security and their protection.

"Sometimes executive officers are carried away by a false sympathy for the criminal. Sometimes they become over desirous of getting a reputation for being merciful. The improper exercise of this power, from whatever cause, may seem to be mercy to the individual, but it becomes the most terrible cruelty to the people who for their own safety have a right to the enforcement of legal penalties in the full measure in all cases where the crime has been proven and the law fairly given. The abuse of this power is a fruitful cause of the crimes against the life and property abroad in the land. Criminals by its abuse are encouraged in the belief that they can evade the penalties of the law by the aid of the executive.

"Those in authority who abuse this power, unwittingly become promoters of crime. When a high crime is committed and the guilt of the criminal is established as required by law, punishment should follow with unerring certainty. In this way only can the people have peace and the law-abiding be protected. He who abuses this power to pardon, be he President or Governor, exhibits his unfi[t]ness for his high station.

"The people demand of all those in official position that they will enforce the law. They have a right to make this demand and to see that it is observed because the peace of the country and the security of their lives and property depend upon it."

At that time Chester A. Arthur, as vice president, had succeeded to the presidency following the assassination of President James A. Garfield. There had been few commutations during either of their administrations, but President Hayes, who preceded Garfield, had commuted the sentences of almost everyone convicted of capital crimes during his term in office. Some of those cases had been heinous crimes prosecuted with incontrovertible evidence, yet the chief executive had seen fit to override the court's decisions. Parker must have been venting his frustration over those decrees.

Edward Fulsom, about twenty years old at the time of his trial, had been born to parents well connected in the Indian Nation, his father being Judge Fulsom of Scullyville and his grandfather Honorable Peter P. Pytentin. On his mother's side, he was connected with the McCurtains (McCurtain County) and the Pages, all well respected in the Nation. He had gone to school at McAlester and later at the district school at Scullyville. After his schooling, he worked as clerk and interpreter in a store and then took up the roving way of cattle hunting and herding for cattle buyers. Cattle hunting in remote areas entailed carrying a gun, but there was no indication that Fulsom was involved in any shooting affray prior to the case for which he was convicted.

Fulsom had known James Hobbs only a short time before August 1881, and they had become partners in the practice of cattle hunting and whiskey running. They made John Stewart's place their informal rendezvous. Stewart owned a house situated on the line between Scott County, Arkansas, and the Indian Territory. The house must have been a combination store, tavern, and gambling house, judging by the events that took place there.

For a day or two before the killing, Fulsom and Hobbs had been seen around the area of Stewart's establishment without any "perceptible reason for so doing." On the afternoon of August 12, 1881, Edward Fulsom and James Hobbs went to Stewart's place, where they played cards and drank. They left, and about three o'clock were found by a Mr. Hill, a neighbor of Stewart's, lying beside the road near his well "in a state of intoxication." The two stayed on Hill's premises until they had had supper and then started for Stewart's store about a quarter-mile away. Sometime after dark, they arrived at the store. Finding it closed, they called for Stewart. Mrs. Stewart, "a young woman in delicate health," answered their call and asked their business. John Stewart then appeared and asked their names, which were given but with protest, "[Y]ou should not make us give our names, for there are strangers here." Stewart admitted the pair to the store and went back for a light. Then, according to a partial confession by Fulsom, they engaged in a game of cards, and in the ensuing events, Fulsom was only a witness and participated in none of the violence.

For some reason a quarrel broke out, either between Fulsom and Stewart or between Hobbs and Stewart. The truth was never ascertained. Stewart was shot seven times and fell dead. The contention of the prosecution was that, as two of the wounds were in the back, they were the first shots fired as Stewart turned to replace a bottle of liquor on the shelf. Massingill, a stranger to the assailants, appeared and started to run. Hobbs pursued him, fired twice, one shot hitting Massingill in the back of the head and killing him instantly. Fulsom then went behind the counter and emptied his revolver of the remaining shots into the breast of Stewart. Further testimony, as reported by the papers, told that after Hobbs had shot and killed Massingill, he beat and mutilated his head with his gun. At that time, Fulsom came out and said, "Don't beat him, shoot him." The defense argued that Hobbs was known to carry two pistols and that he did all of the shooting. But it was revealed that after they left the scene of the murders, they went to the house of a neighbor identified by *The Elevator* as Jesse M. Wright, who lived about five miles away. The same article described how Fulsom had left his bloody boot print on the head and chest of the victim. The writer then tells of the two murderers mounting their horses and leaving the scene whooping and yelling, keeping that up for two miles. At the home of Mr. Wright, Hobbs gave the man his pistol and three cartridges and asked him to reload it. Fulsom then gave the neighbor his gun for the same purpose, but when the man noticed "blood upon the face and bosom" of Fulsom, he remarked that it looked as if he had been in some sort of trouble. To that, Fulsom replied, "Yes, we have killed two of them." At that reply, the man returned the gun to Fulsom. That description by *The New Era* seems to imply that Wright was repulsed by the circumstances. However, *The Elevator* reported that the murderers stayed the night at that home.

Other circumstances reported in *The New Era* suggested that the killing of Stewart might have been a murder for hire. That paper reported that, according to a partial confession by Fulsom, someone near Waldron, Arkansas, not far from the crime scene, had offered him $750 to kill Stewart but he did not accept the offer.

Among the witnesses Fulsom requested subpoenaed was Jackson Crow, who would himself hang just three months short of six years after Fulsom. In that petition, Fulsom told his version of events, which seems at times to be contradictory. According to the document, Fulsom expected "to prove, by Mrs. Walker who lives near the place of the alleged killing that other men were seen in the vicinity late that evening and at the time defendant and Hobbs passed by her house after the killing that two other men ran by her house at the same time coming from the direction of the place where the killing was done." He went on to challenge Mrs. Stewart's testimony before the Coroner's Court, asserting that her calculations of distances between buildings, people, and herself were incorrect and "that it was so dark that she could not tell a white man from a Negro." By a Mr. Cauthron, Fulsom expected to prove that "Mrs. Stewart stated on the morning after the killing that this defendant did not go out of the grocery house during the shooting and that he abused Hobbs for beating Massingill on the head with the pistol after he had shot and killed him, and that Hobbs threatened to kill Fulsom if he did not attend to his business." Here he appears to admit being at the scene where before he contended that Mrs. Walker would prove that he was elsewhere. By Jackson Crow, he planned to show "that there was a plot between Hobbs and others not known to this defendant, to kill Stewart and Hobbs induced this defendant, to go with him to Stewart's house in order to decoy Stewart out, thinking that as this defendant and Stewart were good friends that he could get Stewart to come out of his house at night and not knowing the intention of Hobbs he was induced to go and that Hobbs had accomplices outside of the house, and that they and Hobbs did the killing."

Because of the peculiar location of the property where the crime took place, there was considerable argument by the defense over jurisdiction. Fulsom, when arrested, had first been taken to Waldron, Arkansas, in Scott County to be tried by state authorities. The U.S. Court, however, issued a writ allowing a U.S. marshal to bring Fulsom to Fort Smith for trial. Defense lawyers argued long but unsuccessfully on the point of jurisdiction. Neither the court nor the jury accepted their argument, and the jury was out about one hour before returning a verdict of guilty.

On June 30, 1882, Edward Fulsom went to the gallows. On that same day in Washington, D.C., one Charles Guiteau, assassin, also went to the gallows. The news of Fulsom's trial and execution had shared the news pages with that of Guiteau, assassin of President Garfield. They had occupied about the same news space up until the time of their executions. Guiteau, however, got more print covering his execution than did Fulsom.

Immediately before and after Fulsom's execution, the local papers described his background, his crime, his visits with his wife, and the baptism of their child by Reverend Berne at the U.S. jail. But, as to the hanging, *The New Era* said, "At precisely eleven o'clock the procession started from the U.S. jail for the gallows and in twenty minutes all was over, Fulsom declining to make any remarks before being launched into eternity." The paper did go on to say that Fulsom was attended by Reverend Berne of the P. E. Church, who administered religious consolations to him. And that, "Thus perished, miserably, a young man who might have been an honor to his people and ornament to society." The article neglected to mention that, although the walk to the gallows began at eleven o'clock and the drop was accomplished at 11:17, the body hung for one hour and three minutes until the pulse stopped. Fulsom's neck was not broken, but there was no contortion or struggle, and he "hung like a statue" (*The Wheeler's Independent*, July 5, 1882). The reporter went on to describe the protrusion and color of Fulsom's tongue and stated that Fulsom was a small man, estimated to weigh only about 110 pounds, and that he had appeared to turn his head just as the drop fell, thereby, changing the position of the noose.

When the body was taken down and placed in the casket, Reverend Berne performed the burial ceremony. After the hanging, Mrs. Page, Fulsom's aunt, entered the gallows area to attend the ceremony, but on seeing the casket, she fainted "and fell heavily on the ground" and was not revived until the services were over. The burial was at Mrs. Page's home at Cedar Prairie, about ten miles from the city.

Fulsom's trial attracted attention only because of the legal wrangling over jurisdiction, and his hanging attracted about only twenty viewers, including physicians and clergy. It should be noted, though, that since July 1878, no one had been allowed inside the garrison walls on an execution day except lawmen, clergymen, reporters, and invited guests and that not all of those were allowed inside the sixteen-foot wooden fence around the gallows.

Edward Fulsom was the twenty-fifth man to hang during Judge Parker's administration and the thirty-second hanged during the existence of the Western District Court in Fort Smith. The gallows would wait for more than ten months, until April 13, 1883, for number twenty-six/thirty-three. But in the meantime, the court would try numerous people for capital crimes, some to have the charges reduced and some to have their sentences commuted to life imprisonment.

Mrs. Stewart would later remarry and be known as Alice B. Eads, the same Alice B. Eads who in 1934 claimed to have been the first female deputy U.S. marshal. Her story is long on imagination and devoid of facts. In fact, there are some outright untruths in it.

CHAPTER 14

CATTLE DRIVES, OUTLAWS, AND A HANGIN'

The years 1882 and 1883 were when outlaw legends were born, or died, as the case may be. On Tuesday, April 4, 1882, *The Journal* of Kansas City, Missouri, ran the headline, "Good Bye, Jesse." Bob Ford had shot Jesse James at St. Joseph, Missouri, the day before. On October 6, 1882, the same paper ran the headline, "Surrendered." On October 5, 1882, at Jefferson City, Missouri, Frank James surrendered himself and his weapon to Governor Thomas Crittendon. Also on October 6, the following telegram was sent from New York City to Kansas City:

> To Mr. Speers, Chief of Police: Has Frank James surrendered? Let me know immediately. Bob Ford.

And down at Fort Smith in February 1883, the U.S. District Court for the Western District of Arkansas convicted Sam and Belle Starr for horse stealing. But in between all of those events, Robert Massey was tried in December 1882 in the Western District Court for the murder of Edmond P. Clark, a young man not quite twenty.

The story of Massey and Clark sounds like the outline of a B-grade Western or a dime novel. In 1881 they drove a herd of cattle from Dodge City, Kansas, up to Dakota Territory. After delivering the herd, they started back to their homes in Texas, Massey being from Grayson County and Clark from Comanche County. While passing through Indian Territory about December 1, 1881, they camped near the South Canadian about 225 miles west of Fort Smith. While encamped, Massey shot Clark through the head and dragged his body to a hole about fifty yards from the camp and concealed it. He then burned Clark's saddle, coat, shirt, leggings, and other belongings but kept his gun, belt, and horse, turning his own worn-out horse loose. Massey then went on his way, thinking the evidence disposed of, little knowing Clark had sent a letter to his parents telling them he would be home for Christmas.

Edmond Clark had written his family from Abilene, Kansas, that he would be home for Christmas. When Christmas came and went and no word was heard from his son, Clark's father began making inquiries and placed ads in several Kansas newspapers describing the young man. In mid-February 1882, a man named Bean was hunting in the Chickasaw Nation when he saw wolf tracks leading to a hole in a creek bank. Following the tracks, he found a body hidden by debris. At first he thought it was the body of an animal, but on removing the covering, he found the naked foot of a man. When he and neighbors uncovered the body, they found that it had been shot in the back of the head, the bullet exiting over the right eye. The body had been stripped of clothing except for pants and a red bandanna around the neck. One member of the group who had seen the description of Clark in the newspapers wrote to Mr. Clark suggesting that the body might be that of his son.

Mr. Clark immediately set out to investigate, taking a picture of Edmond with him. His inquiries revealed that his son and Massey set out together from Kansas and were seen together along the way. At the scene of the murder, in a pile of ashes, were found the irons of the saddle, a hull of a cartridge, some shirt buttons, the buttons from a rain slicker, copper fastenings from the leggings, and some buckles. Clark's boots and a spur were found a few steps from the fire. The belongings were carefully gathered, and the elder Clark, satisfied that Massey had killed his son, set out in search of him. Mr. Clark found his man in April about twenty-five miles from Fort Sill, arrested him without incident, and turned him over to authorities to be brought to Fort Smith.

Edmond Clark's pistol was found at the camp where Massey had been located in the possession of a man to whom Massey had traded it; it was identified by the letter "E" cut in the ivory handle and Clark's name scratched in the nickel plate on the butt. Massey had traded Clark's horse to his brother-in-law when he returned to Texas. On the horse that he had traded for, he set out again into the Territory.

The evidence against Massey was circumstantial, but the chain of evidence was complete, even to arriving at the date of the murder, due to the work of Mr. Clark and the Marshals Office. Massey and Clark stopped two nights with two cowboys about thirty-five miles from where the murder would take place, and those men identified Clark's boots and the ivory-handled pistol with the letter "E." Apparently, from the various newspaper reports, they stopped at more than one camp, and in at least one, Massey used the alias "Bob Burns" and called his partner "Bill Dixon." At that camp, Massey told a Mr. Smith that the reason for the assumed names was that he had killed a man in Dakota. He then gave Mr. Smith his right name. Massey and Clark were next seen at a camp about ten miles from the killing, Massey riding a brown horse that seemed exhausted and Clark on a gray mare. At that camp, according to one report, Clark and Massey got into an argument and Massey told someone that he would blow Clark's head off. Massey was next seen a few days later at a ferry about twenty miles from the murder scene, alone and riding a gray mare. He went on to his home in Texas, where he swapped the mare for another horse.

Massey was defended by Messrs. Mallette, Barnes, and William M. Cravens, who entered for him a plea of self-defense. Massey claimed that he and Clark argued the morning of the day of the killing over money Clark owed him. The argument later escalated to the point that Clark fired three shots at him. Massey then fired the fatal shot that hit Clark in the head. His explanation for the wound being in the back of the head was that Clark had turned his head at that moment. The prosecution's counter to that claim was that Clark had been asleep, using his saddle as a pillow, the bullet had pierced the saddle and blood had stained the other articles and that was the reason for the burning of those items. Massey said that he had kept the horse, gun, and belt for the money that Clark owed him and burned the rest to avoid being caught. When asked why he did not burn the boots, he replied that he had intended to but was excited and must have overlooked them.

The jury was given the case late Saturday evening, December 9, 1882, and deliberated until about eleven o'clock in the morning on Monday, December 11, before delivering the guilty verdict. When the verdict was read, Massey's mother, who had attended the entire proceeding along with his brother, George, was almost prostrate with grief.

On February 1, 1883, Robert Massey along with John Jacobs, who was also convicted of murder in December 1882, was sentenced to hang on Friday, April 13, 1883. Jacobs would be more fortunate than Massey and have his sentence commuted.

On February 19, 1883, Sam and Belle Starr were convicted of horse stealing and sentenced to the federal prison at Detroit, Michigan. By the way the articles in the papers of the day were written, it appears that Belle was not as well known in Fort Smith as later historians would lead us to believe. The articles give the impression that she was someone about whom the reporters had heard a lot but had little first-hand knowledge. Many sentences in the articles begin, "It is said that..." The event did get a lot of print space in one paper, though, for several reasons. Tom Starr, the patriarch of the Starr clan, rated some notice because he had become notorious as a partisan in the "bloody vendetta" between the Ross and the treaty factions in the Cherokee Nation. Secondly, a woman convicted for horse stealing was unusual, and even more so, a husband and wife convicted together. And beyond that, the husband got one year for one count of horse stealing, and the wife got two years for two counts. Those things alone would have rated at least a paragraph, no matter what the names of the subjects.

On March 19, 1883, Sam and Belle Starr, along with twenty other prisoners, Deputy Marshal Barnes, and four guards, departed for Detroit Prison. *The Wheeler's Independent* reported, "Belle Starr had a repugnance to the expose in marching off with a squad of prisoners, she was courteously furnished with a well dressed guard and escourted [sic] to the depot in bon ton style." (The fact is that all guards were "well dressed," especially when transferring prisoners. They had been so since 1881 when U.S. District Marshal V. Dell had ordered military-style uniforms for them.)

Massey's representatives made the usual appeals to the president for pardon or commutation to no avail. During his incarceration, he received the care of Reverend D. McManus and two ladies of the Episcopal Church and was baptized. He slept soundly the night before his execution. At eleven o'clock the morning of Friday, April 13, 1883, Chief Deputy C. M. Barnes read the death warrant. The procession of deputies, guards, prisoner, minister, and physicians then started to the gallows. McManus, who walked beside Massey on the left, began the reading service, the *miserere* and *de profundis*, the others in attendance reverently removing their hats as he read. Massey, being handcuffed, asked guard Williams to remove his hat. "Although he was going to his doom, no man in the party walked more erect, nor with a firmer, steadier step than the condemned Massey" (*The Elevator*, April 20, 1883).

On the scaffold, McManus continued the service. Massey sat, stood, or kneeled, and calmly looked at the gallows, rope, and spectators. When the religious services were done, Massey's counsel, DuVal, Cravens, and Thomas H. Barnes, as well as the jailer and the guards, shook his hand. Massey remained composed. He began a conversation with his counsel, requesting them to make a public statement after his death denying his guilt. Barnes, thinking he wished to speak, said, "Mr. Massey, if you have anything to say, please speak up so that all may hear you." Massey stepped to the front of the platform and spoke in "clear, strong, unfaltering tones," claiming as before that he had killed in self-defense, and although the evidence was against him, he was innocent. He was then placed under the crossbeam and on the trap, his hands and feet bound, the black cap and noose put in place. Barnes by the wave of his hand signaled jailer Burns, who sprang the drop at 11:37 a.m., and in twelve minutes, Massey's pulse ceased.

The hanging was private, as all hangings had been since July 1878 when the platform was lowered and the wooden fence raised in anticipation of Carolina Grayson's execution. Besides the guards, there were only a few spectators (twenty by one report), including the reporters. Among them was Edmond Clark's father, who had come from Texas to witness the execution. It was the second time in two years that a father had tracked down his son's murderer and witnessed his execution.

After the body was taken down, Captain John Williams, who was sent by the Massey family, took charge of the body, which was placed in "a neat coffin" and buried in the city cemetery where Reverend McManus performed the burial service.

The gallows would have a respite of just more than two months before it was called into service again.

CHAPTER 15

"THREE LIVES FOR SIX"
(*The Fort Smith Elevator*, July 6, 1883)

Last Friday [June 29, 1883] the three condemned
men, Martin Joseph, Wm. H. Finch and Tual-is-ta, [sic]
expiated their crimes upon the gallows.
— *The New Era*, July 5, 1883

The aforementioned three, plus one lawman who was tried for
murder and convicted of manslaughter, represent some of the diversity
of men tried for capital crimes in the U.S. District Court in the court
terms from November 1882 through May 1883. These four make up
only about a third of the people indicted and tried for capital crimes
during that time period.

WILLIAM H. FINCH

William Finch was a remarkable man among soldiers at that time.
Born a slave in Georgia, he joined the U.S. Army after the Civil War. At
the beginning of the events that led to his trial, he was a tailor at Fort
Sill, Indian Territory. One account has him belonging to the Twenty-
fourth Infantry at Fort Sill, and another says that he had been a member of the Twenty-fifth Infantry and was not in the Army in July 1882
but a tailor at the post. Finch was reputed to have been a very good
tailor and must have educated himself extensively, judging from his
long and eloquent speeches and letters during his sentencing and his
wait for execution.

In July 1882, the post commander summoned Finch to answer for
some minor infraction. Instead of reporting to the officer, he stole a
horse and fled to Texas, where he was captured by civil authorities.
Sergeant Johnson and privates Grimky and McCarty were detailed to
return the prisoner to Fort Sill. A short distance from the post, twenty
miles or so, the detail stopped to rest around two or three o'clock in the
afternoon. After they had eaten and smoked, Johnson and Grimky lay
down and went to sleep, and the prisoner, shackled only at the feet,
feigned sleep. Private Jerry McCarty went to a nearby spring to fill the
canteens. At the first opportunity, Finch grabbed a carbine and pistol
and shot Johnson with the carbine and Grimky with the pistol. On
hearing the shot, McCarty returned in time to see Finch shoot Johnson.
McCarty watched from the safety of some bushes while Finch took the

keys from Johnson's pocket and freed himself. Finch then hid two carbines in the grass, saddled and bridled a horse, took a carbine, a pistol, and provisions, and "flew over the plains to Caddo." At Caddo he took a train to Dennison, Texas, where he was arrested, then taken to Fort Smith.

After Finch left the camp, McCarty returned to find Grimky dead and Johnson dying. Johnson told McCarty that Finch shot him and then Grimky and sent him to the fort for a doctor. McCarty set out for Fort Sill after spreading a sheet over Johnson, as asked, to keep the mosquitoes off. He arrived at the fort about eight o'clock that evening and related the facts to the authorities. About midnight, a detachment of teamsters, a doctor, and McCarty started for the camp. They did not find the camp until about nine o'clock the next morning, and there they found Sergeant Johnson dead. The bodies of the murdered men were placed in the wagon and returned to the fort, arriving there the evening of the same day.

Finch was tried in February 1883 and was defended by DuVal and Barnes. His defense was that McCarty had killed the other two and freed him. He claimed that he had defected from the fort in the first place to escape the tyranny of the commanding officer. The jury was out but a few minutes before returning the guilty verdict.

TE-O-LIT-SE
AKA TUALISTA, TEE-O-LIT-SA, TUAL-ISTA, TUALISTO, TOLETSO

In March 1883, following Finch's conviction, Teolitse, a Creek Indian, became the next candidate for the gallows. Teolitse had been seen on July 6, 1881, following a white man named Emanuel C. Cochrane at a distance. Cochrane was traveling through the Indian Territory on his return to his home in Texas from Eureka Springs, Arkansas, where he had received treatment for his chronically sore eyes. He was walking, carrying his boots, and had wrapped his sore feet in cloths to protect them from the hot road. About twenty miles south of Okmulgee in the Chickasaw Nation, the murderer rode up behind Cochrane and, with his rifle, shot him in the head, dismounted, and robbed the victim of his few dollars. The body was found the next day, the face partly eaten by hogs.

The murder was a mystery for a while until Cochrane's brothers offered a $200 reward and Deputy Marshal Beck began working on the case. Beck was assisted by citizens of the area, and the trail led to Teolitse. Another Creek Indian, John Sinner, was called on to parley with the suspect and eventually got the story from the murderer himself. Beck then obtained a writ for the arrest of Teolitse, but when he went to serve it, he found that Teolitse had been found guilty of horse stealing by his people's tribal court. The sentence was whipping, and when the suspect was released from the whipping post, Beck served his writ and arrested him for murder. Teolitse was brought to Fort Smith in August 1882, more than a year after the murder was committed. He languished in the jail until March 1883 when he was tried. *The Fort Smith Elevator* reported, "He was ably defended, but the evidence was so overwhelming that a defense was scarcely necessary."

MARTIN JOSEPH, A.K.A., "BULLY" JOHNSON

The crime of Martin Joseph was an extreme example of wantonness, but the crime and the collection of evidence have been "elaborated on" over the years. The stories in the newspapers of the time came not only from evidence and from people associated with the events, but also from Joseph's own confession.

Martin Joseph, "an Indian Negro" residing in the Chickasaw Nation, was in the business of horse stealing in partnership with Bud Stephens, white, and Henry Loftis, black. In April 1882, the three men went to the woods in the Arbuckle Mountain region of Indian Territory to build a corral to contain the proceeds from their planned foray. One account has Joseph and Stephens stringing a rope around a circle of trees to form the corral while Loftis was somewhere else. Another has all three together and Joseph and Loftis collaborating in what took place. In Joseph's confession, he said that Loftis shot Stephens behind the ear and then Joseph went to the camp where they had left Mrs. Stephens, "a comely young woman of eighteen" (age given as sixteen, seventeen, and eighteen in other articles). He told her that her husband had been injured and was calling for her and took her up on the horse behind him to go to the place. Instead of going to her dead husband, Joseph took the woman to a cave where Loftis joined him, and they both raped her. Joseph then shot her as she sat crying with her apron over her face. They threw her body into the cave and threw in after her some clothing, saddlebags, and a quilt.

Some time later, Joseph, while intoxicated, told the story to William Loftis, brother of Henry Loftis, and the tale spread but was disbelieved. Later Joseph got into an argument with Henry and accused him of telling their secret and killed him too. That was the story as related by the newspapers. The depositions of witnesses and Joseph's application for witnesses tell quite a different story. The stories all vary in content, but all agree that the shooting of Henry Loftis occurred at the home of July Joseph, Martin Joseph's father, and was the result of a dispute over a pawned saddle, although it may have had other roots.

George Bruner was at Joseph's home for Sunday dinner when Joe Factor, to whom he had loaned three dollars and accepted a saddle in

George Winston
Judge Isaac C. Parker's bailiff

pawn, came to the house to demand return of the saddle. Factor was accompanied by Henry Loftis. There was a disagreement over the saddle, and Factor said he would rather leave than cause a disturbance at July Joseph's house on Sunday. Henry Loftis said that he would sooner burn in hell than leave without the saddle. Loftis pulled the gun from Factor's scabbard, ran behind a tree, and pointed the gun in the direction of the house and Bruner. Martin Joseph then shot Loftis. On those events, all witnesses and Joseph agree. Joseph claimed that he shot Loftis from the porch and shot him through the neck and from the front. He asserted that the witnesses he requested would refute the government witnesses' stories. In their depositions, all but one of the witnesses for the prosecution said that Loftis was shot in the back. However, their stories have some variances. The one who appears to have said Loftis was shot from the front has the bullet entering at the place the others have it exiting. Some witnesses said there were powder burns on Loftis's coat. But one has a distance between the two men too great to produce powder burns. The documents present a very confusing series of events. However, it became a moot point because Joseph was tried and executed for the murder of Mrs. Stephens.

Joseph apparently left the country and, suspicions being aroused, a party went to the cave to verify the story. The party discovered the bones and clothing and went to Mr. Henderson, a merchant in the area, who alerted U.S. Deputy J. M. Mershon, who took a posse to the cave to investigate. At the cave, a young man named John Spencer, a guard for Mershon, (not Deputy Mershon himself) was let down into the pit and discovered the remains of Mrs. Stephens covered by rattlesnakes. He signaled the men at the top and was drawn up where he "obtained a pistol and descended to the bottom of the cave and commenced war upon the snakes" (*The Elevator*, April 13, 1883). Spencer proceeded to gather up the bones and clothing and brought them out. The party then went to find the location of the murder of Bud Stephens and collected as many bones there as they could find. The evidence, bones and all, was displayed on a table in the courtroom during the trial in April 1883.

> Who can imagine the thoughts that must have passed through the mind of the culprit when, on the witness stand, the attorney for the government placed in his hands the skull of the murdered man. It required a second bidding for him to take it.
> — *The Fort Smith New Era*, April 12, 1883

The trial lasted five days, and the jury, after being charged by Judge Parker, was out thirty minutes. When the jury of seven black men, including the jury foreman, Allen Bobo, and five white men re-entered the courtroom, "it required no prophet to foretell what the verdict would be" (*The New Era*). "[T]here was a deathlike stillness in the crowded room. Everyone present who knew anything of the facts in the case said in his heart of the jury, when the verdict of guilty was announced by the court in each case, 'well done, good and faithful servants'" (*The Elevator*).

SAM PAUL

Just a few days after Martin Joseph's conviction, a sergeant of the Indian Police stood before the jury and heard himself pronounced guilty, not of murder, with which he was charged, but of the reduced charge of manslaughter. It was not unheard of for lawmen to be charged and tried for crimes. Apparently, if there were any questionable circumstances in killings involving law officers, investigations were conducted and charges filed if applicable. In March 1883, Jimmy Jones, chief of Indian Police of the Kiowa and Comanche Indians, was tried for murder and acquitted, and some years later, one of the most effective and most famous deputy marshals would be tried for shooting his cook.

Sam Paul, the sergeant convicted, may not have been the most exemplary lawman, although an Indian policeman for a number of years. In gleaning what little information is available from the National Archives, this is the chronology that appears, muddled and overlapping as it may seem.

On December 1, 1877, a warrant was issued for Sam Paul and One Jake for the murder of John Farrell on November 1, 1877. The warrant was served on December 5, 1877, signed by J. M. Mershon. In the same month and week, on December 6, 1877, a warrant was issued for Mrs. Briley, first name unknown, and Sam Paul for on or about October 17, 1877, introducing spirituous liquors into the Indian Territory. That warrant was served December 7, 1877. A warrant issued on June 27, 1882, was served on June 28, 1882, for Sam Paul and four others for the murder of One Smith in June 1881. There is nothing in the archives to indicate the outcome of the case of introducing liquor, and in the murder cases, there are only the depositions of witnesses. If Paul had been convicted in the liquor case, there would have been only a fine, and since he continued on as a lawman, he was never convicted on the murder charges in those two cases.

In July 1882, things took a turn for the worse for Paul. On July 5, 1882, Sam Paul and Jim Ross (two others were named in the warrant but their names do not appear on later records) were arrested on a warrant issued on May 29, 1882, for the murder of John Hawkins on or about May 10, 1882. This murder charge was the one for which he was convicted in April 1883. The only records of the proceedings in the National Archives are copies of the warrants and summonses and the depositions of the witnesses. The newspapers of the time gave no account of the two trials Paul and Ross received, only one-sentence statements that they were in progress. However, the results of the second trial and the sentence did get some ink because both the verdict and the penalty were surprises.

In November 1882, Paul and Ross were tried in a trial that resulted in a hung jury. They were retried in April 1883, the case being given to the jury on Friday, April 13, 1883. The jury deliberated all that day and the next and finally returned a guilty verdict about midday Sunday, April 15, 1883. No records of the trial exist, only the depositions of witnesses. The statements of defense witnesses are only to confirm that Sam Paul was a second sergeant of Indian Police, Union Agency, and a constable in Pickens County, an elected office. All of the witnesses for the prosecution were connected somehow with the victim, John Hawkins, but their testimonies were consistent.

William Hawkins, nineteen-year-old brother of the deceased, testified that before daylight on Saturday, April 22, 1882, John Hawkins was awakened by someone calling his name from outside his house. He went outside, saw no one, and returned to the house but was called a second time and told whoever was calling to come to the house. Ten to twelve armed men, who were in the bushes, came to the house and told Hawkins that they wanted to take him to Governor Birnie's house to identify someone they were holding there. John and William Hawkins mounted and went with the group to Birnie's and then were told that they were being taken to Tishomingo. However, they were taken along an indirect route, and on the way, they stopped. Paul, Ross, and two others took John off the road. While they were gone, the remainder of the posse tried to make William think that they would hang him from a limb if he did not give them information about two other men.

While that was happening, there were four rapid gunshots followed by two shots, and Sam Paul reappeared and told William that they had killed his brother.

Sam Paul, after the shooting, went to the Crocket home and told them that he had shot John Hawkins, then went to the home of William Spicer, father-in-law of Hawkins. He told both families he had shot Hawkins, who was barely breathing when he left him and might be saved. Paul said that Hawkins had grabbed the barrel of his rifle; it discharged and he shot him while he was trying to escape. Testimony of William Spicer and others who went to retrieve the body and who examined the area did not completely agree with Paul's description of the action.

The newspapers had not given much notice of the trial, it falling in the same week as Martin Joseph's sensational trial, but they did note the surprising sentence. The court gave Sam the maximum sentence allowed—ten years in prison and a $500 fine—and *The Elevator* rose to his defense. *The Elevator* described Paul's reason for arresting Hawkins in the first place. In that version, he was in Tishomingo on business and "was summoned to go with the sheriff to protect the governor from assassination by a band of desperadoes who were threatening his life." How that put him in charge of a group that arrested Hawkins is not explained. But the article had previously stated that Paul, being a constable and sergeant of Indian Police, had instructions from Agent Tufts "to be active in suppressing disorder and the arrest of notorious thieves and criminals depredating in the territory." *The Elevator* mentioned Paul's service as a lawman and his many friends, both in the Indian and white communities, and called for his pardon before he ever was sent to prison. Colonel DuVal, one of Paul's counsels, told Judge Parker that the jury, at the time of agreeing on a verdict, had agreed to sign a petition to the court asking for mercy. In February of the next year attorneys DuVal and Cravens, *The Elevator*, and local citizens were still petitioning for a pardon.

Paul, when asked if he had anything to say as to why sentence should not be pronounced against him, gave "in a clear and distinct voice, a little tremulous at first," a speech of which "an imperfect synopsis" was printed in *The Elevator*.

> In the first place I am not guilty of the crime. I did not shoot. I drew my pistol when the deceased had seized my gun and would have shot me, probably, if he had not dropped it. I was forced by the summons of the sheriff to go out on that expedition to enforce the law and I did what I thought was right. For doing this it is possible that I am guilty in the eyes of the law, but

my conscience is clear as to actual guilt and it is hard to be disgraced and have a stigma cast upon my family whom I tenderly love and to be separated from them for years. I was acting under instructions as an officer with orders from my superior when this thing occurred. Suppose Marshal Boles, or yourself we will say, had been in charge of a posse and they had killed a person who had seized your gun and was attempting to escape. Would it have been right to send you or the marshal to hell? I think not. I shall apply for pardon and when the petition is presented to you and Col. Clayton I shall ask your clemency, then your and his signature.

Judge Parker then addressed the prisoner, telling him that he had no complaint, that he had two fair trials, and had been ably defended. He added that there had been "an utter disregard of human life in the Indian country" and that it was necessary to make an example. Parker also told Paul that his mistake was in taking his prisoner from the road and that he did not believe that he intended to kill him but that he (Paul) had no right to do what he did.

The prison time and fine were not the total of Sam Paul's problems. The sentence had not been only ten years and $500, it was ten years, $500 and costs. The costs were $2,017.15, and on May 12, 1883, there was a judgment against Sam Paul for $2,517.15—and that at a time when the average income in the United States was less than $500 per year.

THEIR DOOM PRONOUNCED
— *The Elevator*, May 11, 1883

On Saturday, May 5, 1883, five days after Sam Paul's sentencing, the three murderers, Finch, Teolitse, and Joseph, were sentenced "to be hanged by the neck until they were dead." First to stand before the bar was William Finch, "looking somewhat delicate from his long confinement." When asked if he had anything to say as to why the sentence of death should not be pronounced upon him, Finch launched into a long and eloquent speech of several minutes that evidenced an education far beyond what would be expected of an enlisted man of the U.S. Army in 1863. His speech was "clothed in elegant phraseology, evidently prepared with great care and committed to memory. He indulged in insinuations against the judge, jury and prosecuting attorney and made the usual complaint of not having a fair trial" (*The Independent*, May 9, 1883). In conclusion, he asked the judge to recommend him to the mercy of the president. In answer, the judge admonished Finch not to cling to the last hope of escape from punishment and advised him to use the time he had left to prepare to meet his maker.

Teolitse next came before the judge and heard his sentence through the aid of the interpreter, Grayson. He had nothing to say in his defense, and the judge, as he had with Finch, advised him to spend his time seeking forgiveness and preparing for his fate.

Martin Joseph, when asked if he had anything to say, replied that he was not guilty of the crimes. *The Independent* had a different opinion, which it expressed in this way:

> The atrocity manifest in the crimes committed by Joseph have left no sympathy for him in the public mind. No apology or excuse whatever can be entertained in his behalf even by a fanatical philanthropist. His advocates must have blushed when they pleaded for him before the jury. The crack of his neck under the rope will be music in the ears of justice, and we can hardly believe that any benefit of clergy will be of future avail to him.

EXECUTION

On Friday, June 29, 1883, at eleven o'clock in the morning, Chief Deputy Barnes entered cell No. 1 at the garrison and read the death warrants to the three condemned men. Teolitse had confessed to his crime shortly before the final hour, adding that Cochrane was not the only man he had killed, and showed the interviewers four buttons sewn on his hat, each representing a killing. Martin Joseph, too, confessed to all three murders and gave details of the crimes. At 11:10, the condemned and the usual accompaniment of guards, deputies, clergymen, reporters, and invited guests started the walk to the gallows. At the gallows, the usual ceremony of prayers, singing, and handshaking was observed with Finch and Joseph joining in the singing. Then all of the men were asked if they had any last words. Teolitse only pointed to his heart and shook his bowed head. Joseph said he had no statement to make. Finch, however, in a manner that belied his slave/soldier history made a "very mannerly bow" and stepped to the front of the platform. At that time, Teolitse collapsed and had to be helped to a seat.

Finch's speech was quoted in *The Elevator* on July 6, 1883, "in substance as follows":

> My friends, we meet here this morning upon a very solemn occasion and words are inadequate to ex-

press my feelings as I stand here before you. I make this statement because I think it is my duty and after that I can take the noose as freely as did Socrates when he drank the cup of hemlock. If I had been permitted to say anything at my trial I would not make a murmur now, but as I was not allowed to speak in my own behalf then I deem it now my duty to myself, to you and to my God to either confirm what I have said before or retract. When I do this I feel that I can die with a clear conscience. I taken that horse and left the post to escape the commander's tyranny and rather than be taken back there I taken that gun and killed those men to make good my escape. And now I have done all I can do; my conscience is clear, and when I am gone people may picture me as black as Nero, Tiberius and Caligula those tyrants of old. But no matter what the world may say, I ask you gentlemen of the press, for the sake of those dear ones I leave behind, especially that little boy there (his young brother) not to calumniate my character. Let me see the picture once more, and then I am ready to go beyond that unfathomable abyss of eternity.

Finch was handed a photograph of his sister, which he took in both hands and gazed at for a while, then exclaimed, "God bless that dear girl. May she ever live to cherish my fond memory." He then returned the picture; hands were shaken all around with ministers, physician, guards, and deputies. Finch then indicated his brother, "a bright negro boy," and said, "I hope this will be a warning to you, boy." When the cap was drawn on Joseph, he "began to quail." Teolitse had appeared weak and sick from the time they had left the jail and had to be supported until the fatal drop.

At 11:35 a.m., the drop fell. Teolitse never quivered and was dead in three-and-a-half minutes. Finch and Joseph's "bodies and limbs writhed and twitched convulsively for several minutes after they dropped below the platform." Joseph was dead in six-and-a-half minutes, Finch in nine. Forty people observed the execution, among them members of Finch's family, who had his body shipped to Georgia.

Shortly before the execution Finch had written four letters, one each to his father, his sister, and his two brothers. His letters were as long and as expressive as his speeches. He apparently had acquired an education beyond that of the average person of that day. How he had done so would be interesting to know.

CHAPTER 16

THREE DOWN, THREE TO GO
John Davis, Thomas L. Thompson,
and Jack Womankiller executed

On Friday, July 11, 1884, three of six prisoners convicted of capital crimes in the U.S. Western District Court walked to the gallows. By July 3, 1884, the other three had been spared the death sentence.

The period from July 1883 to July 1884 demonstrated the diversity of cases, difficulties, and decisions the court encountered. In July 1883, Mat Music was convicted of the rape of a six-year-old girl and made motion for retrial. In October, John C. Barr was charged with murder and convicted of manslaughter. The week of December 2-8 saw forty-four prisoners brought into the jail.

The next week, some trials were postponed because witnesses could not get to Fort Smith due to a flood. On December 18, 1883, a jury returned a verdict of guilty against the first woman to be convicted of a capital crime in the Western District Court. In its February 21, 1884, edition, *The New Era* reported that the grand jury had returned sixty true bills, seven for murder, and that seventy-five prisoners were in the U.S. jail. Those are just samplings of the articles relating to the court that appeared in the local papers.

MAT MUSIC

The Elevator on July 20, 1883, reported, "Mat Music a negro man about 35 years of age" was convicted on Saturday, July 14 of "a beastly outrage on the person of a little colored girl about six years of age." In the commission of the crime, "he ruined the health of the little girl for life, imparting to her a loathsome disease." The crime took place on Caddo Creek in the Chickasaw Nation, where the child was living with Music and his wife, the Musics having no children of their own. Music's only defense was that there were others who had the same opportunity that he did. Reportedly, the chain of evidence was too strong for the jury to render a verdict other than guilty. A motion for a new trial was made, but in May 1884, *The Elevator* reported that the motion was still pending, "which accounts for his sentence not having been passed long since."

Music and five others were sentenced on the previous Monday, April 28, 1884, to hang on July 11, 1884.

FANNY ECHOLS

Next to be convicted of a capital crime was Fanny Echols, the first woman to be so convicted in the U.S. Court of the Western District of Arkansas (*The Elevator*, May 2, 1884). On Tuesday evening, December 18, 1883, the jury returned a verdict of guilty of the murder of John Williams against Echols. "She had been, a long time previous to the killing, unlawfully cohabiting with her victim and disturbances between them seem to have been frequent occurrences. The last row terminated in the death of John at the hands of Fanny, and may yet result in the breaking of her neck." "She is a bright, well formed girl, about 25 years of age" (*The Elevator*, December 21, 1883). The couple lived at Eufaula, Creek Nation, and in July 1883, they had had one of their frequent arguments in Fanny's bedroom. There was a gunshot heard by other residents of the building, and when they entered, they found John lying on a pallet with a bullet wound to the chest. The bullet had penetrated John and the pallet and was embedded in the floor. The prosecution's argument was that he was killed while he slept or while he was "lying on his back in an unsuspecting attitude when he received the wound." Fanny's defense was that if she had not killed John, she would have been dead herself—that Williams was trying to get the pistol himself to shoot her.

DAN JONES

Saturday, December 22, 1883, Dan Jones was convicted of killing his cousin, Bill Jones, on August 6, 1879, in the Choctaw Nation. Both men were outlaws who had fled into the Territory from Scott County, Arkansas, to avoid arrest. On the fatal night, Bill's wife or mistress was awakened by a gunshot and found Bill lying dead by her side. The bullet had struck him in the cheek and traveled up into his head. Dan stood by the bed with a light in his hand, and Bill's pistol was found near the head of the bed with one chamber empty. The shot was not fired from outside the house, and there was no one inside the house except Dan, his wife and children, and the woman sleeping beside Bill. Dan's defense was that, "Bill shot himself in his sleep, it being asserted that he was in the habit of flourishing his pistol around in his dreams, imagining that he was fighting with officers of the law who were pursuing him."

Besides the circumstantial evidence the prosecution offered jealousy or revenge as motive. Dan Jones, during 1876, had been in a Texas prison for embezzlement, and during that time, Bill had looked after Dan's wife and two children. However, when Dan came home, he "found a third child, which he could not account for." Bill acknowledged that he was the child's father, and the matter seemed to have been resolved, and the two were partners until Bill's death. "The supposition is that a spirit of revenge rankled in the bosom of Dan, which caused him to quietly arise from his bed that night and slay his wife's traducer" (*The Elevator*, May 2, 1884).

Curiously, Dan Jones was not arrested for the killing, but about nine months before his conviction for the murder, he was brought to the U.S. jail on a charge of larceny and was convicted. The court suspended the larceny sentence, and while in jail, he was indicted for murder. The circumstances surrounding the case were stronger arguments to the jury than those offered by Jones's attorneys, Cravens and Barnes. The lawyers argued forcefully for a new trial but were overruled by the court.

THOMAS LEE THOMPSON

On Friday, February 22, 1884, exactly two months after Dan Jones received his conviction, the jury rendered Thomas L. Thompson, a white man, the same verdict. His trial for the murder of James O'Holerand lasted from Wednesday, February 20, until Friday afternoon when the jury returned the guilty verdict. The two men had known each other only a short time and lived together in a remote cabin near Stonewall, Chickasaw Nation. About September 20, 1883, O'Holerand disappeared. Probably no one would have missed him as the two lived in such a remote place and O'Holerand was not known in the area. But Thompson made a great show of inquiring about his missing partner. Thompson told neighbors that O'Holerand had started for Texas to get a load of whiskey and was to be back in twenty days. O'Holerand, who suffered chronically from fevers and chills, was sick when he left, and Thompson was worried about him. Thompson's stories had inconsistencies, though. One, he was in possession of O'Holerand's horse and saddle for which he claimed to have traded. He then had different accounts of that trade. Next, he had said that the horse, saddle, and bridle had been found in a field. All of those things caused concern among the neighbors, but no one made an inquiry until Thompson made another mistake.

While O'Holerand was missing, Thompson hired a man to fill in a dry well on their place. When the man approached his job, he noticed that a large amount of ashes had been dumped into the well and a powerful stench was coming from it. He related that information to the people at Stonewall, who went to the site to investigate. Thompson told the investigators that a hog was in the well, but they doubted his story, remembering his other inconsistencies. Thompson was placed under arrest while the party excavated the well, and he was told that he would be released if they, in fact, found a hog. Thompson then confessed to having killed his partner but claimed self-defense.

Thompson said that O'Holerand had a violent temper and would fly into a rage at the slightest provocation. On the day of the killing, Thompson had made some soup and O'Holerand had complained that it was too salty and that Thompson was trying to poison him. The argument escalated, and O'Holerand started after Thompson with a knife. Thompson ran outside, and O'Holerand pursued him around the house with an axe until Thompson grabbed a corn fuller (a maul-like instrument for pulverizing corn) and hit him in the head. However, when the body was retrieved, it was found to have a stab wound near the heart as if the victim had been lying down when stabbed. Thompson asserted that he did not know how the wound got there. Also the corn fuller was found to have blood on the handle end, indicating that Thompson already had blood on his hand when he picked it up. The arresting party believed that Thompson had stabbed his victim while he lay sick in bed, dragged him to the yard, and clubbed him.

The prosecution contended, and the jury agreed, that Thompson had killed O'Holerand to obtain his property. Thompson stuck to his self-defense story. Before his death, he wrote a letter to be published in *The Elevator*, relating in detail how he became acquainted with O'Holerand. In it, he described how they came to live where they did, the terms of their partnership, and O'Holerand's health and temperament, and he gave a minute account of the killing. He always claimed not to know how the knife wound got in O'Holerand's chest unless it happened while the investigating party was undressing him.

JOHN DAVIS

The day after *The New Era* announced Thomas Thompson's conviction, *The Elevator* announced the conviction of John Davis, a full-blood Choctaw about nineteen years old. Davis was convicted on February 27, 1884, of the murder of William Bullock of Howard County, Arkansas, in June 1883. "The jury returned a verdict in less than ten minutes after going out" (*The Elevator*, February 29, 1884).

William Bullock, father of "four motherless children," started across Indian country from Arkansas with a drove of cattle in the spring of 1883. After disposing of the cattle, he started on the return trip on foot. On June 27, he met John Davis in the Red River country. During a conversation, Davis came to believe that Bullock had some money and apparently decided to kill and rob him. As Bullock traveled on, Davis detoured through the woods, planning to strike the road ahead of his intended victim. But on reaching the road, he found that Bullock was still ahead of him. He tried again with the same result. On the third try, he got ahead of Bullock and waited behind a log. When his victim came in range, Davis fired, hitting Bullock in the left breast, the bullet going out his back. In Davis's own words, "The white man slapped his hand twice on the wound and hollered." Davis reloaded and shot Bullock, then lying on the ground, in the head and robbed him of sixteen dollars, a small pocket pistol, coat, and the saddlebags that Bullock carried. He took the dead man's boots, put them on his feet, leaving his at the scene, dragged the body to the side of the road, and left it. Afterward, Davis went home and told Ina James, the girl with whom he lived, of his deed.

On June 30, three days after the murder, local residents found the decomposed body, but nobody could identify it, so they buried it near where it had been found. On July 1, Davis went to a neighbor's home to borrow a saddle, saying that he was going to a store in Texas. Late that night he came back whooping drunk, shooting off his pistol and carrying two quarts of whiskey. He showed the neighbor Bullock's pistol and thirteen of the sixteen ill-gotten dollars, having spent three dollars on the whiskey. And he related the details of his crime. Shortly after that, he was arrested by the Red River County sheriff.

Bullock's friends, in the meantime, had begun to worry about him and had started to retrace his route and make inquiries. When they heard of the unidentified man being buried, they went to the place, disinterred the body, and identified it as Bullock's.

Davis never seemed to consider the killing and robbing of a white man as anything of great consequence and never seemed to realize the grave situation that he was in. "The condemned has taken the matter very coolly, his future seeming to trouble him very little. He could most always be seen at the bars of his prison with a contented smile on his countenance though he has had little or nothing to say in regard to the murder" (*The Elevator*, July 11, 1884).

JACK WOMANKILLER, A.K.A., GALCATCHER

Jack Womankiller killed a seventy-three-year-old white man, Nathaniel Hyatt, on May 7, 1883, and was convicted of that crime on Wednesday, March 5, 1884, just eight days after John Davis's conviction. Womankiller never denied his guilt after his conviction, and no effort was made "to save his neck."

On May 3, 1883, Hyatt left his home in the Cherokee Nation not far from Maysville, Arkansas, to look at some land about three miles from Maysville. On May 7, he was seen walking on a road between Maysville and his home with Womankiller riding along with him. Womankiller was drunk and carrying two small kegs of whiskey. When the two arrived at the Teehee home, about four miles from Hyatt's residence, Womankiller stopped to eat, but Hyatt walked on. When asked why Hyatt did not stop, Womankiller replied that it did not matter, that he was going to kill him anyway and to watch for the buzzards circling. No attention was paid to his drunken boasts until May 10, when they did see buzzards and found the decomposed body of Hyatt. He was lying under a tree with his coat folded under his head and one hand under his head as if asleep, his cane leaning against the tree. He had been shot in the left side and in one eye, and the money he was known to carry was missing. Not far from the body, they found Womankiller's hatband and one of the whiskey bottles. The hatband was identified as one that had fallen off Womankiller's hat at Teehee's. At that time, he had picked up the hatband and stuck it in his pocket.

Womankiller applied for three witnesses, and, "By said witnesses deft. can prove facts going to establish that he was not present at the place of the killing alledged [sic]. Also that he has not made the statements or confessions attributed to him in reference to said killing."

Whether those witnesses appeared is not known. If they did, the government witnesses were more convincing to the jury. The chain of evidence brought about Jack's arrest, and while in jail at Tahlequah in the Indian Territory, he admitted to a friend that he had killed Hyatt. Womankiller was ably defended, but he "had boasted of the deed, and this, together with the circumstances related, formed a chain of testimony that could not be broken, and which will probably break Jack's neck" (*The Elevator*, March 14, 1884).

DOOMED

Monday, April 28, 1884, "dawned cloudy and gloomy — just such a morning as is calculated to depress the spirits of all mankind" (*The Elevator*, May 2, 1884). And six people, Music, Echols, Jones, Thompson, Davis, and Womankiller, had another reason to be depressed — on that day Judge Parker would pass on them the sentence of death by hanging to take place July 11, 1884.

At nine thirty that morning, Judge Parker ordered the marshals to bring in the first three prisoners. The marshals then brought in Thomas L. Thompson, Jack Womankiller, and John Davis accompanied by the guards and two interpreters.

Thompson was first to stand before the judge, and when asked if he had anything to say before sentence was pronounced, he replied only that he had killed the man but did not cut him.

Womankiller was next given his sentence through an interpreter and had nothing to say except that it was all right.

Davis next stood up and received his sentence through an interpreter. By his remarks, it appears that he still did not realize the seriousness of his situation—he asked the court to be light on him in passing sentence.

The three condemned men were removed, and Dan Jones and Mat Music were brought in to receive the same sentence.

Music was first up and denied his guilt. In angry tones, he told the judge that if the laws of the United States hanged innocent men, then he would have to stand it.

Dan Jones asserted his innocence and said that his case had not been half investigated. He had had a motion before the court for a new trial, which had been overruled just before sentence was passed.

Fanny Echols, the first woman convicted of a capital crime and sentenced to death in the U.S. District Court for the Western District of Arkansas, was the last brought in. "She was plainly though neatly dressed and wore a nicely laundried sun bonnet." She said that she herself would have been killed had she not done what she did, and that she always thought a person had a right to defend oneself. She showed no emotion as she listened to her sentence and Judge Parker's address that he gave to all whom he sentenced to hang. On being removed from the courtroom, however, she broke down and was taken to her cell crying.

MINUTIAE

The newspapers of the day noted whenever the marshals brought in prisoners, how many, sometimes their names, and on occasion, their crimes. On June 13, 1884, between the sentencing and the execution of the condemned, these words appeared in *The Elevator* in the paragraph listing Deputy Farr's prisoners. "Mollie Speaks is a very pretty girl about 14 years of age. Her crime is the poisoning of an infant about three months old which she had been employed to nurse at the home of Mrs. Skaggs in the Choctaw Nation, about the 21st of March, by giving it lye. She acknowledges that she gave the stuff to the little one by dipping her finger in the box and putting it in its mouth."

In August of that year, the grand jury ignored Mollie's case, meaning they did not return a true bill, a bill of indictment.

UNCONDITIONAL PARDON AND COMMUTATIONS

After sitting in a U.S. jail for most of a year, much of that time pending the results of a motion for a new trial, Mat Music must have been elated on Monday evening, June 30, 1884, to learn that President Chester A. Arthur had granted him an unconditional pardon.

However, in that same communication, the president denied clemency for Fanny Echols and Dan Jones. It was reported that Judge Parker immediately telegraphed the U.S. attorney general informing him that both he and Prosecuting Attorney Clayton recommended commutation in Dan Jones's case "and his neck may yet be saved."

Jones's wife and children visited with him through the bars of the jail every day, and it was reported the he looked very downcast and haggard as the day of execution approached.

Up until the end of June, none of the condemned had appeared to make any preparations for their deaths or the hereafter. But on the same day that Music received his good news, Echols was baptized in the river by "the minister of the colored Baptist Church of this city." Jack Womankiller had "made no religious demonstrations" until the previous Thursday or Friday, "when he espoused the Baptist faith." He was baptized on the same morning as Echols, apparently by the same minister in a "large box or tank, which the government furnishes for such occasions" (*The Elevator*, July 4, 1884).

On Thursday, July 3, 1884, Jones and Echols had reason, if not the opportunity, to celebrate the Fourth of July. On that day, they received word that their sentences had been commuted to life in prison.

The Last Sunrise
Tomorrow's sun will rise for the last time to three men languishing in the U.S. Prison here and under sentence of death for murder committed in the Indian Territory.
— *The New Era*, July 10, 1884

The three remaining doomed men rose early Friday morning "to prepare for their graves." They had each been furnished "a suit of black alpaca [sic] clothing, clean white shirt, shoes, etc." (*The Elevator*). Early that morning, their spiritual advisers had come: Reverend Mr. Berne, Episcopal, for Thompson; Reverend Mr. Butt and Mr. Parke, Methodist, for Davis; and Reverend Mr. Moore, Baptist, for Womankiller. The morning was spent in religious exercises until nearly eleven o'clock, when Chief Deputy C. M. Barnes came and read each man his warrant. At eleven o'clock, "the ponderous doors swung open," and the prisoners and guards came out and were joined by the clergy and reporters waiting outside. On the walk to the gallows, Thompson and Davis walked erect, but Womankiller walked with his chin on his chest, "eyes steadfastly riveted on the ground."

They ascended the steps to the gallows and took their seats on the platform. Reverend Berne went first and performed the ceremonies of his church with Thompson, bid him goodbye, and left the scene. Reverend Butt next made some remarks and offered a prayer for the condemned, followed by Reverend Moore on behalf of Womankiller.

111

Moore stated that Womankiller had asked him to say that he was guilty and was very sorry for what he had done, that he was willing to die to atone for his wrong, and that he did not think that he had been unjustly dealt with. Then at Womankiller's request, a song was sung, and the ministers said their good-byes and left. The three men stepped on the trap. Thompson made a few remarks, but the Indians had nothing to say. They all stood erect and displayed no fear. Their legs and arms were pinioned, the black caps adjusted, and the trap sprung. The drop was six feet, and all their necks were broken, and they were "pronounced pulseless in 14 minutes." After sixteen minutes, their bodies were placed in their coffins, and by one o'clock were buried on the reservation, and these unfortunates joined the thirty-six who had gone before them on the gallows.

As mentioned before, Thompson gave Reverend Berne a sealed letter that *The Elevator* published in its entirety on July 18, 1884. In the letter, he described his partnership with O'Holerand and gave his version of the killing. Thompson also requested that the club he used to kill O'Holerand be his grave marker with this inscription:

T. L. Thompson
Born the 10th day of April 1850
This club prolonged my life from the 20th
of September 1883 to the 11th of July 1884

His request was not granted.

According to *The Elevator*, the hanging went off with such efficiency and decorum that it was not noticed outside the garrison walls and some in town did not even know that it had taken place. The newspaper reported that no more than fifty attended.

The New Era on July 17, 1884, reported the execution in this way:

> The execution last Friday of the three men convicted of murder in the Indian Territory took place in the old garrison. Everything passed off quietly. The bodies were buried on the reservation. Bye the bye, why can't such bodies, when unclaimed by relatives or friends, be quietly turned over to the Arkansas University? The thing is done in every country and is perfectly proper, and results in good to science and hence to mankind. At any rate the city should stop the interment of human bodies in ground about to be sold for city lots.

CHAPTER 17

EXECUTION OF WILLIAM PHILLIPS

Wholesale Commutation of Death Sentences
THEY SLIPPED THE HALTER

On Saturday night last [April 11, 1885] the hearts of Mason Holcomb, Fred M. Ray and William Meadows, three of the men to be hung next Friday, were made glad by the news that President Cleveland had commuted them to imprisonment for life.

— *The Elevator*, April 17, 1885

On the following Monday evening, April 13, 1885, William Dickson had the same reason for rejoicing when news of his commutation arrived. William Phillips, however, had only hope of reprieve, which he held onto until the last hours of his life on April 17, 1885.

All five men mentioned had been convicted of murder. Holcomb's and Dickson's cases were not unusual, and Phillips's was a case of man and father-in-law disagree, man kills father-in-law. The case of Ray and Meadows, though, was a little different than the typical murder case and deserves commentary before the story of the ill-fated Phillips.

In November 1884, Fred M. Ray, his son, Joe (age listed variously as twelve and fifteen) and William J. Meadows (aged variously as sixteen, seventeen, and eighteen) were on trial for the murder of an old black man in the Cherokee Nation about August 1 of that year. According to the November 28, 1884, edition of *The Fort Smith Elevator*, reporting the trial proceedings after the jury verdict, all of the principals in the case lived at a farm rented by Henry Meadows. The owner, George Alberti, employed the victim, Finn Morgan, a man of about eighty years known as "Old Finn," to do small chores. It was rumored that Old Finn carried a considerable amount of money, and it was for that money that either Ray or Meadows killed him.

There were several articles in the papers descending in sensationalism to the final piece after the trial that is probably nearer the truth. One article has Fred Ray, Joe Ray, and Meadows confronting Finn and demanding his money, and the father encouraging the son to fire the fatal shot. According to a later article, Fred Ray went to the house and asked Meadows if he wanted to make some money and told him to bring a pistol. They went to where Finn was doing his chores, and young Ray, observing the proceedings, ran back to the house, and when the report of the gun was heard, he cried, "They've killed Old

113

Finn." That version is disputed by Meadows in his testimony. After killing Old Finn, they buried him in a shallow grave. A day or so later, hogs or other animals "exhumed the body," so they attached a rope to the body, dragged it to a lake, weighted it, and threw it in. The murder occurred Friday, and on Monday, Fred Ray went to a barbecue held by the black residents in the area and inquired after Finn, saying he was missing, and Ray was the most diligent in a search for him. When the body was found, circumstances indicated that Ray might be the murderer. Young Joe Ray was said to have confessed immediately, the statement being taken down by Deputy Marshal Mershon. That statement is not on file at the National Archives with the other depositions concerning this case, and later testimony shows that all Joe could have confessed to would have been knowledge of the crime.

William Meadows, according to the newspapers, supposedly confessed after Joe Ray did, but his deposition, on file at the National Archives, denies his guilt. In that statement, Meadows, citing Florence Meadows as witness, claimed Fred Ray had come to him in the Meadows home and induced him to go with him to make some money, not stating his intentions. He said that when they found Finn Morgan, Ray killed him without Meadows's participation. Fred Ray, in his testimony, disputed Meadows, saying the only pistol on the place belonged to Meadows. Ray claimed to have been asleep on the porch when he was awakened by the gunshot and cited Florence Meadows as witness to his veracity, saying that she was in the kitchen talking to his son, Joe.

Whatever the truth might have been, the jury made its own deductions and acquitted Joe Ray, who was reported to have appeared unconcerned during the trial, sitting with his attorney, chewing his gum, and observing the proceedings. But they convicted both Fred M. Ray and William J. Meadows. And on Saturday, January 31, 1885, Judge Parker sentenced both men to hang on April 17, 1885.

The attorneys for both men immediately applied for a new trial, and in Ray's case, secured petitions signed by many acquaintances in a county in Missouri and one in Arkansas, where he had lived for about ten years in each, attesting to his good character. In Meadows's case, a petition was obtained from a minister and acquaintances who had known him for ten years. Those petitions apparently had the desired effect, for, as stated before, both men's sentences were commuted to life in prison. However, the date in *The Elevator* appears to be wrong. On April 17, the paper states, "On Saturday night last..." which would have been April 11. Existing copies of the pardons and commutations read, "Done at the City of Washington, this Fourteenth day of April, A.D. 1885, and of the Independence of the United States the one hundred and ninth. (signed) Grover Cleveland." In Meadows's case, the president cites his age as a reason for the commutation, and in Ray's, lack of conclusive evidence. Both men signed their acceptance of the terms April 22 and were admitted to the Detroit prison April 26, 1885.

WILLIAM PHILLIPS

On the morning of April 17, 1885, William Phillips still hoped for the message from the president that never came. He had been convicted of the murder of his father-in-law, William Hill.

Phillips and Hill had previously lived in Franklin County, Arkansas, where Phillips had persuaded Hill's fourteen-year-old daughter to run away with him. The couple went to Fort Smith where a minister "pronounced them man and wife on the famous 'Grem's Green.'" Hill did not approve of the marriage or of Phillips, but to make the best of it and to be near his daughter, he moved to the area where Phillips had located, near Fort Smith in the Cherokee Nation. The two rented jointly, but life near Phillips became so intolerable for Hill that he moved to another part of the same farm. One day, Hill went to get farm implements that Phillips had, and a violent argument erupted. The old man ran across a field, and as he did, Phillips fired at him, wounding him in the ankle. Hill went to the U.S. commissioner at Fort Smith and filed a complaint for assault with intent to kill. Phillips was indicted by a grand jury and bonded out and continued to make violent threats.

Catherine Hill, wife of the deceased, William Hill, testified in the proceedings before the commissioner that:

> On the morning of Monday last, Sept. 8th/84, Deft. Phillips came by my house and abused me right smartly. Mrs. Mathews & Deft. Phillips wife & my little children were the only ones present. My husband William Hill was not at home. This was about nine or ten o'clock in the morning. He came up & tried to make his wife go home. His baby was there sick & we did not want him to take the baby out in the sun. Deft. stayed there about a quarter of an hour. When he got on his horse and was going off he swore he would kill Hill before daylight next morning.

Mrs. Hill's deposition goes on to describe the events of the night of September 8, 1884, and how someone put a shotgun through a crack in the house and shot William Hill in the head while he slept. Besides Mrs. Hill, fifteen other witnesses for the prosecution testified in the same proceedings. All fifteen tell of seeing Phillips either with a shotgun or riding in the vicinity of the murder or both.

As soon as the murder was discovered, Phillips was arrested with a man named Lackey and William Hill's son, Bob. Bob was a suspect because he had had an argument with his father some time before and was living at another location at the time of the murder. However, Bob Hill and Lackey were among the fifteen witnesses for the prosecution and were released September 11 at the end of the proceedings before the commissioner. Phillips maintained until the end that Bob Hill had done the killing, but he and his attorneys were not persuasive enough. On Monday, January 19, 1885, the case was given to the jury. On Tuesday, it returned a verdict of guilty. The court wasted no time in sentencing; on Saturday, January 31, 1885, Phillips was sentenced to hang.

Phillips was so sure he would receive a commutation that he "made no preparations to meet his fate." But on Friday morning, his last day, when all but he had received commutations, he sent for a minister. Reverend T. J. Hendrickson responded, but Phillips did not give up hope until about eleven o'clock, when a dispatch arrived from the president saying he would not intervene. Phillips then sent for Colonel Walthen, one of his attorneys, with whom he had a long conference. He asked Walthen to have his body taken to the home of a Mrs. Gann, where Mrs. Phillips was staying, then shipped to Ozark to be buried beside his first wife. He told Walthen to sell a cow he had at Gabe Payne's place to cover the expenses. "About 11:30 o'clock a first class dinner was sent over to him by order of Col. Walthen and he ate heartily, devouring most all that was sent and appeared to enjoy it." The time of execution had been set for three o'clock, and Phillips spent the remaining time "in religious exercises" and visiting with his friends.

Just before three o'clock, the jailer, Deputy C. M. Barnes, entered the cell and read the death warrant. Phillips said his good-byes and "marched forth to death" accompanied by Hendrickson on one side and Barnes on the other. On the scaffold, the proceedings were brief, the minister offered a prayer, and the condemned man stepped onto the trap. When asked if he had any last words, he said he did not. The black cap and noose were adjusted, and he seemed to realize "his awful condition and certain doom," for he began to recite the Lord's Prayer, and as the words, "Thy will be done," were uttered, the trap fell. His neck was broken, and in fourteen minutes, he was pronounced dead.

Just before going to the gallows, Phillips had given Chief Deputy Boles a lengthy written statement still asserting his innocence and blaming Bob Hill. Bob Hill, he claimed, had done the deed using Lackey's shotgun, and several witnesses had sworn falsely. On the gallows, Phillips handed jailer Barnes a folded note intended for his wife. The note read, "Mary, my slipers is to tite. i want you to take them of to knight and lay them in the coffin. it is the last request i can make of you, don't fail to take me back tomorrow. Long farowell."

CHAPTER 18

JAMES ARCINE
AND WILLIAM PARCHMEAL
Executed June 26, 1885

The gallows got but a short respite. After disposing of William Phillips in April, it was again called to duty on June 26, 1885, for James Arcine and William Parchmeal. The case of Parchmeal and Arcine had actually gone to trial before Phillips's but through delays and retrials, the cases had leap-frogged each other until Phillips's verdict and execution preceded Arcine and Parchmeal's.

Henry Feigel, referred to in the newspapers variously as German, Swiss, or Swedish, and in testimony as "the Dutchman," had been known around Tahlequah, Cherokee Nation, for about fifteen years. On November 25, 1872, after having his boots half-soled, he left Tahlequah, walking in the direction of Fort Gibson. The next day he was found brutally murdered; he had been shot, his head crushed with a rock, his boots, coat, and overshirt taken. He had been dragged off the road into the brush. The murder aroused attention for a while, but because the victim had no relatives in the area, interest waned and the case was nearly forgotten. However, there were some in the area who had information that they had not forgotten. And in 1883, Deputy Marshal Elias Andrews, who was working in the area, became interested in the case and began work on it. After some investigation, he arrested James Arcine on Sunday, March 30, 1884, and lodged him in the U.S. jail at Fort Smith. Andrews continued work on the case, and on Monday, August 4, 1884, brought in William Parchmeal.

Arcine and Parchmeal must have been more elusive characters than the newspapers indicated. In their archives file, there are several arrest warrants issued to different deputies at different times. Most of the warrants have the notation "not served."

Both Parchmeal and Arcine were full-blood Cherokees, and all statements and testimony were given through interpreters. Several of the half-dozen or more witnesses were also Indian, and their testimony was taken through an interpreter. Two of them complained of being misquoted or misunderstood. One witness was recalled and gave additional testimony and stated that he did not like the interpreter whom he had the day before, adding that the interpreter either did not seem to understand what he was saying or that he did not know how to translate it into English. Some of the witnesses testified that Arcine had told them of the killing within a short time of the event, yet no one reported the crime to authorities.

Parchmeal, when arrested, confessed to being a witness to the crime and took Andrews to the spot where it had occurred. But he claimed that he was only an unwilling witness and that Arcine planned and carried out the whole affair. Parchmeal said he had had no part in it except to help drag the body off the road. Two witnesses at the proceedings before the commissioner testified that Parchmeal had told them of the killing a short time afterward and that he was an unwilling participant. Arcine, according to Parchmeal, had told him that he knew where they could make some money and persuaded him to go along. When they spotted Feigel on the road, Arcine said that there was their game, and when they approached Feigel, Arcine shot him. In fact, Parchmeal said that he had tried to run when Arcine shot Feigel, but Arcine threatened to shoot him too. Arcine then smashed Feigel's head with a rock, and the two of them dragged him off the road. Feigel had only twenty-five cents, which Arcine took along with the boots, coat, and shirt.

Arcine denied from the beginning and through the trial any involvement in the event and blamed Parchmeal for the whole killing and robbery. The case came to trial in the November 1884 term of court, twelve years after the crime. Arcine said that he was only a boy at the time. He requested four witnesses who he said would testify that he was only eight or nine years old at the time and was at his home fourteen miles away. However, his mother said that she could not testify to his exact age, only that he was born sometime before the war. When he was brought into jail, he gave his age to the jailer as thirty-three, and that age was entered, thus making him about twenty-one at the time of the murder. Arcine denied as false the testimony of other witnesses who said that he had told them of killing Feigel and having his boots. Those witnesses described in detail when and where Arcine had told them that he had killed a white man on the Gibson road. Thomas Horn testified that he had asked Arcine why he had done it and Arcine had replied, "Because I am man."

The case went to trial on Wednesday, December 24, 1884, and lasted through Monday, January 5, 1885, having consumed thirteen days when it was given to the jury. The jury was out until "a late hour in the evening" on Thursday, January 8, when jurors were discharged, having reached no agreement. They were deadlocked—ten for conviction, two for acquittal. The trial was then rescheduled for March 15, according to *The Elevator*. However, March 15, 1885, was a Sunday, so that is probably an error on the part of the reporter. Whatever the case, on Saturday afternoon, March 28, 1885, another jury returned a verdict of guilty after a trial that lasted about ten days. Parchmeal and Arcine were sentenced shortly thereafter to hang on June 26, 1885.

The Elevator reported after that trial—when somewhere near the facts were known—that the killers had overtaken Feigel about two miles southwest of Tahlequah where they killed and robbed him. Arcine took the hat and boots, and Parchmeal took the coat and overshirt. The twenty-five cents they took back to Tahlequah and bought ammunition, which they divided, then went their separate ways.

Testimony by the defendants was about the same in both trials, with each proclaiming his innocence and blaming all on the other. Attorneys for both men did their best to convince the jury of their client's story. Arcine was defended by Marcum, Tiller, Wolfberger, and Hallum. Marcum spoke for five hours trying to convince the jury that their client was not at the scene at the time of the murder and that Parchmeal "was trying to save his own neck by placing that of Arcine in the noose." But in the end, prosecutors Clayton and Grace prevailed. Defense attorneys immediately filed appeals for a new trial, listing six reasons including error in charge to the jury and that the verdict of the jury "was contrary to the law and not supported by the evidence."

On Wednesday, June 24, two days before the execution date, Arcine sent for one of his attorneys, Judge Tiller, "to make his last statement on earth." In it he claimed that Price Cochran and Parchmeal had committed the murder and went on to describe two other murders that Cochran had committed. Parchmeal made no statement until Friday, June 26, the morning of the execution day, when he sent for Chief Deputy Barnes and admitted that he hatched the plan and had gotten Arcine to go along. But, he said that Arcine did the shooting. "Then Arcine came to the front and knocked all the romance out of his previous statement by acknowledging that he was guilty." He said that Parchmeal had the pistol and gave it to him to shoot Feigel, which he did four times, then Parchmeal smashed his head with a rock. The two of them then dragged the body into the brush, and he took only the hat, which he wore for about a year, then gave away.

Both men were baptized on the Tuesday of the week of their execution by Reverend Sam Dean, who accompanied them to the gallows.

At two o'clock on the afternoon of the June 26, 1885, the prisoners were taken from the jail and "proceeded to the place of execution during the prevalence of quite a heavy shower" that had started while the death warrants were being read to them. They ascended the scaffold "with the indifference and stoicism so peculiar to the Indian race evincing no sign of nervousness or fear." After a hymn and a prayer by Reverend Sam Dean, they stepped onto the trap. Facing the moment of their impending death, both confessed their guilt and said that they were ready to accept the consequences. The statements were taken down by the court stenographer, Professor Saunders.

All preparations made, arms and legs pinioned, and black caps in place, the trap was dropped and the necks of the two men broken. After the bodies were cut down, they were taken to the city cemetery for burial.

CHAPTER 19

A NEW GALLOWS
FOR NEW CUSTOMERS

The Execution of Joseph Jackson and James Wasson

The men who mounted the twelve steps to the gallows on April 23, 1886, walked up and onto a completely new platform and gibbet. By April 1886, the old gallows, last used nine months before, had become dilapidated and was replaced, allowing Joseph Jackson and James Wasson to be the first of forty-four unfortunates to take those twelve steps on a new structure. On Friday, April 23, 1886, the day of their execution, this paragraph appeared in *The Elevator*:

> The new gallows is put up in a more neat and sub-stantial manner than the old one was. The platform is 16 x 20 feet, supported by solid oak columns 12 x 12 inches square, the cross beam is of solid oak 9 x 11, 16 feet in the clear and resting on two upright columns of solid oak sixteen feet high and about 12 x 12 inches square. The beam is braced on top by heavy timbers, the ends of which rest on the upright columns. The trap door is sixteen feet long and three feet wide. The drop is six feet.
>
> Note that the length of the trap is sixteen feet. Al-lowing two feet for each person no more than eight people could be accommodated, not twelve or any of the other numbers that have been attributed to it.

Now that *The Elevator* has clarified the capacity of the gallows, another myth should be addressed. During the time between the execution of William Parchmeal and James Arcine and that of James Wasson and Joseph Jackson, many others were tried in the U.S. District Court. Among them were Deputy Marshal Bass Reeves, murder, Belle Starr (again), horse stealing, and Bluford "Blue" Duck, murder. People who write fiction in the name of history have made Blue Duck into kind of a dime novel bad man and "sweetheart" of Belle Starr. Blue Duck, from all appearances, was such a minor character that he never rated one exclusive paragraph in the newspaper. He is mentioned only along with the prisoners with whom he was brought in, his accomplice, the people convicted in the same week, and those sentenced at the same time. In the paragraph listing him among the prisoners brought in by

Deputy Marshal Andrews, four sentences describe his crime and capture. He happened to have been tried in the same period that Belle Starr was indicted on several counts of horse stealing. Their famous photo was probably taken at that time, likely at the same studio where the well-known picture of Starr, armed, mounted on a horse, and guarded by Deputy Marshal Tyner Hughes, was taken. Belle and Blue Duck may or may not have been acquainted. At that time, Belle was married to Sam Starr and lived at Younger's Bend in the Eufaula area of Indian Territory. Blue Duck lived in and his crime was committed in the Flint District, just west of Siloam Springs, Arkansas. The story that Belle hired expensive lawyers to obtain a pardon for Blue has no credence. He was defended by Thomas Marcum of Marcum, Rutherford and McDonough, lawyers who were public defenders for many who appeared before the U.S. District Court. It is true that he was sentenced to hang, commuted to life at Southern Illinois Penitentiary at Menard, Illinois, and eventually pardoned. However, his pardon was March 22, 1895, six years after Belle Starr was murdered and about six weeks before he died on May 7, 1895. The man was dying of consumption (tuberculosis) and simply may have been sent home to die. At that time, there was no parole system, so the only way to be released from prison was to serve out the sentence or be pardoned. And that long paragraph is probably more than the total of print Bluford Duck ever got in the Fort Smith papers, such a minor player was he.

JOSEPH JACKSON

Joseph Jackson's case is relatively simple. According to newspaper reports written from testimony in the court and the U.S. district attorney's description of the crime, Jackson had abused his wife for a long time and finally murdered her. He was indicted July 8, 1885, his trial began September 7, 1885, the guilty verdict rendered September 14, 1885, and he was sentenced January 30, 1886, to hang on April 23, 1886.

In an almost illegible letter dated March 29, 1886, Jackson's attorney pleaded to President Grover Cleveland for a pardon. Citing the character of the witnesses who testified for the court, he stated, "I am assured that malice actuated most of them and that the man is innocent of the charge. Jackson prays a pardon."

U.S. District Attorney Monte H. Sandels replied to the defense attorney's plea in a letter to the U.S. attorney general dated April 13, 1886, with these words:

> Sir,
> Referring to the application of the Negro Joseph Jackson, for pardon. I have to say that he was a mur

derer long before he committed the crime of which he is now convicted. That neighbors and employer had often interfered to prevent his murdering his wife. That she finally moved up from Red River to within sixteen miles of this place and was employed as a cook by Mr. J. F. Tibbetts of Oak Lodge, I. T. That Jackson came up to that place, went into Tibbetts kitchen and shot her to death while she was washing dishes. That he robbed her of what little she had and went off and told various neighbors that his wife was very sick and asked them to go down and nurse her. He left.

The character of witnesses appearing against him was far better than the average. The testimony was indisputable and his guilt is palpable. My opinion upon the facts is that he has no claim to execution clemency either in the present case or in others upon which he has not yet been tried.

Respectfully
M. H. Sandels
Dist. Atty.

The district attorney's letter pretty well sums up the events of the case. Jackson shot his wife with a shotgun and afterward brought another woman to do some housework on the pretense that his wife was ill. On their arrival, they found the body of the murdered wife and Jackson "feigned great surprise and immediately gave the alarm." However, his past brutal actions caused him to be arrested, and the truth became known. *The Fort Smith Elevator* speculated, "he wanted her out of the way so he could take unto himself another dusky damsel of the vicinity with whom he had become smitten."

JAMES WASSON

Jim Wasson, who was brought here from Texas quite sick a couple of weeks ago, is now all right and is better pleased with his quarters in the U.S. jail than he was with the Texas prison.

— *The Elevator*, December 19, 1884

James Wasson's story was the kind of stuff that inspired the writers of Western novels, a bad man doing bad deeds and a reputation that deterred anyone from wanting to attempt his capture.

In November 1881, near Harney in the Chickasaw Nation, Wasson and Johnny McLaughlin appeared at the house of a Mrs. Brooks, "a

123

widow lady of some wealth," and asked to see Henry Martin, who was living there. Martin was not present, having gone to a store a short distance away. When informed of this, Wasson and McLaughlin, who were both armed with pistols and were "under the influence of whiskey" mounted and rode off in the direction of the store. A few minutes later, several gunshots in rapid succession were heard, and shortly after Martin's horse came up minus Martin. Some men at the home went in the direction of the shots and about 200 yards away found Martin's body "perforated with several bullets."

Even though Wasson and McLaughlin were the prime suspects, they were not arrested, "notwithstanding a deputy marshal was at the time camped near the scene." The two culprits left the Territory and went to the Panhandle country of Texas for a while. After about eighteen months, Wasson returned to the Territory, "but as he was known to be a dangerous and desperate man and one whose ill will no man cared to engender, he was not molested and rode around the country at will, merely keeping a little shady when a deputy marshal was known to be in the locality, and none of them cared to attempt his arrest under ordinary circumstances" (*The Elevator*, April 30, 1886).

It appears that Wasson assumed the lifestyle of ordinary inhabitants of the Territory, for on July 28, 1884, he joined a posse of men headed by Almerine Watkins in pursuit of two men and some stolen horses. After the stock was recovered the posse celebrated the event with whiskey, and during that time, Wasson and Watkins got into an argument that ended with Wasson shooting Watkins. Watkins's widow, reportedly a very wealthy woman, immediately offered a $5,000 reward for her husband's killer, dead or alive. Even though the promise of reward put a number of men on his trail, Wasson successfully eluded them, and eventually the chase was abandoned. Mrs. Watkins then posted a standing reward of $1,000 deposited in a bank in Dennison, Texas, for Wasson dead or alive. On September 28, 1884, he was arrested near Muskogee, Indian Territory, by Indian Policeman Simps Bennett and was taken to Texas, where he was incarcerated at Dallas and for a time was too sick to travel. When he had recovered sufficiently, Wasson was taken by Deputy U.S. Marshal J. A. McKee of Dallas to Fort Smith, arriving on December 2, 1884.

Wasson was indicted on two counts of murder and was tried and convicted on the first, the murder of Henry Martin. That conviction made it unnecessary, at the time, to try him on the murder of Almerine Watkins. The papers reported that Mrs. Watkins was present at every term of the court after Wasson was indicted and that she employed counsel to assist the district attorney in prosecuting the case. It was said that Mrs. Watkins spent more than $7,000 in bringing Wasson to justice. Wasson protested his guilt in both cases, claiming self defense in the case of Watkins and blaming McLaughlin in the killing of Martin. He blamed his conviction on prejudiced witnesses persuaded by the widow's wealth. His attorneys immediately petitioned for a new trial and, that failing, sought clemency almost until the hour of his death.

John McLaughlin remained at large until after Wasson was convicted but spent fifteen months in the federal jail and was given three trials. The first two trials resulted in hung juries. The November 12, 1886, edition of *The Elevator* reported:

> As we go to press the Johnny McLaughlin murder case is in progress. The court is holding night sessions in order to get through with it as soon as possible, as under the present ruling juries on murder cases are not allowed to separate during the progress of the trial.

November 19, 1886:

> The case of the United States vs. John McLaughlin, charged with murder, was taken up on Monday evening of last week [November 8] and occupied the court until a late hour Monday [November 15] night, when the jury took the case after receiving a forcible charge from Judge Parker. They are out as we go to press with little or no probability of agreeing.

November 26, 1886:

> **THE THIRD TIME CHARMS**
> At the close of our last report, the jury was still out in the John McLaughlin murder case and Harry Warfield and Joe Hendrick were on trial for larceny. Just after we went to press the McLaughlin jury brought in a verdict of acquittal, much to the surprise of everybody, as they had been out since Monday night and a disagreement was generally anticipated.

The article goes on to say McLaughlin's acquittal was a great relief to his relatives, who were among the most prominent and wealthy in the Indian country. They employed for him the best of counsel in attorneys DuVal, Cravens, and Barnes. The writer of the article felt that Wasson should have been respited until the outcome of McLaughlin's case, "for either his jury or the three juries that have served on McLaughlin's case made a mistake." If Wasson had been respited, he might have been cleared of Martin's killing and then convicted of the killing of Almerine Watkins, for which he had really been arrested. But, the Watkins family, through use of their money, got together all the evidence and witnesses necessary to hang Wasson. Those witnesses could not then appear in McLaughlin's case and refute themselves.

COMMUTATION FOR SIX, EXECUTION FOR TWO

Eight men had been sentenced to hang on Good Friday, April 23, 1886, but in the early part of that week, all but two received word from President Grover Cleveland that their sentences had been commuted to life in prison. Wasson and Jackson continued to have hope of reprieve, Wasson until the last moments, but none was forthcoming.

Up until the evening before the execution, Jim Wasson had been confident of a commutation or "respite." On receipt of the telegram announcing that the president would not interfere, he "was greatly unnerved and could not talk about it without crying." He felt it was very unfair that he should die when all but Jackson had been allowed to live. He denied his guilt, citing prejudice and perjury on the part of his enemies, of whom there should have been plenty if the stories of his reputation are true. He never denied killing Almerine Watkins but claimed it was for self-preservation and not of malice. Thursday night, the eve of his execution, he was awake most of the night and "until a late hour paced the floor of his prison bewailing his fate." On Friday morning, he still clung to some hope. Congressman Rogers had been telegraphed with a request to intervene on Wasson's behalf. Wasson was so confident he would receive some reprieve or clemency that when a minister called on him, he declined his services, saying that he thought that he could do him no good. The hanging was postponed until two o'clock awaiting an answer from Congressman Rogers. In the meantime, Wasson lay on his bunk with his hat over his face.

"Jackson was morose and out of humor, having little to say to anyone." He, too, refused the offer of a spiritual adviser, saying that if anyone could get him out of his predicament, it would be all right, otherwise no one could do him any good.

When two o'clock came and no telegram had arrived, Marshal Carroll, several deputies, and jailer Pryor entered the jail and presented each condemned man new clothing, including underwear, socks, shoes, shirts, neckties, collars, and suits. "They proceeded at once to dress, and assisted by their fellow prisoners were soon ready to be lead forth to death" (*The Elevator*, April 30, 1886). Wasson's bidding of farewell to the other prisoners reportedly left nearly every man in the jail weeping bitterly. Johnny McLaughlin, Wasson's alleged accomplice, was the last to say his farewell with a long embrace. After Jackson had dressed and

126

made his preparations, he approached Marshal Carroll and asked if there was any hope for him. When told that there was not, Jackson went to his bunk and attempted to cut his throat with a piece of an old saw that had been sharpened. He caused considerable bleeding but otherwise inflicted little damage.

Farewells accomplished, the prisoners were taken to the box or anteroom between the jail and the exit. There they were read the death warrants, then a light pair of handcuffs was placed on each man, and with a deputy on each side, they were lead forth to the gallows. *The Elevator* reported that, "All day there had been crowds of people flocked around the jail endeavoring to get a peep at the condemned men." And now they passed "through a line of several hundred spectators drawn up on either side of the walk leading from the jail."

After arriving on the gallows, Wasson, in what was believed to be a delaying tactic, asked for a minister, and one came forward and conducted appropriate services. Both Wasson and Jackson talked freely during the preparations, but neither said anything significant about their crimes. Wasson, to the last, denied anything to do with the murder of Martin. He said that McLaughlin, who was yet to be tried for and acquitted of the same crime, would "come clear." Wasson, although he stood up bravely, wept while he was being pinioned and placed on the trap.

> At 3:40 p.m., the drop fell and the job was complete, the necks of both men being broken. They remained motionless and died without struggling a particle. In less than twenty minutes, they were pronounced dead, and their bodies were cut down and placed in their coffins. An autopsy was performed on Wasson, during which his brain was removed; it was found to weigh fifty-one ounces.
>
> — *The Elevator*, April 30, 1886

CHAPTER 20

SPROLE AND JAMES HANGED
"They Meet Death Without a Murmur
and Have Nothing to Say"
(*The Weekly Elevator*, July 30, 1886)

Calvin James's crime appears to be one of a man coveting his neighbor's goods — illicit goods, but his goods nevertheless. On a Friday in late July 1885, James, Henry Reuben, and Albert Kemp left their homes in Chickasaw Nation, Indian Territory, near Tishomingo to go to Texas. Tony Love left his home later that same day, and all four men arrived at Joe Minow's Grocery at Thompson's Ferry on the Red River within a few hours of each other. Then, according to statements of witnesses, arresting officers, and the accused, they crossed back over the Red River on Friday and camped in a field. On Saturday, Henry Reuben (this name appears as Roby on some documents) and Albert Kemp were riding ahead, while James and Tony Love were riding side by side in the rear, Love carrying four gallons of whiskey in two containers. Kemp, according to the deposition of Zeddick Jackson, an arresting officer, said that the men in the lead heard a pistol shot and turned to see Love slumping over his saddle horn, blood running out of his face. Calvin James then ordered Reuben and Kemp back to help him. Kemp refused, saying that he did not think that James was going to do such a thing. James replied, "God damn it to hell what you standing talking so long for? Come back here and let us get away with this thing." Kemp stayed where he was; Reuben went back, and he and James led the horse and dead rider off the road and came back with the booty of whiskey.

Tony Love did not arrive home as he had said he would on Saturday, but on Monday, his unsaddled horse came home. On Tuesday, Love's father set out to look for him. On Saturday, a week after he had been expected home, Wash Taylor heard that he had left the Red River a little ahead of James, Reuben, and Kemp. Taylor and Andrew Colburn overtook the three suspects at Cherokee Town and arrested Albert "Abb" Kemp first. Abb at first denied any knowledge of Love's whereabouts, but when confronted with the information that they had been seen leaving the store together, he told Taylor that as soon as they arrested James and Reuben he would tell all. Shortly after, Henry Reuben rode up, and Taylor "threw down on him" and told him he was under arrest. Reuben drew his pistol, and Taylor told him to put it away or he would kill him. Andrew Colburn then threw down on him, too, and as he turned to look, Taylor hit him over the head and grabbed his pistol. About that time James came up, and they arrested him, too. James too denied any knowledge about Love and said that they had come home by a different route. The lawmen and suspects then started for home, and it was during that ride that Abb Kemp related the details of the killing and robbery. Kemp told his story to Zeddick Jackson as well as Taylor, and both versions are consistent. After Calvin James had shot Tony Love and ordered the other two to help him, Abb stayed in the road while Reuben went back, and he and James led the horse and dead rider off the road, unsaddled the horse, and turned it loose.

The lawmen left James and Reuben in the custody of "old man Peters" then went, with Abb Kemp directing, to the site of the killing. From there they followed a trail to where the body was left. It had apparently been put between two logs. It was eleven days after the killing, and hogs or wild animals had torn the body to pieces, so they gathered up the remains, including the head with the bullet hole in it. They took the remains back to old man Peters and showed them to James and asked him if that looked anything like Love. James still denied any knowledge or involvement.

From Peters's place, members of the arresting party continued to Caddo where they turned over custody to Deputy Mershon. Apparently all of the arresting party continued on as guards with Mershon, for in the night a guard went to Taylor with a message from Reuben. Reuben, who was shackled to James, wanted to be taken a distance from the others where he said that he would tell all about the event. Taylor refused his request for obvious reasons. Taylor, while at Caddo, had asked all three when they were together who had done the killing. James and Reuben replied that he would find out when they got to Fort Smith. Later they both said that Kemp shot Love because he owed him and would not pay him. However, when the critical time came, both Reuben and Kemp testified against James, and both went free.

On November 10, 1885, James and Reuben petitioned for witnesses who they said would prove that Kemp had made threats toward Love concerning a debt and that two of those witnesses would state that they had bought some of the whiskey taken from Love. Further, they claimed that Kemp had told the witnesses how he had obtained the whiskey. On March 26, 1886, the defendants requested a continuance because those witnesses, although subpoenaed, had not appeared. A later newspaper article reported that the continuance was denied.

LINCOLN SPROLE

Lincoln Sprole was described by at least three witnesses as a peaceable and quiet man and by his jail mates as one with limited mental abilities. But in his argument with Benjamin and Alexander "Ellick" Clark, father and son, fear or anger pushed him past his peaceable limit. Sprole and the Clarks were among a number of people who farmed neighboring lands around Pauls Valley, Chickasaw Nation, Indian Territory. Benjamin Clark was known to have a terrible temper, as verified by J. W. Solomon, who had known him in Texas and stated that he had always been in difficulties there. Ellick Clark was said to have been even more volatile than his father.

In May 1885 Sprole and a man named Perry, with whom he lived and farmed, got into an argument with Ben Clark that was precipitated by a disagreement over a plow bolt. The hostilities progressed to the point that late one evening Ellick Clark went to the house of J. W. Solomon and demanded a pistol. When Solomon refused, Ellick jumped off his horse and said, "John, by God I am going to have it." Being familiar with his neighbor's house, Clark went inside and got the gun. Solomon later followed Clark to his place and got the gun from Ben Clark, who said that he did not know why Ellick had taken it since they had plenty of guns of their own. It was then that Solomon learned of the seriousness of the dispute and described Clark as the maddest man he had ever seen.

Solomon found that Clark was in a rage because he was told that he could not water his horses at Perry's place. Clark swore that he would water his horses there the next day or shoot someone. Solomon tried to quiet Clark and get him to go up to Perry's and "quash the fuss," but he would not listen. He told Clark that Perry and Sprole were afraid of him and might kill him, but nothing would calm him. So Solomon went to Perry's house, where he found Sprole armed with a rifle and Perry with a shotgun and the doors locked. They would not let him in but raised the window, and both expressed a desire to end the argument. While Solomon was talking, Ellick Clark arrived and watered his horse. Solomon talked to the boy and tried to get him to promise not to come back "until the fuss was stopped." While he was talking, Ben Clark stepped out from behind a gatepost holding a shotgun and told his son to come along. Clark said later that the reason he had gone to Perry's was to show them that he could water his horse and if anyone had stuck his head out, he would have "blowed it off." Solomon argued with Clark for a long time, and finally Clark agreed to go up the next day with his coat off in his shirtsleeves to show that he was not armed and "fix it up with Mr. Perry."

Early the next morning, Solomon saw Ben and Ellick Clark passing in their wagon and asked where they were going. Ben said they were going to White Bead Hill to get his son a suit of clothes. Shortly afterward, Sprole rode to the McCracken home and obtained a saddle, then rode past Solomon's house in a run. When he got to Solomon's house, he hit his horse with a quirt and went by at full speed. He had a rifle across his saddle. About three hours later, John Unland came driving Clark's wagon and calling for Solomon and McCracken to come quickly. They found Ben Clark in the wagon mortally wounded and learned that his son had been shot, too. They found young Clark at the scene of the attack shot in the knee and the upper right chest. Both Clarks said that Sprole had shot them. When Ben Clark was shot, the horses ran, and Ellick jumped out to stop them. It was then that Sprole shot him in the knee then advanced and shot him again on the ground.

Both Clarks were taken to their beds, Ben dying later that day. In the meantime, Sprole had gone to the McCracken place and acted as if nothing had happened. When asked if he regretted what he had done, he replied that he was not sorry for anything. Alexander Clark lived on for seventeen days, sometimes rallying and forgiving Sprole and other times pledging to kill him.

Sprole left the Territory for Kansas where he had relatives. In Kansas, he was arrested and taken to Fort Smith.

Prisoners Sentenced

On Friday last Judge Parker passed sentence of death on Lincoln Sprole, Blue Duck, Kitt Ross and Calvin James, execution to take place July 23d. Sprole was sentenced twice, having been convicted of two murders. None of them had anything to say why the sentence of death should not be passed and took the matter with great indifference. All are young men.

— *The Elevator*, May 7, 1886

Duck, Ross, and James petitioned for new trials, with Duck and Ross being granted one but James denied. Sprole expected a commutation from the president but none was granted, so by July 23, 1886, only James and Sprole remained. *The Fort Smith Elevator* reported:

On Friday last, in accordance with the sentence of the court, Lincoln Sprole and Calvin James paid the dreadful penalty prescribed by the laws of God and man for the crime of murder.

Sprole was taken to the Catholic church on the evening preceding his Friday execution, where Reverend Lawrence Smythe baptized him. On the way to the church, he was taken to a barbershop and was shaved. The paper reported that he seemed to enjoy the outing, it being the first time he had been out for more than a year. James was baptized in the jail on Friday morning by Reverend A. J. Phillips of the African

Methodist Church. Sprole slept soundly on his last night on earth and "partook of a hearty breakfast on Friday morning."

Early Friday, people began to gather around the front of the jail, trying to see the condemned men, and before the time of execution arrived, a large crowd had gathered. At one o'clock jailer Pryor and two deputies entered the jail with a complete change of clothing for each condemned man. "They soon arrayed themselves, assisted by their fellow prisoners, and announced themselves ready." Sprole made a touching farewell that caused him to weep "while tears forced themselves to the eyes of many of his companions." James appeared little affected. They then removed to the anteroom, where Deputy Marshal Carroll read the death warrants.

The procession then started for the gallows with a guard on either side of each prisoner and Reverend Smythe in front of Sprole and his guards. On the scaffold, Smythe conducted religious services with Sprole while Reverend Phillips attended James. On the trap, when asked if they had any last words, Sprole shook his head, and James also declined. The arms and legs of the men were pinioned, the caps put in place and the trap sprung. Both necks were broken, and both men died without a struggle. The whole affair from the time they left the jail occupied less than twenty minutes. Sprole was buried in the Catholic cemetery, and James was taken to the potter's field. James had a wife and children in the Territory, but neither his nor Sprole's people visited them.

CHAPTER 21

KITT ROSS EXECUTED

"Calm and Stoical He Meets His
Fate, and Without a Murmur Dies"
(*The Weekly Elevator*, August 13, 1886)

When Kitt Ross stepped on the death trap August 6, 1886, and asked, "Is this where you want me?" it was the nineteenth time that one or more men had met justice at the end of a rope at the Fort Smith garrison. He was the forty-seventh man to die. He had been sentenced to hang on July 23, 1886, with Sprole and James but was respited for two weeks until August 6.

Ross, part Cherokee with the appearance of a white man, was about twenty-five years old with a long memory and bad habits. Sometime in 1882, Ross, in a drunken condition, had gone to the home of Jonathan Davis and ridden his horse into Davis's house—or tried to. Davis expelled him "in a violent manner." Over the next three years the men had met on many occasions and appeared to be on friendly terms, at least as far as Davis was concerned. But apparently, somewhere in the recesses of Ross's mind the old grudge lurked, and on December 20, 1885, alcohol brought it forward. On that day, both men were at a store at Choteau, Cherokee Nation, Ross again "in a drunken condition." As the two men left the store, Davis in the lead, Davis commented, "Looks like we might have some snow, Kitt," whereupon Ross drew his pistol and shot Davis twice in the back with no word of warning. He then ran away, dropping his pistol and losing his hat as he ran. Davis pursued him about seventy-five yards, shooting at him twice without effect.

Jane E. Evans stated in her deposition that she heard shots and heard someone running past her house, and then another person came by and said, "Let me in—I am shot. Kitt Ross shot me. I am shot bad." She told the person that there were no men in the house and that she could not help him. The wounded man then turned in the direction of Whitaker's store and hailed Whitaker, who helped him to the store. Both Whitaker and R. P. Lindsey talked to Davis before he died, and he stated that Kitt Ross had shot him. Both men quoted Davis as saying that he did not mind dying but he hated to be killed by such a scoundrel as Kitt Ross.

The local citizens got together a reward of $150 for Ross's capture, and six weeks later, he was apprehended at Shawneetown. He never denied the killing and offered only the excuse that he was drunk. The excuse of drunkenness seems to be refuted in the testimony of Riley P. Lindsey, wherein he quoted a boy named Bird Delay. In his statement, Lindsey said that he was in the hotel at Choteau in Indian Territory when Bird Delay came and said, "Kitt Ross has shot Davis." Delay also said that Ross had told him he was going to do some dirty work and kill Davis. Ross allegedly told the boy to go away, as he did not want him to be a witness against him. From the documents that exist, it appears that Bird Delay was subpoenaed but never found. His subpoena states that he lived in Galena, Stone County, Missouri. The subpoena was returned with a letter saying that two people named Delay were found in the vicinity of Webb City, Missouri, which is about thirty miles northeast of Galena, but no Bird Delay.

On the evening before his execution, Ross was taken to the Catholic Church and baptized. On Friday morning, his last day on earth, he arose at his usual hour after sleeping well. During the morning, he was visited by Miss Lizzie McCabe, who lived in Fort Smith and who just the day before had learned that Ross was her first cousin. "She remained with him until nearly noon, offering such consolation as only a woman can offer when in sympathy with those in distress."

The hour of execution was set for one o'clock, and just before that time, Ross talked at length with Marshal Carroll about the details of his crime, but there was no material difference from what had come out at the trial. He said that whiskey was the beginning and end of his troubles with Davis.

Because Reverend L. Smythe, Ross's spiritual adviser, was detained, the execution did not take place at one o'clock as scheduled. Ross was not taken from the prison until nearly two o'clock, and for about ten minutes before he was told to prepare for death, he paced the jail rapidly from one end to the other. On his walk he was accompanied by another prisoner with whom he talked, at the same time smoking the traditional cigar.

He had been given the customary suit of burial clothes the day before, and when he arose on Friday morning, he put them all on except the shirt and collar so that he would not soil the shirt. When informed that his time had come, he immediately finished dressing. He then said his good-byes to the other prisoners and stepped into the anteroom of the prison where he listened attentively as the death warrant was read. By that time Reverend Smythe had arrived. After the reading, the heavy iron door was opened, and Ross stepped out to make his death march to the gallows. He took the walk between two guards and with firm step. He ascended the stairs to the gallows unassisted.

After the usual religious ceremonies, Ross stepped forward onto the trap, placed his feet where indicated and asked, "Is this where you want me?" After that he stood perfectly still while his arms and legs were pinioned, reciting the Lord's Prayer in a low tone. While he was still praying, the black hood was drawn over his face, the rope adjusted, the trap sprung, "and the murderer of Jonathan Davis was launched into eternity, a victim of his own base disposition."

Court had been adjourned that day because of the execution, and few attended the event. Marshal Carroll, who never stayed on the scene for the actual drop, had left the gallows area. "Ross displayed remarkable composure all through the dreadful ordeal, appearing perfectly resigned to his fate, and was less nervous than those who were executing him."

CHAPTER 22

LUST, REVENGE, BAD TEMPERS SEND FOUR TO THE GALLOWS
T. J. Echols, James Lamb,
Albert O'Dell and John Stephens
January 14, 1887

The President having declined to interfere in the cases of the unfortunate men mentioned above, they will to-day suffer the extreme penalty of the law in accordance with the sentence of the court passed upon them October 30th last.
— *The Fort Smith Weekly Elevator*, January 14, 1887

In that October 1886 sentencing, six men were condemned to hang, but John W. Parrott's sentence was commuted to five years in prison, and Patrick McCarty had been respited to April 8, 1887. So on that bright, winter morning in January, the four men prepared to meet their doom that afternoon. On the previous day, Thursday, January 13, Echols, O'Dell, and Stephens were escorted to the Catholic Church where they were baptized by Reverend Lawrence Smythe and given the last rites of the church. From that time until the execution, they "made earnest efforts in behalf of their souls." James Lamb listened to the advice of Reverend M. D. Cato of the Methodist Church and was baptized into the M. E. Church South on January 2, 1887.

JOHN T. ECHOLS

The Elevator described Echols as "an intelligent man who had borne a good character as a peaceable and law-abiding citizen" up until the time of the crime and one whom "from his general appearance no man would for a moment suspect him of being a murderer." But on Friday, August 20, 1886, the jury, being out for only a short time, returned on its first ballot a verdict of guilty of the murder of John Pettenridge.

Echols, born in Fulton County, Georgia, was thirty-five years old. He lived with his wife and five children in the Chickasaw Nation after immigrating to Arkansas in 1870 and living in Sebastian County for three years. In 1887 his father, stepmother, and several brothers and sisters still lived in Sebastian County.

Echols and Pettenridge lived in the Chickasaw Nation near White Bead Hill. In February 1886, Echols traded a horse to Pettenridge for a

136

pony, two yearlings, and a Winchester rifle. The pony and rifle were delivered at the time of the agreement, but the yearlings were on the range and were to be "gotten up" by Echols. He found one but failed to find the other. On the morning of February 16, Echols sent word to Pettenridge to find the animal or he would take back his horse. Pettenridge sent word back that he could not attend to it that day but would as soon as he had time. Pettenridge was hauling logs to build a house, and Echols and his brother-in-law went to the woods where Pettenridge was working and encountered him on his wagon starting home with a load of logs. Hot words were exchanged, and Pettenridge, who was unarmed, moved as if to get down from the wagon when Echols fired at him, the bullet going through the brim of his hat. The horses bolted when the shooting began, and Pettenridge jumped from the wagon. Echols fired again, and Pettenridge fell wounded. Echols fired three more shots as his victim lay on the ground.

National Archives records hold subpoenas for several witnesses and show four actually testified. But when Echols took the stand on his own behalf, he denounced all evidence of the prosecution's witnesses as false. He said he did not go to the woods to confront Pettenridge but was horse hunting and happened to pass that way. He claimed both he and Pettenridge were on the ground during the argument and that Pettenridge flew into a rage, drew a large pocket knife and charged at him. He said he shot in self-defense, knowing Pettenridge to have used his knife more than once on other men with fatal results. Echols stated in his petition for witnesses that William Neal "will testify that the character of the deceased, John Pettenridge, was that of a dangerous and lawless man." Echols said he fired five shots in rapid succession while Pettenridge was standing and never fired after he fell. Witnesses first on the scene who examined the body stated Pettenridge's knife was still closed in his pocket. Since death was almost instantaneous, it was not credible that he closed it and put it there after he was shot.

Echols, like most other condemned men, applied for executive clemency, but on Saturday, January 1, 1887, a telegram was received saying that the president would not interfere with the court's decision. At first Echols was completely undone by the news but later began to make his arrangements for his demise.

JOHN STEPHENS

John Stephens, "a fine looking mulatto, twenty-eight years of age," was convicted September 2, 1886, of a triple murder that occurred near Bartlesville, Indian Territory, in the Delaware Reservation, Cherokee Nation. Stephens was born in Iroquois County, Illinois, and, for twelve years prior to the murder, he had lived in the Indian Territory, where he had a wife and child.

On Saturday, May 29, 1886, several people were called to the homes of Anna Kerr (misspelled "Carr" in *The Elevator*) and Dr. James T. Pyle. At Kerr's home, they found her and her son, Louis Winter, bludgeoned to death in their beds with an axe. At Pyle's home, the doctor lay mortally wounded, also with an axe, and his wife's head had been bashed in at the rear. She would survive the attack after fourteen pieces of her skull were removed. The attacker also assaulted a hired man, bruising him and cutting his leg, and struck a little girl with a board.

The witnesses who deposed made little mention about evidence found at the Kerr home. But at the Pyle home, they found the evidence that, though circumstantial, would convict Stephens. On the evening of May 28, Stephens borrowed a horse and saddle blanket from Charlie Whitefeather and rode off in the direction of Kerr's home. At the Pyle home, survivors thought their assailant might have ridden off to the south, as indicated by the dog's barking. Upon investigating in that direction, officials found where a horse had pawed the ground; nearby were a saddle blanket, later identified by Whitefeather, and a foot rag. When arrested, Stephens had in his coat pocket a foot rag that appeared to be a mate to the one found. Stephens had worked for Whitefeather, who stated that he had seen the suspect in possession of foot rags like those found but never saw Stephens use them to wipe the horse's collars, as Stephens claimed he had done. Also, at the Anderson house, where Stephens had been staying, a horse was found staked out, and Whitefeather identified it as the one loaned and not returned.

The arresting party, four of whom deposed, did not state why they went the next day, Sunday, to the Anderson home and arrested Stephens. Apparently he was immediately suspected. Stephens claimed to have been at the Anderson home all Friday night. However, when other members of that family were questioned, they said that he had not arrived until about eleven o'clock Saturday morning. Also, two other men who Stephens said could vouch for him said that he was not there and did not arrive there until about noon. Then Stephens said that he had started to the home of a man named Johnson who owed him money. He had stayed all night at the home of John Capps and had breakfast there and then proceeded to Johnson's. At the time he was arrested, he was not told why he was being arrested, even though he had asked. But on arrival at the Johnson house, Mrs. Johnson asked why he was arrested and he replied that he supposed that it was for murder. Up until that time, no one had mentioned murder.

The reasons for the murders appear never to have been absolutely determined. It was thought, however, that Mrs. Kerr's husband, from whom she was separated "and on very bad terms," was behind that murder. Mr. Kerr was arrested, but the grand jury ignored the case and did not deliver a true bill. Some time prior to the murders, Stephens had been arrested for larceny — accused of stealing Pyle's cattle — and Pyle testified against him. Andrew H. Norwood, a member of the arresting party, said he had heard Stephens had threatened Pyle's life.

The Elevator of September 10, 1886, stated, "Stephens seemed entirely unconcerned when the verdict was announced; evidently anticipating that he was a doomed man." More likely, even though he may have anticipated the verdict, he expected to appeal and get clemency.

LAMB AND O'DELL

It would be hard to describe the crimes of James Lamb and Albert O'Dell more effectively, or more colorfully, than *The Fort Smith Weekly Elevator*, so the following is verbatim from its January 14, 1887, issue:

James Lamb and Albert O'Dell

These young men were convicted of the murder on the 18th of last September, the jury returning a verdict in a few minutes after the case was given to them. The circumstances surrounding the case were of a most revolting character, presenting the most striking illustration of human depravity ever held up to the public gaze. The evidence showed that in the fall of 1885 Edward Pollard and George Brassfield with their families were tenants on the same farm near Lebanon, Chickasaw Nation, and that Lamb and O'Dell were engaged picking cotton there. Mrs. Pollard and Lamb became infatuated with each other, as did also Mrs. Brassfield and O'Dell, which resulted in criminal intimacy between the two couples. The young men became so bold in their attentions to the two faithless wives that their conduct became the neighborhood gossip. They made threatening demonstrations toward Pollard and Brassfield and the latter, fearing his life was in danger, fled the country when O'Dell forthwith took possession of his family. Pollard was not so easily driven off and continued to remain at home. On the afternoon of the 26th of December, Mrs. Pollard sent her husband to Lebanon some two miles away to get some coal oil and coffee, while Lamb on the same day went to engage a preacher to come and marry O'Dell and Mrs. Brassfield, the ceremony to take place the next day. Pollard went to the store on foot, made his purchases and started home and that was the last ever seen of him alive. Late that night Lamb and O'Dell went around to different places in the neighborhood making inquiries for him, saying his absence was alarming his wife, but insinuated that he had deserted her the same as Brassfield had his family. The next morning the preacher came and after performing the marriage ceremony for O'Dell and Mrs. Brassfield, was requested by Lamb to perform a like ceremony for himself and Mrs. Pollard, saying Pollard had deserted her and never would return. The preacher declined, however, and that afternoon the whole outfit packed up and left that section in one wagon, going to a more remote part of the territory. About two months after their departure the dead body of Pollard was found in a ravine about three quarters of a mile from where he had lived. He had evidently been waylaid as he was going home from Lebanon on the evening he was sent by his wife to the store. He had been shot in the head. Suspicion was at once directed to Lamb and O'Dell as his murderers, and it was evident from circumstances before and after his disappearance that a conspiracy had been entered into by Lamb, O'Dell and the two women to get rid of both Pollard and Brassfield, either by killing them or by frightening them out of the country. Deputy Marshal Mershon being camped in the vicinity when the body was found, at once began to work at the case, and becoming satisfied that the suspected parties were the murderers, at once took their trail and located O'Dell and his paramour at a point on Buck Horn Creek, about fifty miles from the scene of the murder. He arrested O'Dell some distance from the house where they were living, early in the morning, and learned that Lamb and Mrs. Pollard had become alarmed and left for a more obscure locality a day or so previous. Leaving O'Dell in [the] charge of his posse, he went on to the house and arrested Mrs. Brassfield, who feigned great surprise when told it was for being accessory to the murder of Pollard, saying she did not know that he was dead. Mershon then told her there was no use making any denials, "[F]or," says he, "I have O'Dell already in irons and he has told all about it." This threw the woman off her guard and she began to cry, saying

140

if he had told it himself she could not help it if they hung him. O'Dell was then brought to the house, and finding that Mershon had, by strategy gotten a confession from Mrs. Brassfield, acknowledged that he had assisted Lamb to drag the body off and conceal it, but further than this was not a party to the crime. After securing O'Dell and Mrs. Brassfield, he left them in [the] charge of a guard and took the trail after Lamb, coming upon him at a late hour the same night in a lonely cabin in the woods, about forty miles from where O'Dell was arrested. Lamb denied everything and laughed at the idea of being arrested, displaying a bravado surprising in one of his age. O'Dell in making his statement to the officers, even told where they hid Pollard's hat and the can of coal oil, which were afterwards found at the place indicated by him. He said they took the package of coffee home and made use of it. Mrs. Brassfield had three children and Mrs. Pollard one. While at the Marshal's camp after the arrest, Brassfield visited them and took possession of his two oldest children, while the brother of Pollard came over from Texas and got Mrs. Pollard's child, taking it home with him. The wicked quartette [sic] were lodged in jail here on the 15th of April last and on examination before the United States commissioner O'Dell and Lamb were bound over for murder, while the women were held as witnesses. Mrs. Brassfield remained in jail up to the close of the trial but Mrs. Pollard gave bond and went to Livingston County, Mo. where her relatives live, and before returning to court, gave birth to a child of which Lamb was the parent. A few days previous to the trial Mrs. Brassfield gave birth to twins, both boys, the offspring of her debauchery with O'Dell, though both of them died.

When on trial, Lamb and O'Dell each employed his own lawyer and, in the words of *The Elevator*, "prosecuted each other." Lamb testified that O'Dell shot Pollard as he was approaching the house after dark thinking that it was Brassfield coming back. O'Dell testified that Lamb did the killing. Both admitted to having assisted in dragging away and hiding the body. Both of the women, however, stated that O'Dell was at the house when shots were heard and that Lamb was absent. Mrs. Pollard maintained that she did not know that her husband was dead until she was arrested, saying that Lamb had led her to believe that he had deserted her, as Brassfield had his wife.

The prosecution's belief was that there was a conspiracy to kill both men and that Brassfield had foiled part of their plot by fleeing. The prosecution held that they were both equally guilty, regardless of who actually did the killing. The jury apparently agreed and was out only a short time in delivering a guilty verdict.

> The case developed not only murder but larceny and bigamy, they having not only robbed their victims of their families, but all other movable property they possessed, besides living in a state of debauchery revolting in the extreme, both couples most of the time occupying the same room.
> — *The Elevator*, January 14, 1887

Judge Parker, when passing sentence, opined that the wives were equal conspirators and should be standing in the dock with the men.

Lamb was twenty-three years old and was born in Crawford County, Arkansas. He had lived in the Indian Territory fourteen months at the time of the crime. O'Dell was twenty-six and was born in Franklin County, Alabama, and moved as a child to Texas. He had lived in the Territory two years.

THE GALLOWS

By the Saturday preceding the execution, all of the condemned had received word that the president would not interfere with the court's decision. At that news both Lamb and O'Dell broke down in tears as Echols did on receipt of his notice. Lamb soon recovered, though, and spoke of his situation, saying that he was not afraid to die and if not for his mother, he would go to the gallows willingly. He felt that the president should pardon O'Dell since he did not take part in the actual killing, saying that his life should be sufficient to atone for Pollard's.

Lamb's statement was relayed to Attorney General Garland, who wired District Attorney Sandels to interview Lamb and report his opinion of anything he might say in O'Dell's behalf. That was done, but nothing more than what was brought out in court was found.

> Friday morning dawned bright and beautiful, the sun rising for the last time on the four unfortunate men whose names appear above, throwing its bright rays into the gloomy prison as if to cheer the inmates who

142

would in a short time bid farewell forever to four of
their fellow prisoners and see them led forth to die.
— *The Elevator*, January 21, 1887

Reportedly Echols, Lamb, O'Dell, and Stephens slept well the night
before their execution and spent the morning talking to callers and
meeting with spiritual advisers. Lamb, O'Dell, and Stephens talked
freely about their situation, but Echols had little to say and appeared to
prefer seclusion. O'Dell, when asked if he realized his death was immi-
nent, answered, "O, yes sir, I fully realize my position, and know that
time is short, but I can't help it, and I feel resigned, though I don't think
my punishment is just" (*The Elevator*, January 21, 1887). Lamb said he
was ready to die but would save O'Dell if he could. Stephens, while
resigned to his fate, berated the newspapers for misrepresenting his
case, saying a true account had never been published. Lamb ordered a
large meal, which was brought to him about eleven thirty. He "partook
with apparent relish," saying he did not want to go to the gallows hun-
gry or thirsty. He invited the other three to share his meal, which they
did, "not a scrap being left." After the meal all four smoked the customary cigars then dressed in the suits provided for the occasion.

After being led to the anteroom, the condemned were read the
death warrants by Deputy Marshal John Carroll and handcuffed.
O'Dell, Echols, and Stephens knelt on the scaffold with Reverend L.
Smythe. Lamb sat by himself on a bench and trembled from nervousness and the January cold. Occasionally he made eye contact with an
acquaintance and acknowledged them with a nod and smile. The services finished, the men stepped onto the trap and were asked by Carroll if they had any last words. Stephens asked only that the marshal
not let the doctors cut his body. Lamb offered a few words, advising
people to keep out of bad company and out of Indian Territory. Reverend Cato walked onto the platform and shook hands with Lamb and
offered words of consolation. "The arms and legs of the condemned
were pinioned, the noose adjusted, the black caps drawn, the trap
sprung, and the unfortunate men launched into eternity, all four of
their necks being broken by a fall of seven feet" (*The Elevator*, January
21, 1887).

The Elevator on January 21, 1887, stated:

> George Maledon prepared everything for the exe-
> cution and adjusted the noose on the neck of each sub-
> ject, and his work was well executed. George has as-
> sisted in the hanging of about fifty men.

Apparently the Maledon myth had already started. The hanging of these four men brought the total hanged at Fort Smith to fifty-one, of which only forty-three took place during Judge Parker's administration. Maledon was not an employee of the court or the U.S. Marshal's Office for at least the first thirteen hangings, Story's seven and Parker's first six, and possibly several more. So unless he participated in hangings in some other place, he could not have "assisted in the hanging of about fifty men."

On the back of each death warrant, the U.S. marshal always wrote a paragraph nearly identical to the following:

> I certify that I have duly served this writ by reading the same to and within the presence and hearing of the within named John Stephens and with the assistance of Deputy Marshal J. C. Pettigrew by hanging the said John Stephens by the neck until he was dead on Friday the 14 day of January 1887 at Fort Smith Ark. And within the Western District of Arkansas in the presence of Dr. J. G. Eberle and others as herein I am commanded.
>
> John Carroll
> U.S. Marshal
> By J. Carnal
> Deputy

Service	25.00
Paid J. J. Little Co. 1 suit clothes	10.60
" C. A. & H. C. Hines 1 coffin	5.00
" L. Smith 1 grave	6.00
" Spencer Ball Hauling corpse	1.00
	47.60

CHAPTER 23

PAT McCARTY'S RESPITE EXPIRES, AND WITH IT, PATRICK McCARTY

Washington, D. C. April 4
U.S. Marshal Carroll
The president declines to interfere further with the sentence of the Court in the case of Patrick McCarty. Acknowledge receipt. A. H. Garland
                 — *The Elevator*, April 8, 1887

When those words were read to Patrick McCarty on the Monday morning preceding his scheduled Friday execution, they extinguished his last ray of hope for a reprieve. He had been convicted of murder in September 1886 and sentenced October 30, 1886, to hang along with Echols, Lamb, O'Dell, and Stephens on January 14, 1887. But for the granting of his appeal for respite, he would have been long gone before April.

McCarty's attorneys had appealed to President Cleveland on the premise that, among other things, they had not had sufficient time to prepare their case. The president then wrote Judge Parker an inquiry concerning the case, to which the judge responded in great detail, saying that the attorneys' statement was "knowingly false," intended to give the impression that McCarty did not get a fair trial. Parker's letter was accompanied by one from District Attorney M. H. Sandels. Both letters went into great detail describing the crime, assigning of attorneys, continuances, and trial.

Judge Parker's letter was published in full in the April 8, 1887, edition of *The Fort Smith Weekly Elevator*, and thanks to him, there is a very detailed account of the crime. Excerpting from the letter, this is the account of the murders:

Brothers John and Tom Mahoney were working on the Atlantic and Pacific Railroad between Tulsa and Red Fork, Indian Territory, in early 1886. In February the brothers had started to Fort Scott, Kansas, in their wagon with a team of mules, a pair of mares, an extra set of harness, "quite a quantity of loose property," and the money they had earned. They had "permitted to travel, ride and camp with them two vagabonds and tramps, Pat McCarty and Joe Stutzer." About seven miles east of Coffeyville, Kansas, McCarty and Stutzer convinced the Mahoneys that the route from there to Fort Scott was across prairie and that wood would be scarce. They suggested that they cook all the necessary food then in preparation for the trip. They told the brothers to go on to bed and that they would do the cooking. When they had ascertained that the Mahoneys were asleep, McCarty took a .38-caliber pistol and Stutzer a shotgun to kill their victims. McCarty shot one of the brothers in the eye, but Stutzer's gun misfired. The shot from McCarty's gun wakened the other brother, and Stutzer killed him with an ax. The next day they hauled the bodies about thirty miles to where they disposed of them by placing them in the drain of a coal pit and covering them. At that place they burned a feather bed and all other items that were bloody. Stutzer's clothes were bloody, too, so he burned them and took some from the Mahoneys' trunk. They camped overnight and the next day drove to near Vinita, Indian Territory, where they camped. That evening Stutzer went into Vinita to determine whether anyone there was from the Red Fork area and could recognize them or the teams and wagon. The next morning they went into town and, representing themselves as brothers John and Joe Ryan, sold the mules and one set of harness for $125, less than half their value. McCarty took $105, gave Stutzer twenty dollars and the mares and wagon, and left for Missouri. McCarty went first to Pierce City then to Dixon, Missouri, where his wife lived with her father.

In March the bodies of the Mahoneys were found by neighbors of the area and buried. The neighbors had, about February 18, smelled burning clothes and feathers, and the remains of such were found nearby. Newspaper reporters circulated the story, and Mrs. Mahoney, on seeing the newspaper reports and not having heard from her sons in quite some time, went to the site, where the bodies were disinterred, identified, and reburied. Mrs. Mahoney identified the remains of the feather bed as one she had made before the boys started on their trip and the burned shoes as her sons'.

Pat McCarty, in the meantime, had been seen around Springfield, Missouri, by people who had seen him at Red Fork and knew that he had left there in the company of the Mahoneys. They also knew that at Red Fork, he had had no money but now he did. Those people accused him of "getting away with the Mahoneys" but they did not know at that time that they had been murdered. All things began to come together, the murder story was circulated, and a law officer at Dixon, Missouri, notified the U.S. Marshal. When arrested, McCarty had a watch in his possession that he tried to pass to his brother-in-law, but the marshal stopped him. The watch was later identified as one that Mrs. Mahoney had given to her husband for Christmas eighteen years before and had passed on to her sons when they left to work on the railroad. McCarty was taken to Vinita, where he was identified, and there he made a confession that he later denied making.

The wagon that Joe Stutzer had taken in his share of the loot was found in the possession of a man near Fayetteville, Arkansas, who said that Stutzer had lived in that area. When he had arrived there from Vinita, the wagon bed was covered with blood. Stutzer explained that with a story very similar to what really happened, except he said he was the one who had picked up two tramps. He said that while sleeping in the wagon, he heard them plotting to kill him, and when they crawled into the wagon bed to carry out their plot, he killed them both. Stutzer left Fayetteville suddenly, leaving the wagon and harness, but taking the mares. The U.S. government offered a reward of $500, but as of April 15, 1887, Stutzer had not been apprehended.

All of the foregoing was brought out at the trial and, while circumstantial, created a chain of evidence that was unbroken. McCarty had no defense. He did apply for witnesses, but one named Childers testified in opposition to McCarty's story about the watch. McCarty claimed to have won the watch gambling, but Childers would not substantiate that story. McCarty requested two people described as "one Dunn." The "one Dunns," despite a diligent search by marshals, were never found and were unquestionably "men of straw." Mrs. Mahoney testified at the trial about how she had found the remains of her boys and identified various belongings, "and everyone in the court room was perceptibly affected." McCarty always claimed publicly that he was innocent, but he reportedly confided his story to a friend in jail, and it did not differ significantly from what the evidence proved to be true. McCarty's lawyers, Vernon and Cooper, did the best they could with what they had, but it was not enough. The case was given to the jury shortly before noon, and soon after dinner, the jurors returned the guilty verdict.

The Elevator described McCarty as "an intelligent young Irishman, full of the humor so peculiar to his nationality, and a man whom a casual observer would never select as a wanton, wicked murderer. He was born in Ireland and raised in England, and we understand says he at one time belonged to the British Navy, which he deserted and came over to this country."

The night preceding his execution, McCarty went to bed at his normal hour but arose about three o'clock, walked the cell for a while, then went back to his cot. He rose at the usual time and was taken to the Catholic church for seven o'clock Mass. He was dressed in a navy blue suit, white shirt, and white tie purchased by the Marshal's Office from J. J. Little & Co. for ten dollars and twenty-five cents. After the service, he returned to his cell, apparently in good humor, and spent the morning talking to callers.

Shortly before two o'clock, Father Lawrence Smythe arrived at the jail and spent a few minutes with McCarty. The prisoner was informed that the time had come for his execution. The death warrant was read to him, and they proceeded to the gallows, "marching with a steady step." He ascended the steps "with as much coolness as though it were an everyday affair with him." Though he was pale from the long months of confinement and his lips and nose appeared a little more pinched than usual, he showed no signs of emotion. On the scaffold, McCarty knelt with Father Smythe and then took his place on the trap, holding a small crucifix. Father Smythe then addressed the approximately seventy-five people within the gallows enclosure. He said that due to reports he had heard in the last few days, he would say "that there was nothing in the laws of the Catholic church to prohibit a member from speaking the truth under any and all circumstances; that a Catholic was always at liberty to unburden his mind of any load that might lie on it from a source crime or under the circumstances of the nature of those in which the condemned was placed." Then McCarty, "standing on the brink of eternity, with the crucifix in his hand," declared that he was innocent and totally ignorant of anything to do with the murder of the Mahoneys. At the request of Father Smythe, he repeated the statement "in a clear and distinct voice, and showing no signs of agitation beyond a very slight tremor of his hand that grasped the crucifix." He went on to say, as many of the condemned did, that possibly malice or prejudice accounted for his conviction, but he forgave everyone and thanked Marshal Carroll and all the officers of the jail who had shown him consideration. When finished, he kissed the crucifix and returned it to Father Smythe and shook hands all around. His feet and hands were pinioned, the black cap put in place while he recited his last devotions. As the rope was adjusted, McCarty asked the executioner to draw it tight. "At exactly 2:07 p.m. the drop fell, the body of the wretched criminal going down like a shot and stopping with that dull horrible sound that always attends such events." His neck was broken, and he was pronounced dead at 2:38 p.m. when the body was taken down and taken to the Catholic cemetery.

McCarty's poignant performance, especially while holding the crucifix and accompanied by the priest's words, caused some who had before believed in his guilt to have doubts. But the writer for *The Elevator* felt, "those well acquainted with the evidence produced at the trial are still of the opinion that he was as guilty as guilty could be and from our own knowledge of the case we are forced to the same conclusion."

CHAPTER 24

THE EXECUTIONS OF SEABORN KALIJAH AND SILAS HAMPTON

The execution of Silas Hampton and Seabron Green (Kalijah) took place in the federal court yard last Friday at 2:33 p.m. There were no special incidents connected with the affair. They were taken from the jail at 2 o'clock and led to the gallows surrounded by guards, and took their places on the death trap without showing the least sign of trepidation. Seabron Green was attended in his last moments by Rev. Lawrence Smythe, and Silas Hampton by Rev. Mr. Massey. On the scaffold there were short religious exercises, after which the condemned men took their places on the trap. Green had nothing to say after this, Hampton said that he had made peace with his God and was ready to go. The trap was then sprung, and the wretched victims of justice dropped to eternity.

That terse paragraph from *The Fort Smith Weekly Elevator* on October 14, 1887, is the shortest description of an execution found up to this point. (The newspaper consistently refers to Seabron Green, once noting that he is also known as "Calija." Court records, however, consistently call him "Seaborn Kalijah," alias "Seaborn Green.")

SILAS HAMPTON

If living today, Silas Hampton, a Chickasaw about eighteen years old, might be a candidate for the "Dumbest Criminals" list. He was convicted in July 1886 of the murder of Abner N. Lloyd, a man of about sixty years old.

Lloyd was one of a group of men contracted to haul hay for the new railroad being built in Tishomingo County, Indian Territory. He was camped for the night near Tishomingo when Hampton murdered him for about seven dollars and a pocketknife.

The murder happened about a half mile from the home of Joseph Wolf. Wolf testified that about eight o'clock on the evening of December 9, 1886, he was sitting by his fire when he heard a gunshot from the direction that the body was later found. Shortly thereafter, Hampton appeared at Wolf's house to return a pony that he had borrowed earlier. He turned the pony loose and threw down a saddle with a scabbard attached to it containing a Winchester. He sat with Wolf for a short time, then left saying that he was going to a nearby store to buy some things. Wolf's brother-in-law, Frank Greenwood, brought the gun into the house where they examined it and found it to contain one cartridge. Charles McSwain, apparently the store owner, testified that Hampton came to the store about nine o'clock that night and bought a pipe, tobacco, and some other items, paying about three and a half dollars in silver coin. When asked where he got the money, Hampton said he got it from J. R. Hearn. When asked how he earned it, he said picking cotton. Hearn later testified that he had paid Hampton only thirty cents. Hampton then denied saying that he had gotten the money from Hearn, claiming instead that Squire Wolf had given it to him, again for picking cotton. But in his deposition, Squire Wolf stated, "I never gave the Deft. a cent of money in my life. Deft. never worked a lick for me in his life."

E. B. Marshall, a guard for Heck Thomas, testified in his deposition that while in camp alone with Hampton that Hampton "commenced crying and went and got holt of an ax in camp." Marshall took the ax away and asked why he was crying. Hampton replied that they said that he had killed a man, and then he proceeded to tell about the event. He said that he had gone to the store to get some things but lacked the money. On his way home he had seen Lloyd, stopped a while, then went home, got his rifle and went back. He sneaked up on the man and shot him through the hind wheel of the wagon. He got seven dollars and a pocketknife. He then went to the store and purchased a hat, shirt, a pair of drawers, and gloves. The storekeeper said that Hampton had spent about three dollars and fifty cents. Marshall also testified that he had overheard Hampton telling Albert Rogers, another prisoner, that he had gotten seven dollars and a knife. When Hampton was arrested, he had on him three dollars and thirty cents and a pocketknife.

Four of the five witnesses who deposed (E. B. Marshall was not at the crime scene) stated that there had been footprints at the crime scene made by boots that had a half sole on one boot and a patch on the sole of the other. Hampton's boots fit this description. Also the affiants described handprints in the soft dirt of gopher diggings that indicated the killer had crawled on hands and knees to the point where he did his deed. That was consistent with the story Hampton had told to E. B. Marshall of sneaking up and shooting Lloyd in the back.

On December 11, 1886, Hampton was arrested by his uncle, Sheriff McGee, at the home of Joseph Wolf, where his trek had started. When he was searched and the money and knife taken from him, he told the sheriff to just shoot him there and get it over with. At the time of Hampton's arrest, Joseph Wolf's wife came out of the house and gave him a quarter that he had given her for a chicken, saying that if that is how he got the money, she did not want it.

On July 9, 1887, the jury was not long in returning a verdict of guilty for Silas Hampton, although he continued to claim not to have committed the crime or have any knowledge of it.

All of the foregoing information is from the proceedings before Commissioner James Brizzolara, February 1, 1886.

SEABORN KALIJAH

Seaborn Kalijah, alias Seaborn Green, an eighteen-year-old Creek Indian, killed Mark Kuykendall, Henry Smith, and William Kelley, posse and guards for Deputy Marshal Phillips, on January 17, 1887, while Phillips was away from camp.

On February 19, 1887, Kalijah made application through an interpreter before Commissioner Stephen Wheeler for seven witnesses. He stated in that application:

> He expects to prove by said witness Mrs. Jersey that the deceased were killed at or near her house and under justifiable circumstances. That the deceased provoked, maltreated and abused this affiant and inflicted upon his person such wrongs and injuries as to endanger his life and cause this defendant to believe his life in imminent peril and so believing he killed the deceased in self defense. In this that defendant was arrested and released by deceased and afterwards re-arrested by them and in so doing the deceased ran over him with their horses and trampled him under foot without reasonable cause or excuse, that they drew their guns and pistols upon him as though they would kill and murder defendant, so that he had reasonable cause to apprehend his life to be in imminent peril.

The statement goes on to say that the other witnesses will prove that "this defendant is a peaceable, law-abiding and quiet citizen." Apparently the witnesses and the evidence did not bear out his story. The description of the crime scene reads more like an ambush than a killing in self-defense.

Kalijah had been, as he said, arrested, released, and rearrested for introducing alcohol into the Indian Territory. At the time of the murders, he was the only prisoner of Marshal Phillips's posse. On January 17, Phillips went to Eufaula on business, leaving his prisoner in the charge of his guards. The next day he returned to find Smith and Kuykendall dead by the fire where they had slept, their heads nearly severed by an ax. A short distance away laid Kelley's body in a pool of blood. He had been shot and mutilated with the ax. Kuykendall and Smith's bodies were roasted from the waist down by faggots from the campfire that had been piled on them. Phillips buried the bodies near the camp and soon after again arrested Kalijah. Kalijah told Phillips that during the night, some men had come into the camp and killed the men and that he had escaped into the woods.

On Friday, February 11, Phillips brought in Doctor Walker, uncle of Kalijah, and Josh Alrovia Ethlo Harjo (later called Ohoola), a relative. They too were charged with the murders of the guards. Some guns had been missing from the camp, and one of the pistols was found under Doctor Walker's house. On February 18 the three suspects were arraigned, and Kalijah entered a guilty plea while the other two pleaded not guilty. The court refused to recognize the guilty plea, and trial was set for the May 1887 term of court. It was thought that Kalijah's plea was made to shield the other two defendants. The reporter for *The Elevator* felt that the evidence, while circumstantial, was stronger against Walker than against Kalijah.

Kalijah stated before the commissioner, as seen in his petition for witnesses, that he alone did the killing, his only excuse being that they had abused him and he feared for his life. Kalijah, Walker, and Harjo (Ohoola) were tried jointly, but Walker and Harjo were acquitted and only Kalijah was convicted on July 13, 1887.

"Doctor" may have been Walker's name rather than a physician's title. *The Elevator* described all of the defendants as "full blood Creek Indians of the most ignorant class," and, "Seabron was a mere boy, not more than eighteen years of age, ignorant and half civilized."

On Hampton and Kalijah's death warrants, the usual list of charges for services appears. Hampton's unmarked grave at the city cemetery cost three dollars as usual. But the price of Kalijah's grave at the Catholic Cemetery was eight dollars, an increase of two dollars since Pat McCarty's burial in April of the same year.

CHAPTER 25

SEVEN SENTENCED, THREE HANG

Jackson Crow, George Moss, and Owen D. Hill

> The execution at the Federal court yard last Friday
> was unattended with any special incident of im-
> portance. The culprits passed rather a restless night be-
> fore their death, praying and singing much of the time.
> — *The Weekly Elevator*, May 4, 1888

On February 10, 1888, Judge Parker passed sentence of death on seven men, but on April 27, 1888, only three would hang. The sentence of William Alexander, the second person condemned to death for rape, would be commuted to life in prison. Dick Southerland received twenty years. Jeff Hilderbrand and Emanuel Patterson were granted a respite of ten weeks. *The Elevator* predicted accurately that Hilderbrand would not live out the respite. He had been in the jail since November 14, 1885, and was in the last stages of tuberculosis. The editor felt that Hilderbrand "should be pardoned at once and allowed to go to his home and spend what little time he may remain on earth."

JACKSON CROW

Jack Crow took the fall, literally, for ten other people, at least one of whom was guiltier than he. On August 7, 1884, Charles B. Wilson was found dead on the road near Kulla Chaha in the Choctaw Nation. As Wilson was a well-known merchant, both in the Nation and in Fort Smith, his murder caused quite a stir.

On August 6, 1884, an election was held in the Choctaw Nation. Charles Wilson and Robert Benton had both run for the office of county representative. According to prosecution witness Adam Morris, Wilson was county treasurer at the time. Wilson was returning from that election on the morning of August 7 when he was confronted by Robert Benton, Jack Crow, Peter Consaw, Ned McCaslin, John Allen, Dixon Perry, Charles Fisher, Jim Franklin, Cornelius McCurtain, Joe Jackson, and John Slaughter. Benton and Wilson exchanged words over a disagreement they had had before the election, and Wilson was killed.

Apparently there had been hostility between Crow and Wilson since the previous December. Deputy U.S. Marshal T. A. (Bert) Brown testified in Crow's trial that he and Wilson had arrested Crow in December 1883 on a charge of murder and had brought him to Fort Smith.

Crow was cleared of that charge but threatened retribution against Wilson. Also, from the testimony of Edmund Pickens, Wilson's nephew, it appears that some problems existed between Wilson and Robert Benton before the election. Pickens had accompanied his uncle to the election, and he quoted Wilson as saying to Benton on their arrival: "I heard you was going to kill me, and if you are I am ready." Benton replied, "I ain't got nothing against you." Pickens also testified that Benton told him later the same day that he had nothing against Wilson.

Pickens further testified that he carried a pistol and a Winchester on the day of the election. When he and Wilson had traveled but a short distance after leaving the election, they were stopped by Charley Fisher and Cornelius McCurtain, acting as deputy sheriffs through the county, and eight or nine other men who arrested Pickens for carrying a pistol. Wilson bonded Pickens out and tried to bond out the pistol and rifle but could not. After Pickens was released, Wilson told him to go home, he would stay all night at a nearby house.

Joseph Jackson, witness for the prosecution, testified that he met with the group of men charged with the killing of Wilson on the morning of August 7 and was told that Wilson was going to be killed that day. Jackson traveled with the group for a quarter of a mile and separated from them, then met Robert Benton, who sent him back for the others. He claimed that he did not follow after the men regrouped, but a short time later heard shots. Jackson "cut out" but was met by some of the men and rode with them about three miles. He then went back to where the shooting was, "and this fellow was dead."

John Slaughter, one of the men originally charged in the crime, testified through an interpreter and told of the whole series of events starting from the evening before when he was invited to Benton's house for supper. His testimony was that the men started in different directions, regrouped, and arrived at the spot where Wilson was stopped by Charley Fisher and Jim Franklin. Benton arrived, and he and Wilson greeted each other with, "Good morning." Benton asked Wilson what office he held (apparently in reference to his carrying a pistol) to which Wilson replied that he was a deputy marshal. Wilson told Benton that he was drunk, "and he hated it mighty bad that he was drunk and toting a pistol." Benton asked Wilson what papers he had to prove his office, then took Wilson's pistol and asked why he had a grudge against him, then the pistol fired. Benton then fired two more times and struck Wilson on the head several times. Wilson fell to all fours and grabbed the gun and struggled with Benton for it. Jackson Crow stepped up and shot Wilson in the back with the Winchester that had been taken from Edmund Pickens the day before.

All of the people involved in the crime except Crow were Choctaw citizens. As Indian citizens committing a crime in their own tribal territory, they were not subject to the jurisdiction of the U.S. District Court. Since they were all prominent citizens, the tribal court dealt lightly with them. In the words of *The Weekly Elevator*: "hence Jack must suffer the extreme penalty of the law while they go scot free, as the Choctaw courts here long ago disposed of their cases by acquitting them." Crow, who had earned the reputation of a bad man in the Territory, was classified as an "Indian Negro," his father being Creek and his mother "a Negress." At the time of the crime, Crow had not taken advantage of the Choctaw Nation's Freedmen Act, which would have put him in the same position as the others, so he alone was subject to U.S. government law.

The Trade and Intercourse Act of 1834, Section 25, states:

> ...That so much of the laws of the United States as provides for the punishment of crimes committed within any place within the sole and exclusive jurisdiction of the United States shall be in force in the Indian country: Provided, The same shall not extend to crimes committed by one Indian against the person or property of another Indian (p. 733).

The act devotes several paragraphs to describing and defining an Indian.

In 1866 at Fort Smith, the tribes that had taken up arms against the U.S. government negotiated new treaties. Some of those treaties, the Cherokee for example, gave Freedmen automatic tribal citizenship. The Choctaw and Chickasaw treaty did not. People of African descent had to apply under the Choctaw Freedmen Act for citizenship. All of the Freedmen involved in the murder had gained citizenship except Jackson Crow. After the murder, Crow went on the scout and remained at large until the winter of 1886, during which time his cohorts attempted to get him registered as a Choctaw citizen. Charles Benton, witness for the defense, testified that he had registered both Crow and his sister with the commissioner because Crow had no horse to go to register. However, his name or any variation of it does not appear today on any Freedmen roll.

In December 1886, Deputy Marshal Charles Barnhill and his posse trailed Crow to the Poteau Mountains where his family lived. On the second day of January 1887, the posse found Crow at his home. Crow would not surrender, and Barnhill continued to besiege the place until one of his feet became frozen. He then got close enough to set fire to the house. Only then did Crow, for the safety of his family, surrender, and the fire was put out. *The Fort Smith Elevator* reported that when arrested Crow was in possession of the murdered man's pistol. Algie Hall, in his testimony at the trial, gave a detailed description of the arrest. In cross-examination, he was asked specifically about whether Wilson's pistol was found in Crow's possession or in the house, and he answered that it was neither. Hall testified that he asked Crow about the pistol and Crow said that he had traded it off.

When brought to the court, Jackson Crow argued on the grounds of jurisdiction, but the court declared that argument invalid since the crime occurred before he became an Indian citizen. The court ruled that blood followed the mother and Crow's mother was a "Negress."

At trial, the facts as stated previously were brought out. Crow's defense was that he had been summoned as a posse by Benton to arrest Charles Wilson who, contrary to the law of the Nation, was carrying a pistol. Wilson resisted arrest, and Benton shot him and that it was Consaw who shot him in the back. "Crow was a man of extraordinary nerve and will power, stubborn as a mule and non-communicative" (*The Elevator*, April 27, 1888). During the trial he pretended not to speak or understand English, and an interpreter had to translate the reading of the sentence. However, when the president refused to interfere in his case, he quickly acquired a good command of the language.

It was regrettable that none of Crow's cohorts paid along with him for the crime. But it was reported that this was probably not his first murder. Several people last seen with him were never heard from again.

GEORGE MOSS

> George Moss was convicted on the 17th of September last (1887) for participating in one of the most diabolical murders that ever occurred in the Indian Territory, and is the last of four men who took part in it. [More hyperbole than fact.]
>
> — *The Elevator*, April 27, 1888

The murder of George Taff was indeed wanton, but "most diabolical," when compared to other diabolical crimes in the Territory, it was not.

On November 26, 1886, Moss, Sandy Smith, Factor Jones, and Dick Butler decided to kill and steal a beef from the range of Red River County, Choctaw Nation. Their plan was to steal the beef and kill anyone who might interfere. They carried out their plan by going to the Red River bottom and shooting a steer belonging to George Taff, a prominent farmer. Unfortunately for them and the farmer, Taff was in the area tending to other stock when he heard the shot. He went to the scene and was shot. Moss's horse ran away during the shooting, the

156

men abandoned the beef and escaped in their separate ways, and Moss went home afoot. Taff's failure to return home caused alarm, and the next day a search party was organized. In a short time, the searchers found the body and Moss's horse, which was grazing in the bottom and still wearing the saddle and bridle. Moss was soon arrested and informed on the other three. Moss and Smith were turned over to a deputy marshal working in the area and were brought to Fort Smith for trial. Jones and Butler were registered citizens of the Choctaw Nation and as such did not come under the jurisdiction of the U.S. court. The local citizens, knowing that the culprits probably would never be punished under tribal law, took matters into their own hands. They took the murderers to the exact spot where they had killed Taff, riddled them with bullets, and left the bodies where they fell. Sandy Smith had tried to escape on the way to Fort Smith and was shot and wounded by the deputy marshal. He died of those wounds on the day of the trial, leaving only Moss to expiate his crime according to U.S. law.

Moss, in his application for witnesses, asserted that said witnesses would state, "that Defendant Moss was hung up by the neck to make him confess to the crime until he was almost dead." Moss made three separate applications for witnesses, all proclaiming his innocence. Obviously, they availed him nothing to convince a jury.

OWEN D. HILL

Owen Datus Hill came to grief largely because of his mother-in-law. He might never have been caught after his escape if he had not written a fifteen-page letter to his landlord inquiring after the condition of his wife, whose throat he had slashed. The letter, which is on file at the National Archives in Fort Worth, is marked in the upper left corner, "Ex A." The letter, presumably, might have been all the evidence that the prosecution needed. It is not just a detail of the why and how of the crime, it is almost a complete biography of the man.

The letter dated July 30, 1887, Kansas City, Missouri, tells that Hill was born in Alabama and that he was now twenty-seven years old, so he possibly could have been born to slave parents. He was taken to Cincinnati, Ohio, when he was two and was raised there until he was seventeen, when he moved to Arkansas. In 1881 he was in bad health so he left Washington, Arkansas, and went to Hot Springs, Arkansas. After two years there, he was in better health, and he met and fell in love with Vinna Anderson. They made a "true engagement" to each other to "marriage" and did "marriage." Just before they were to marry, he was told that his intended was already "marriage," so he confronted her, and she confirmed that she had been. Not long after she and her first husband were married, her mother moved in with them.

After three or four weeks, trouble started between her husband and her mother and grew worse and worse until she could no longer stand it and she moved from Little Rock to Hot Springs.

Hill and Vinna moved to Fort Smith and were married and "had no trouble whatever and lived as loven as two people could live." In February 1887, Vinna got sick. For three months, Hill nursed her and their baby, even quitting his work so that he could tend to them. After Vinna was well, he sent her to visit her mother in Muskogee in Indian Territory. In early 1887 the mother-in-law invited Hill to come to Muskogee and consider making a crop with her, which he did around February 20, 1887.

At Muskogee, Hill liked the country and rented forty acres of bottomland and began to live peacefully. But after a while, his trouble started with his mother-in-law to the point, as he said, "She just try herself and see how mean she could be." Eventually Hill told the mother-in-law that she could no longer live in his house and she moved. But Vinna still would visit her mother, and for days afterward, she and Hill would argue. One day he slapped her during an argument over her giving her mother some tobacco.

On the morning of June 25, 1887, Hill went to the field to work. When he later went into the house to get water, he found his wife and child were gone. Hill went to his mother-in-law's home, and when he arrived, Vinna's cousin was standing in the yard with a gun. He told Hill not to come any farther, and both the cousin and mother-in-law told Hill that his wife was going to live there now. Hill went back home and was troubled all night and the next day by the situation. Not owning a gun, Hill borrowed a shotgun, and on June 26, went back to the house with the gun and a razor, intending to bring his wife and child home or kill his wife and himself. He was confronted at the door by his mother-in-law, whom he beat with the shotgun until he broke it. Believing that the old lady was dead, he then pursued his wife into the bedroom and then into the yard, where he slashed her throat and broke the razor. Now, having no weapon to kill himself, he took the child to his landlord's home and watched from the woods until he was sure the baby had been found. He then caught the train and fled to Kansas City.

Once in Kansas City, he wondered whether his wife had survived the attack and wrote the letter that became his undoing. In the letter, he said that if his wife were not dead, he would try to get her "away from any of her peoples and then my wife will be as good to me as she ever was and so will I to her." If she were dead, as soon as he got some money, he would come back and "die the death of a dog." According to the report in *The Fort Smith Elevator*, he need not have wondered whether his wife was dead. The paper reported that he had nearly severed her head from her body. His mother-in-law, whom he thought he had killed, had survived the attack and was present to testify against him.

In the days preceding the execution, all of the condemned accepted religion to some degree. Jackson Crow and George Moss were visited constantly by Reverends R. C. Tyler and S. M. Fisher. Crow and Moss, however, remained morose and uncommunicative with reporters and others. Crow appealed for executive clemency and was stoic on receiving the denial. Moss did nothing to try to save himself from hanging. Hill was baptized in the Baptist faith, and he applied for commutation of sentence, but when he received the denial, he exclaimed, "Thank God, thank God, I am ready to die." When visited by a reporter from *The Elevator*, Hill was walking the corridor of the jail and whistling a tune, apparently at ease. He expressed that in five days he would be free of worldly cares and gave the reporter several unsealed letters, asking that they be mailed on the day before the execution. All were dated April 26, 1888, and a long and intimate one to his mother, brothers, and sisters was published in full in *The Elevator*. One letter was to his mother-in-law in which he blamed her for all his troubles, but whom he forgave.

HANGMAN'S DAY

On the morning of the execution day, the prisoners were quiet and spent much of the morning shaking hands and saying good-byes. The spiritual advisers were with them, and Hill's sister spent part of the morning with him. At twelve thirty that afternoon, Marshal Carroll entered and read the death warrants. Then the march to the gallows began. Hill sang and prayed alternately and on his breast wore a large card with the letters "M. S. B." made from the hair of his mother, brother, and sister. The card was buried with him. Hill's sister accompanied him to the gallows and stood on the platform until the fatal drop. On the scaffold the usual religious ceremonies were carried out and the final adjustments made. The necks of all three men were broken by the drop, and death was almost instant. The bodies hung for about half an hour and then were taken down and placed in coffins. Hill's body was turned over to his sister, who arranged his hands and closed his eyes after the body was placed in the coffin. The other two were buried in the potter's field.

CHAPTER 26

GUS BOGLE
"Launched Into Eternity Protesting His Innocence"
(*The Elevator*, July 13, 1888)

Gus Bogle, a young black man from Denison, Texas, is another of the people around whom a "gallows myth" has grown. Contrary to the myth, he did not hang in slow strangulation for eight hours. According to *The Fort Smith Weekly Elevator* of July 13, 1888, "His neck was not broken by the fall, and he died of strangulation after a few convulsive struggles." Apparently death came in minutes, not hours. Gus was, however, "considered one of the hardest cases in the jail, and when the verdict was read he was surrounded by deputy marshals and guards, who conducted him back to jail with great care" (*The Elevator*, May 18, 1888).

On June 27, 1887, William D. Morgan, a coal miner suffering from consumption, left his home between Atoka, Choctaw Nation, Indian Territory, and Denison, Texas, to seek a climate more agreeable to his condition. He left with $115 in his pocket, undecided at the time where he would go. He told his wife, Ann, that he might go to Colorado or Galveston, Texas. Morgan appears never to have made it past Denison. On June 28, he wrote his wife that he had reached Denison, everything was all right, and he hoped that the children would be good. That same day he went to the store of Waterson, Star & Co. and purchased a hat, which he wore, and several other items that he expressed back to his home. The clerk testified that Morgan had been drinking but was not drunk, but it appears that he went on a spree later.

Around three o'clock the next afternoon, Ann Morgan received a parcel containing the items William had purchased at the store and the cap that he had worn when leaving home. But about an hour earlier, Charley LeFlore had come to the house bearing a valise belonging to William Morgan and containing his clothes and a leather strap. His body had been found at Blue Tank, Indian Territory, between Denison and his home. He had been strangled and beaten to death.

Neither the court records nor the news articles make clear how Bogle was developed as a suspect. Of the four who were arrested and charged with the crime, he was the only one none of the witnesses knew by name. Nevertheless, he was arrested in Denison on June 30. He, of course, denied being present, knowing the victim, and having any knowledge of the event. He also made confessions that varied as to details and later said that those were coerced. It appears that there may

160

have been an attempt to hang him. It was mentioned several times in the trial but no details or confirmations were given. While in jail at Muskogee, Bogle named William Netherly, Thomas Wright, and Dennis Williams as accomplices. Those three were known to the railroad conductors and brakemen as bootblacks in Denison. But none of them were identified as the ones at the scene by those who knew them.

D. D. Cannon, railway conductor from Denison to Muskogee, testified that on the night of June 28 the train stopped at Armstrong switch (Blue Tank), and the brakeman, hearing a noise in one of the cars, put four black men and an Indian (actually the white man, W. D. Morgan) out of the car. "Two of them looked to be about twelve and the others looked to be about eighteen, there was two small ones about the same size and two large ones about the same size." One of the blacks claimed that the white man had been kicking them and had two bottles of whiskey in his valise. The white man was described as being intoxicated, but none of the black men appeared to be. When asked if he recognized any of the defendants as the ones he had put off that night, Cannon pointed to Gus Bogle as the only one who had drawn his attention that night. Bogle had objected to being left, saying that he did not know the country and wanted to ride. The train left with the conductor watching to see that no one reboarded.

J. W. Carey, the attendant, who lived at Armstrong switch, heard people arguing and cursing after the train left around one o'clock in the morning, and it went on until the next train arrived about three o'clock. The next morning, his mother-in-law showed him the body of a man lying a short distance from their house. The man had been strangled with a strap that lay nearby and beaten. He had no shoes or hat, his pockets were inside out, and his vest had been pulled over his head. In one of the confessions that he later recanted, Bogle described buckling a strap around the man's neck and beating him. He said that he got ten dollars and the hat but later threw away the hat and money.

John Whalen, cousin of the jailer at Muskogee, was sleeping in the jail the night that Netherly was brought in and placed in the cell with Bogle, who was already there. Whalen awoke in the night to hear Bogle and Netherly arguing about the killing. Bogle told Netherly, "You got the shoes and as much money as I did." And Netherly said, "No, I didn't and I had nothing to do with it." And the argument went back and forth in that tone until Whalen went back to sleep.

The beginning and end of Gus Bogle's case went rapidly. The murder occurred on June 28, and he was arrested June 30. Nine days after the murder, the proceedings before the commissioner (hearings and depositions) were held, and on July 16, he arrived at the jail at Fort Smith. Had it not been for a request for witnesses and a continuance of trial, he would have been tried in the fall term of court. As it was, he was tried in May 1888. The case was given to the jury on Thursday evening, June 10, and they were out but a short time before delivering a verdict of guilty for Bogle and acquitting "his three companions who were mere boys." Convicted on June 10, he was sentenced June 26 to hang on July 6. At the sentencing, Judge Parker addressed Bogle in much the same words that he did all of the men he condemned, except at one point he said, "You are evidently not in a fit condition to stand before the dread tribunal where you must soon answer for the crimes and wrongs committed by you. You cannot appear there with a hope of pardon for these crimes unless you do that which the great God has commanded shall be done. Before mercy and forgiveness is extended there must be penitence and sorrow."

Penitence and sorrow Bogle did not show. *The Elevator* reported:

> His keepers represent him as being one of the most contrary and singular men ever in the jail, and one who appeared to delight in annoying others. For several nights last week, after being locked in his cell for the night he would whoop and yell like a lunatic for hours for no other purpose than to annoy the other inmates and prevent their sleeping. When remonstrated he would reply that he would soon be dead anyway and they could not hurt him for making noise.

Though admonished by some ladies who visited him on Saturday before his execution, he did not seek a religious adviser. Later, though, he made arrangements with Elder Wade of the Colored Methodist Church for baptism, but when the time came, he deferred it until Thursday, the day before his execution. When Thursday came, he asked to delay until Friday morning but was told by the jail officials that would not be possible, so there was no baptism. Bogle's mind was on saving not his soul, but his mortal being. A few days before the execution, he tried to persuade a trusty to smuggle him out of jail in a barrel that had contained sawdust for the spittoons. The trusty, having more to lose than to gain, declined.

> Thursday night—his last night on earth—he slept little if any, walking his cell the greater portion of the night. He had been restless for some days past and was constantly changing around from one cell to another, being allowed to occupy a cell with some other prisoner, as it was evident that he dreaded to be alone.
>
> — *The Elevator*, July 13, 1888

On the morning of his execution day, Bogle was among the first to leave the cell and ate heartily of a good breakfast. He then met with a spiritual counselor but was very restless. Afterward he walked the corridors of the jail until time to prepare for the execution. When brought the usual clothing given the condemned — underwear, black suit, white shirt, and shoes — he put on the pants, coat, socks, and shoes and handed back the vest, saying it was too hot for it and too much trouble to put on the shirt.

About ten minutes before Bogle was to be taken out, guard John McNamee was careless enough to stop in the corridor to talk to two other guards with his holstered pistol on the side close to Bogle. Gus grabbed the pistol and ran into a cell. Emanuel Patterson, sentenced to hang but granted a respite, was lying in the cell, and when he saw the situation, he wrestled the gun from Bogle and slid it under the bars to the officers. After that, Bogle was not allowed the opportunity to try anything else. The guards knew that he had said that once outside he intended to make a break so that they would have to shoot him.

When jailer Pettigrew began to read the death warrant, Bogle told him that he did not need to because he saw no use in it but, nevertheless, he listened while it was read. The iron door was opened and, surrounded by "a bevy of guards," Bogle proceeded to the gallows. There was a brief religious service, and Bogle took his place under the noose. There was no perceptible change in his countenance until the hangman began pinioning his legs. His face assumed an ashen color, but he never flinched. When asked if he had any last words, he replied that they were executing an innocent man and that he had nothing more to say than had been already stated. The black cap was placed over his head, the rope adjusted and the trap sprung. Dr. J. G. Eberle pronounced him dead a short time later.

Note: The name "Bogle" was consistently misspelled in the newspapers and on the early government warrants and subpoenas. Most of the later documents and Gus's own signature on the application for witnesses spell the name "Bogle," not "Bogles."

CHAPTER 27

HIS BOOTS WERE HIS DOWNFALL
Richard Smith, January 25, 1889

Richard Smith made all of the usual protestations and lies and even tried to induce his boots to lie but they did not cooperate, nor did his in-laws.

On Wednesday, March 28, 1888, Thomas Pringle went to the woods about 400 yards from his home in Towson County, Choctaw Nation, Indian Territory, to cut boards. Hattie Seals, who lived at the Pringle home near Shawnee Town, had gone along to assist in chipping the bark from the boards and was standing only a few feet from Pringle when a single rifle shot was fired from behind some trees. Pringle was hit in the right shoulder, the bullet ranging downward. He fell mortally wounded, and his first words to Hattie when she went to his aid were that he was going to die. Pringle told Hattie to tell his brother to kill a man named Murphy with whom he had "had a fuss" at a dance about a week before. But Murphy had not threatened to kill Pringle. After Hattie had tended to him awhile, Pringle instructed her to go for some Indian men who "lived tolerable close." Hattie and the men carried Pringle to his house, but Thomas Pringle died before they could get him there.

Charles Pringle, brother of the deceased, was informed about noon the day of the murder and went to the site and looked for tracks. He found where a man had stood behind a tree and indications that he had crawled up to the tree. The tracks were distinctive in that they showed the imprints of large tacks in the soles of the boots, twenty in the right and fourteen in the left, with three in the shape of a "V." Also, one boot was broken, allowing the big toe to protrude and the sock to make a fabric imprint in the soil. The wearer appeared to have walked a few steps and then run toward a pond or lake where the trail ended. The next day Charles Pringle and three others found the same boot tracks on the other side of the water going in the direction of Richard Smith's house and at Smith's house.

It was determined by the search party that they would arrest Smith the next day, but then they learned that he and his brother-in-law, Charles Mitchell, had gone to Wheelock, Indian Territory, to a funeral. The following day, Smith was arrested, still wearing the boots but with the tacks removed from the left and the heels removed from both boots. He claimed that he had removed the heels three weeks earlier, but all of the witnesses testified that they could tell that the boots had not been worn long since the tacks and heels were removed. Also, William Henry testified that Smith had come to his house wet up to the waist on the day of the killing. Henry and Smith went to the field where Henry was burning brush, and Smith asked Henry to help him remove the heels from his boots. They were later found where Henry said that they had thrown them. Smith removed the nails from the sole of the left boot but kept them. In the words of Henry, "He wanted them nails."

All of the foregoing information is from the depositions at the proceedings before the commissioner, and judging from the list of affiants, it appears that all of Smith's in-laws, his neighbors, and all of the evidence were against him. Still he maintained his innocence. But in a confession to Deputy Marshal J. N. Ennes, which he later denied making, Smith implicated his brother-in-law, Charles Mitchell, as an accomplice. Mitchell supposedly told Smith that he should kill Pringle. The assumed motive for the killing was a quarrel that Smith and Pringle had on the previous Sunday. Smith had traded Pringle a cow for a gun, but Pringle later learned that the cow belonged to Smith's employer, not Smith. They were to meet and go to the employer's house to clear up the matter later, but in the meantime, Pringle was murdered.

Charles Mitchell did not even get as far as a grand jury indictment. He was discharged as a suspect at the commissioner's hearing. Charles, along with his brother, Samuel Mitchell, also a brother-in-law of Smith, and a host of others were all witnesses against Richard Smith, and the testimony of each corroborated that of the others. In August 1888, it did not take the jury long to bring a verdict of guilty of murder.

The August 18, 1888, issue of *The Elevator* carried this article:

> At noon on Tuesday last, while most of the guards were at dinner, Turnkey Casey, who was in charge of the lower tier of cells, where all those charged with murder are confined, unlocked the door leading into the guard room to pass a bucket of dinner in for one of the prisoners. About the only prisoners in the corider [sic] at the time were Carroll Collier, a white man, and Dick Smith, a negro murderer. Collier was standing at the door, and when Casey unlocked it he attempted to pull it open so he could pass out. While he and Casey were struggling in the door, Dick Smith came up and grabbed Casey's pistol from the scabbard. At this juncture Mike O'Connell, one of the guards, arrived on the scene and fired a pistol shot into the cell, which was followed by another shot from Dick McStravick, who was on the steps leading to the second story, which caused Smith to drop Casey's pistol, though neither of

the guards shot to hit any one. At this time Collier was standing right over Casey's pistol, and was ordered to shove it out under the bars with his foot, which he did, and thus ended the excitement. During the shooting the other prisoners in the jail were hugging the corners of their cells closely.

On Saturday, November 3, 1888, Judge Parker pronounced the sentence of death on Richard Smith and set the date of execution for Friday, January 25, 1889.

The headline of *The Elevator* on January 25, 1889, read simply, "NO. 60." However, the newspaper was mistaken; Richard Smith was number fifty-nine. The paper had been mistaken more than once before, sometimes getting the number executed off by as many as four. Presumably the newspaper staff, as others did later, mistook the name George Young Wolf Six-Killer, executed October 10, 1873, to be two people. Nevertheless, whether he was number fifty-nine or sixty, Richard Smith was just as dead by one thirty on the afternoon of January 25.

Smith had accepted the Catholic faith, and on the morning of his last day, after arising early and partaking of a "hearty breakfast," he spent the rest of the morning in prayer. He appeared to be resigned to his fate. At twelve thirty that afternoon, jailer Pettigrew entered the jail, announced that the time had come, and put the handcuffs on Smith. He was then taken into the corridor where the death warrant was read. Reverend Lawrence Smythe accompanied him to the gallows, where the ceremonies were brief. On the death trap, Pettigrew asked Smith if he had any last words. Reverend Smythe handed him a small crucifix, and while holding it, Smith once more declared his ignorance of the killing of Pringle and stated that an innocent man was being hanged. His arms and legs were pinioned, the black mask was placed over his face, the trap was sprung, and a drop of eight and a half feet broke his neck. He was pronounced dead in fifteen minutes.

CHAPTER 28

THREE SENSELESS MURDERS, TWO HANGINGS

Malachi Allen and James Mills

April 19, 1889

Neither Malachi Allen nor James Mills was a stranger to the U.S. District Court for the Western District of Arkansas. Mills appeared before the court in 1882 and 1885 on liquor charges and in 1882 and 1888 for larceny and had an 1883 warrant for failure to appear.

MALACHI ALLEN

Malachi Allen, alias Nole Chil, was charged in 1884 with assault with intent to kill. From the depositions available in that case, Allen appears to have been a man who intended to have his way, even if it required violence. He had loaned ten dollars to John Kemp on the promise that Kemp repay him as soon as possible. When Kemp went to repay, he found that Allen had taken his cow and intended to keep it. Allen told Kemp not to take the cow back, but Kemp said the cow was not part of the deal and took her. The next morning, Allen rode his horse to Kemp's door and went in shooting. He must have had as little control of his weapon as he did his temper. The first shot was so close Kemp had powder burns on his hands. Allen fired a total of five shots and never struck Kemp. Kemp ran into the next room and fired back through the crack in the door with his Winchester, prompting Allen to run for the fence. Kemp followed Allen into the yard and attempted to fire two more times, but his father restrained him.

Allen, in his deposition, told a different tale. He said he had gone in peace to work out the matter and that Kemp had come out shooting. The depositions of other witnesses and the evidence did not bear out Allen's story. The fact that he had a pawn note from Kemp, who could neither read nor write, did not lend to his credibility either. However, for some reason, it appears that Allen was not convicted of assault.

The killings that led to his execution seem to be further proof of Allen's volatility. They occurred after Sunday church services when four men were arguing over a saddle. Allen was not a part of the group, but he heard his name mentioned, approached the men, and told them to keep his name out of it. One of the men responded, and Allen went to his wagon and got a rifle. He pointed it at Cy Love and pulled the trigger, but the gun did not fire. Shadrack Peters, who was nearby, told

167

Allen, "Put down your gun and fight fair, Cy has got no gun." Allen then turned on Peters, also unarmed, and told him that if he wanted to take up the argument, he would kill him, too. Peters replied that if he wanted to kill him then to do so. Then Allen fired and killed Peters. He then fired on Nero Russell and shot twice at Jack Peters, missing both men. Cy Love ran around the church building. Allen followed and shot him in the back, killing him. According to witnesses, Allen's rifle was the only gun present.

Deputy Marshal John A. McAllister sent the following letter to U.S. Marshal John Carroll next day:

> Paul's Valley I. T. July 2nd, 1888
> Col. John Carroll, U.S. Marshal
> Yesterday, July the first a Negro named Melikies Allen shot and killed Silas Love and Shed Peters, both Negroes near Winewood I. T. The witnesses are Lawrence Love, Lige Blue, Mat Russell & Nero Russell.
> The killing was done at the church. There was only one gun there. That was the one Allen had. The two Negroes he killed was unarmed and did not know Melikies Allen was mad or had anything against them. Both men are shot in the back. I hunted him all day yesterday after the killing and last night. Allen has three brothers and a cousin that is with him. They are all armed now and say they will not be taken alive. I am going after them today. Please send warrant at once.
>
> > John A. McAllister,
> > Deputy Marshal

The newspapers made a longer and more exciting story out of Allen's pursuit and capture than Deputy McAllister did, but they neglected to tell how fast this man worked. Later the same day, still July 2, McAllister sent this letter to Carroll:

> Paul's Valley I. T. July 2, Inst.
> Marshal Carroll, I wrote you this morning for a writ for Melikies Allen, a Negro, for double murder. I stated that I was just starting to capture him. We found him about one mile from where he done his shooting, near a branch that runs through the prairie. When he saw us he ran his horse to the branch and got off the horse and behind a tree and began shooting at us. He shot three shots at us before we commenced shooting

at him. We fired several shots without any effect. He fired about ten shots and we got him surrounded. He left the tree and took the open prairie tho [sic] in high weeds and grass. One shot struck his left arm and broke it and one struck his left foot in the bottom but didn't amount to much. He then surrendered. We brought him to Paul's Valley about 12 o'clock. His arm was shot so badly the doctors had to amputate it. He is getting along fine. Please send writ at once. He killed Silas Love and Shed Peters, both Negroes, yesterday, July 1st near Winewood I. T. Witnesses, Lawrence Love, Nero Russell and others, all Negroes. You will see in the information I sent this morning.

If Mr. Thomas is there tell him to send me the writ for Bud Bennett, a Negro from Stone Wall. I have him arrested, or if the writ is there send it or if the information is there send writ. Please send me writs for all the cases I have sent.

Yours Truly,
John A. McAllister, Dept.

In the first week of January 1889, Allen went to trial in Fort Smith. In his application for witnesses, he asked for a number of people whom he said could verify "that he was attacked by the deceased and others, some of them with knives — and beat and bruised — and that he shot in his own necessary self defense." At the trial, however, his attorneys, Duval and Cravens, based their defense on insanity. *The Elevator* reported, "Allen has conducted himself in a 'cranky' manner since his incarceration, but at the time of the killing he had sense enough to make a desperate and shrewd flight when the officers overtook him." On Thursday, January 5, 1889, the jury took about twenty minutes to return a verdict of guilty.

JAMES MILLS

No motive is given for James Mills's murder of John Windom either in existing archives documents or the period newspapers. There is one mention in *The Elevator* that the men might have had an argument on an earlier occasion. Without a motive, or maybe even with a motive, the events make no sense. The whole story involves a group of people with unfathomable — or a total lack of — logic.

Mills either lived or boarded at the home of his victim. On Friday night, December 9, 1887, James Mills, Tom Robbins, John Windom, and Windom's twelve-year-old stepson, Phillip Lincoln, went hunting for coon and skunk. When the only witness, twelve-year-old Phillip Lincoln, deposed, he said Windom was walking along in front of Mills and listening for the dogs when Mills shot him. Then Tom Robbins, who was walking behind Mills, stepped up and shot Windom twice. Mills shot Windom in the back, the bullet coming out his breast. Robbins turned him over and shot him first in the mouth then in the breast. They left Windom where he fell and started back to the Windom house. On the way, the men told the boy that if he told anyone what happened they would kill him too. The trio went back to the house and told Windom's wife, Eliza, some story explaining her husband's absence. Phillip Lincoln testified his mother, Anna Edwards, Sylvia Lincoln, George Coody, George Lincoln, and Robin Bruner were at the house when they returned and that Eliza Windom, James Mills, Tom Robbins, George Lincoln, and Anna Edwards stayed there all night. The next morning Lincoln went to a neighbor's house and told what had happened. That day Eliza Windom, James Mills, and others went out and found Windom's body and brought it home.

Peter Lincoln, Phillip's father, said in his deposition that Tom Robbins told him that they were walking along when Mills pulled out his pistol and shot Windom then told him (Robbins) to shoot him and that he shot him twice. Robbins gave no reason for the shooting.

Eucum Bruner, in his sworn statement, said that he went to the Windoms' the day after the killing and asked Mills if he killed Windom and he said, "Yes." Bruner asked Mills if he would show him where the body was. They went in a wagon, and Mills drove to the spot where the body lay. Bruner said, "I told Jim that it was a pity they killed him and Jim said he had to do it to save himself. He did not say why he had to do it to save himself." Bruner and other neighbors formed a posse and attempted to arrest Mills and Robbins. In the process, Robbins was shot "in the fleshy part of his leg" but Mills escaped. Robbins was taken to the jail at Fort Smith, where he died from infection in the leg wound. He had been indicted but not tried.

On the back of the true bill indictment No. 2386, "United States v. James Mills} Murder," is this notation dated November 10, 1888: "We the jury find the defendant, James Mills, guilty of murder as charged in the second count. R. A. Caldwell, Foreman."

On Saturday, February 2, 1889, Judge Isaac Parker, acting on "United States v. James Mills, Indictment for Murder No. 2386," sentenced Mills to hang on April 19, 1889. Mills's attorneys immediately filed for a retrial citing the usual charges—that the jury's verdict was not according to law and the court erred in its instruction to the jury.

On the same day, the same sentence was pronounced on Malachi Allen, with Judge Parker giving one of most the scathing addresses to the condemned man. In part he said:

We scarcely ever have a case in court which exhibits the moral depravity and wickedness in your case. You have wickedly, wantonly and without any just cause taken the lives of two of your fellow men, for which high crimes against the law of your country you are called on to pay the penalty due an offended and violated law. You not only killed the two men I have named, but you fired on two others. You made every endeavor possible to kill the officers who pursued you to bring you to justice. These acts done wrongfully and wickedly by you show that you have no regard for human life. You must pay the penalty of the offended law with your own life. But you must do more than this. You must propitiate and satisfy God. A God whose law has been wickedly broken by you.

On that Saturday, four more men were sentenced to hang, but one's sentence would be commuted to life in prison, one would be given an unconditional pardon, and two would be respited to a later date. The following Friday, February 8, 1889, *The Fort Smith Weekly Elevator* ran this article:

On Sunday evening last [February 3, 1889] the notorious Belle Starr was shot and killed near her home by unknown parties. She was riding along the road alone when her assailant fired on her with a shotgun, the shot striking her in the face. As she reached for her gun the assassin fired a second time putting a load of buckshot in her breast and she fell from her horse dead. The frightened animal ran home and the alarm was soon given, but up to this time, so far as we know, there is no clue to her murderers.

Her husband, Jim Starr, alias Bill July, was here attending court as a defendant in a larceny case and received the news by telegraph Monday evening. He at once set out for the scene and will likely be heard from in due time.

And on the next Friday, February 15:

On Saturday last Jim Starr, husband of the late Belle Starr, arrived here, having in custody a man named E.

A. Watson, whom he charges with having murdered Belle, and turned the prisoner over to Jailer Pettigrew.

The Fort Smith Weekly Elevator, Friday, April 26, 1889:

Friday last was a gloomy day, being cloudy and raining, but especially gloomy about the United States court house and jail, where two lives were to be taken according to law and in behalf of justice. Malachi Allen and James Mills were to suffer the extreme penalty of the law for murders committed in the Indian country. The death trap had been carefully prepared and the ropes well stretched for the occasion. The condemned men slept well during their last night on earth, and arose at the usual hour in the morning. They were furnished with a good breakfast of which they partook with apparent relish. During the forenoon they were furnished with neat black suits, white shirts, collars, cuffs and white ties. They made their toilets with great care, assisted by their fellow prisoners.

Until the execution day, Allen had made no religious preparations, but on that morning he asked for a minister. Reverend J. L. Massey of the Methodist Church responded, and Allen was baptized saying that he had repented and was ready to die. Between eleven o'clock and noon, dinner was brought to the men. Allen ate well, but Mills ate nothing and stayed in his cell with Reverend Lawrence Smythe. By noon other ministers had arrived at the jail, and they held services for Allen, who knelt in the jail corridor surrounded by fellow prisoners Henry Miller, George Brashears, Frank Capel, Joe Martin, and Jack Spaniard, all of whom were also convicted of murder.

Services concluded, jailer Pettigrew entered and read the death warrants to the condemned men, who showed no emotion or nervousness. That done, they bade farewell to the other prisoners, the doors swung open, and the walk to the gallows commenced in drizzling rain. The ceremonies on the scaffold were brief. Allen's injured arm was pinioned to his side, and Mills was bound the usual way. The men spoke only to their spiritual advisers, the black caps and nooses were placed, and in a few seconds, the drop fell. Just fifteen minutes passed from the time the walk began until the drop fell. Both necks were broken.

This brought the number executed since 1873 to sixty-one, nineteen of whom were executed under the administration of Marshal Carroll.

CHAPTER 29

"BROKE THEIR NECKS

That's What Hangman Maledon Did for
Spaniard and Walker Last Friday"
(*The Fort Smith Weekly Elevator*, September 6, 1889)

On Monday, April 29, 1889, Judge Parker overruled motions for new trials in the cases of convicted murderers Jack Spaniard, Frank Capel, Joe Martin, William Walker, and Elsie James. All were sentenced to hang on Wednesday, July 17, 1889. This was the first time hangings were scheduled on a day other than Friday since the execution of John Childers on Friday, August 15, 1873. Elsie James was the second woman sentenced to hang by the U.S. District Court for the Western District of Arkansas. But out of those five, only Spaniard and Walker would take the long walk and the short drop.

ELSIE JAMES

The December 16, 1887, issue of *The Elevator* announced that Deputy Heck Thomas arrived on Monday, December 12, 1887, with thirty-eight prisoners, including twelve charged with murder. In those twelve were Elsie James and Margaret James, mother and daughter.

The Elevator of January 13, 1888, describes Elsie James as "quite a respectable looking old Chickasaw woman." However, in later editions, the paper makes light of her weight, which was said to have been more than 200 pounds. She was charged with murdering a white man, William Jones, in early July 1887, near Stone Wall in the Chickasaw Nation.

Jones had gone into the Nation sometime in the months prior to his death looking for land to rent. He was directed to the widow James, and the two made an agreement that he would rent her land, do the farm work, and share the proceeds of the crop. In return he would board at the James home.

Sometime after July 2, 1887, neighbors noticed that Jones had not been seen and questioned Elsie and Margaret James about his whereabouts. At first, they said that Jones had left to find a job around Cherokee Town and that he had said that if he did not find a job there, he would go to Denison and might return around Christmas. Jones was missing for about three months before the truth came out. Bond Underwood, in his deposition, said that in July, he had met Margaret

James on the road and she had told him that her mother killed Jones and that she was afraid of her mother.

When confronted, the two women admitted that, indeed, Jones was dead and that Elsie had shot him. They had a plausible story, and had they stuck to it, they might have gotten off with a plea of self-defense. Elsie claimed that Jones had come at her with a knife so she grabbed a gun from her bedroom and shot him. The home appears to have been a dog-run house with the kitchen separated from the living quarters by a hall or breezeway. Jones had taken a knife from the kitchen and come at Elsie; Margaret, seeing what he was doing, "hallooed" a warning at her mother. Jones yelled something at Elsie in English, which she, speaking only Chickasaw, did not understand. But she understood his intent and turned and shot him. The body lay in the hallway all night, the time of day being near dark.

The next morning the women and Samson Alexander took the body about 300 yards from the house and buried it in a depression where another house had once stood. After the women admitted that Jones was dead, Margaret took some men to the burial spot, where the body was found under about eighteen inches of dirt overlaid with stones from the old fireplace. The skull had been broken into several pieces and was taken to Fort Smith, along with the attached hair, and presented at the deposition hearings and trial. Much was said at the hearings about the skull being broken, but apparently, that was caused when the stones were piled on it at the burial, and the cause of death was shooting.

The James women told their self-defense story to several people before and after being arrested by Heck Thomas. But somewhere along the line, Elsie began to say that she would tell the whole story when she was in Fort Smith. She indicated that she did not feel safe as long as she was near Stone Wall. She then began to tell a story that Zeno Colbert, another Chickasaw, shot Jones in the afternoon and told her to burn the body, but she refused. Colbert then left, telling Elsie James that if she told anything about the killing, he would kill her too. At one time, she said Colbert had shot Jones because Jones had attacked him with a knife. Another story was that both men wanted to marry her.

J. D. Huggins, postmaster at Stone Wall, was among the people who helped bring about the confession of Mrs. James and who dug up the body. He offered another possibility for the killing. On the evening of July 2, 1887, Jones received a letter and opened it in Huggins's presence. Huggins estimated the letter contained between fifty and seventy-five dollars. He was certain that there was a twenty- and a five-dollar bill and that Jones rolled up the other bills and put them in his pocket. It was mentioned several times by witnesses in their depositions that the left pocket of the dead man's pants had been cut out,

There was never a direct statement that he had been robbed, but it was certainly alluded to.

If the Colbert story ever had any credence, it lost it when Lucy gave her deposition. Lucy was an Indian woman who lived with the Jameses. Lucy did not know her last name or where her original home was except that it was far away. She did know, though, what she had heard and seen the day of the killing. She had gone about sundown to get water some distance from the house. While going to the creek, she heard three shots, and when she returned, Jones was lying in the hallway with blood coming from his forehead. The butcher knife, which she recognized, was lying near his hand and his fingers were curled as if holding a knife. The James women told her the same self-defense story that they later told to others. But when questioned before the commissioner about Zeno Colbert, Lucy testified that he had not been there at all that day. Lucy, sometime after the killing, went to live at the home of Bond Underwood.

There are seventy-two pages of depositions from several witnesses. In reading those, it seems that several people knew, could have known, and should have known that William Jones was dead. Samson Alexander and his mother helped with the burial. Lucy knew, and if Bond Underwood did not learn of Jones's death from her, he learned about it from Margaret in July. At the time that Margaret told Underwood of the killing, there were at least three other people present. Still the murder was not discovered until about October 1 when the postmaster at Stone Wall, Heck Thomas, and several others uncovered the body.

The James women, Zeno Colbert, and Samson Alexander were brought into Fort Smith, all initially charged with murder. Alexander was released after the deposition hearings. The grand jury did not return a true bill on Zeno Colbert. Eventually the grand jury ignored the bill against Colbert, and he was released, only to be murdered later. *The Elevator* of December 30, 1887, stated that the grand jury discharged Margaret James, having ignored the bill against her. However, they must have been mistaken in that statement, for she did go to trial in January 1889 with her mother but was found not guilty.

Elsie James owned a good farm stocked with horses, cattle, and hogs, as well as crops. Knowing that she would be confined for some months before being tried, she turned the management of her property over to Mr. Tandy Walker. In March 1888, Elsie James was released on $6,000 bond, more than ten years' wages for the average person in the United States at that time.

In January, the Jameses went to trial, but the jury, after two days of deliberation, announced that they were hopelessly deadlocked—four for acquittal and eight for conviction. On Saturday, March 16, 1889, a new trial of both Elsie and Margaret began and occupied the court for a full week. On Friday, March 22, 1889, the jury returned verdicts of acquittal for Margaret and guilty for Elsie. Elsie, by law, was now a candidate for the gallows, but formal sentencing would not come until April 1889.

WILLIAM WALKER

William Walker was one of twelve accused murderers brought in by Heck Thomas in December 1887 in the same group of thirty-eight prisoners that included Elsie James. He was accused of murdering a neighbor, Calvin Church, just a few days earlier near Durant, Choctaw Nation, Indian Territory. All existing documents give the date of the crime as December 12, 1887; however, that is the date he arrived in Fort Smith. Heck was good but not that good, and the error does not change the basic facts of the crime.

Following is the article from *The Weekly Elevator* dated February 15, 1889, taken apparently from testimony at the trial:

> William Walker, colored, was convicted of murder on Tuesday evening last, the jury being out only a few minutes. He killed another Negro named Calvin Church, near Durant, Choctaw Nation, on the 12th of December, 1887; was arrested immediately after the killing, and has been in jail here since that time. Calvin Church and Bat Gardner were near neighbors. Walker lived at Gardner's. On the day previous to the killing Walker and Church had a few angry words about an axe. On the morning of the killing, Walker, whose duty it was to attend to Gardner's cows, took a Winchester and went to the cow pen, which led him by the house of Church. He attended to the cows, and on the way back stopped at the fence in front of Church's house and called him. Church came to the door and Walker began arguing with him over some trivial matter. Mrs. Church spoke to her husband, telling him to have nothing to do with Walker. Church replied that he was not afraid of him, when Walker spoke up and said: "If you are not afraid why don't you come out here?" Church went into the house, lit his pipe, and walked out to a little store nearby where Walker was standing. Walker began quarreling, and finally told Church that if he ever crossed his path again he would kill him. Church told him he had had guns rubbed up against him many a time and no one had scared him yet. At

176

this time Church was standing with one foot on the store porch smoking his pipe. Walker said: "Maybe you think I won't shoot" and, suiting the action to the word, threw the gun to his face and shot Church in the head killing him. After his arrest he told officers that Bat Gardner had hired him to kill Church, and was to give him $10 and a quart of whiskey; that he had gotten the whiskey, but had not gotten the money. In making application for witnesses lately he claimed that Church was trying to shoot him. At trial he claimed that Church was coming at him with an axe, and also denied having told officers that Gardner hired him to kill the man. Two eye witnesses, however, testified to the murder as we have given it above, and Walker's neck will in all probability be broken in due time. He is a young, ignorant Negro, with scarcely intelligence enough to realize the enormity of his crime.

In addition to the application for witnesses in which Walker claimed Church came at him with an axe, he made another, saying that witnesses would swear that Church had come at him with a knife and that Walker was a peaceable man while Church was a known trouble-maker. In his file, there are no subpoenas for any of the names he lists in the applications. If such people appeared in the court, their testimony did not sway the jury, as can be seen by the quick verdict.

JACK SPANIARD

In April 1886, Marshal Carroll was, for the first time, instructed by the U.S. attorney general to offer a $500 reward for the capture of a criminal. Rewards were offered for Jack Spaniard and Frank Palmer, who had murdered Deputy Marshal William Erwin, and for Felix Griffin, Erwin's prisoner, whom they rescued. Official notice was posted in the April 30, 1886, edition of *The Weekly Elevator*.

Spaniard, one-fourth Cherokee and raised in the Cherokee Nation, was thirty-six at the time of his trial in 1889. But, he was not a stranger to the U.S. District Court for the Western District of Arkansas. In 1879, he was indicted for assault with intent to kill, accused of attacking with a butcher knife one Tobe Johnson, "a Negro and not an Indian." There is not sufficient information to determine the outcome of that case, but apparently Spaniard challenged the court's jurisdiction. In his application for witnesses, he claimed that his witnesses would prove that Johnson was a "Cherokee citizen, an Indian in law, and not a Negro." If he could prove that—both men being of the same tribe and the crime

(Left) Cemetery where Jack Spaniard is buried. (Right) Spaniard's grave marker.

committed in that tribe's nation—the case would have fallen to tribal court.

Spaniard continued in his lawless ways, associating with robbers and horse thieves. On April 12, 1886, Deputy Erwin was at Webbers Falls, Indian Territory, with Felix Griffin, one of Spaniard's partners in crime, in custody and on his way to Fort Smith. Spaniard was also in town, and it was hinted that he would rescue Griffin. Erwin left with Griffin before noon and went to the home of the prisoner's mother and had dinner. After their meal they left, intending to stop at the home of Wesley Harris for the night and proceed to Fort Smith the next day. After noon, Spaniard and Frank Palmer, both on one horse, left town heading in the same direction as Erwin and Griffin. At Mrs. Griffin's home, they obtained another horse and continued along the path of the deputy and prisoner. At the Canadian River, they asked the ferryman, who knew both Spaniard and Palmer, if the deputy and prisoner had passed over. On being informed that they were about an hour ahead, the pursuers pushed on, followed by a dog belonging to Palmer. Several witnesses observed Spaniard, Palmer, and the dog along the road that day and testified to the identity of the dog but not the men. About seven miles from the ferry and a quarter-mile from Harris's house, they overtook Erwin and Griffin and killed the deputy before he could return fire. Harris heard the shooting and early the next morning went to the scene and found Erwin dead. Erwin's fully loaded pistol was still in its holster, evidence that he had not had a chance to defend himself. The killers left him as he fell, not disturbing anything about his body or his possessions.

The same morning that Harris found Erwin's body, Felix Griffin and another man crossed the Canadian River near Belle Starr's home and ate dinner there. A ferry operated on the river near there, and the dog, which had followed the men to the ferry, did not cross and was taken by the ferryman, W. W. Wagner.

Spaniard and Palmer immediately were developed as suspects, and a $500 reward was offered for each. Griffin was soon arrested and brought to Fort Smith, but the grand jury ignored the murder charge, indicting him only on the robbery charge. He was in jail but a short time before making bond and returning to the Territory and his old habits. One year after the murder of Erwin, Griffin was killed in a horse pen one night while in the act of stealing horses.

On March 17, 1888, Spaniard surrendered to Deputy Marshal James Pettigrew and was jailed at Fort Smith, where he remained until his trial and execution. Palmer was never heard from again, and it was presumed that he either was killed or left the Territory permanently. The dog stayed with Wagner and was a prominent figure in the trial. All of the witnesses who testified to seeing two men pass along the road that day testified that the dog looked very much like the one they had seen, but none would swear positively that this was the animal.

Pearl Younger and Eddie Reed, daughter and son of Belle Starr, both testified that the man who came to the house with Griffin was not Jack Spaniard. But only they swore in that manner — all other witnesses disputed their testimony.

SENTENCED TO HANG

On Monday, April 29, 1889, Judge Parker overruled motions for new trials and sentenced Jack Spaniard, William Walker, and Elsie James to hang. Spaniard stood first, and when asked if he had anything to say as to why sentence should not now be passed, he replied that he was not guilty and did not deserve to hang.

William Walker replied to the same question, "Yes sir, I have to say a little something. I am not guilty. Of course the court found me guilty. I am not guilty. That is all I have to say."

Elsie James heard her sentence through an interpreter. "She protested her innocence vigorously, and as the remarks of the judge were conveyed to her, she had an answer for each sentence propounded to her and talked all the way through, declaring her innocence after the sentence of the law had been pronounced" (*The Elevator*, May 3, 1889).

RESPITE

Death warrants were issued on the day of sentencing, but just before their appointed final day arrived, the president granted a respite for all of the condemned in order to investigate their cases more thoroughly.

On the back of Elsie James's death warrant is this notation:

> This writ returned not executed by reason of a commutation of sentence by the President of the United States to imprisonment for life. This July 30/89
>
> Jacob Yoes
> U.S. Marshal

The executions of Spaniard and Walker were moved to August 9, and on Thursday, August 8, Spaniard received a second respite. Judge Parker immediately telegraphed Washington requesting the same consideration for William Walker. On Friday, hours before the hanging, a telegram granting the request came.

On Monday, August 19, 1889, a telegram arrived from Washington stating the president would not interfere further in the case. The execution date for Spaniard and Walker was set for Friday, August 30, 1889.

EXECUTION

The Fort Smith Weekly Elevator, September 9, 1889:

> As announced Jack Spaniard and Bill Walker were hung last Friday in accordance with the sentence of the court pronounced some time ago. Spaniard slept but little during his last night on earth, but the negro, Walker slept soundly, retiring about his usual hour. The execution was conducted quietly, nothing unusual occurring, except that Spaniard got a little stubborn and refused to come out when the hour for departure to the gallows arrived. He begged jailor Pape to shoot him, and said he did not believe in this hanging business. Three deputies were sent in to bring him out when he seized a camp stool and threatened to brain the first man that laid hands on him. Finally he succumbed to reason, and went forth to death, meeting it bravely. Neither of the condemned had anything to say on the gallows concerning their crimes. Both their necks were broken and not so much as twitched after the drop fell.
>
> Spaniard's body was turned over to relatives and taken to Webbers Falls for burial, while Walker's remains will moulder in the potter's field.

CHAPTER 30

"GALLOWS FRUIT"
(*The Elevator*, November 1, 1889)

Judge Parker will today pass death sentence on nine men convicted of murder during the term of court just closing; Sam Goins and Jimmon Burris, Choctaws, who murdered Houston Joice in the Choctaw Nation in November, 1888.

Harris Austin, Chickasaw, who murdered a white man at Tishomingo, in 1883.

John Billy, Thomas Willis and Martin James, Choctaws, who murdered A. B. Williams in the Choctaw Nation, in April 1888.

Jefferson Jones, Choctaw, for murder of Henry Wilson, in the Choctaw Nation, in March 1889.

George Tobler, Negro, who murdered another Negro at a dance in Choctaw Nation.

Charley Ballard [Bullard], Negro, who killed Walker Bean near Gibson Station, Cherokee Nation, in March last.

We are unable to state at this writing what the date of execution will be. This is the largest number ever before sentenced at one time.

— *The Elevator*, November 1, 1889

One week later, in the next edition of the same paper, it was announced that Judge Parker had set the date of January 16, 1890, as the execution date and, as there were no mitigating circumstances in any of the cases, that they would all probably hang. On that date, however, only six of the nine would meet the ultimate fate.

CHARLEY BULLARD

Charles Bullard, by his own admission, killed Walker Bean on March 6, 1889, near Gibson Station in Cherokee Nation, Indian Territory. According to the report of *The Elevator*, Walker Bean was "a quarrelsome, overbearing man, a 'bulldozer' in every sense of the term." The evening before the killing, the two men had been in an argument and separated. The next day, Bullard acquired an old musket and went to the site where Bean was at work as a section hand on the M. K. & T. railroad. Bean was unarmed. The hostilities renewed, and "Both men used very abusive language to each other and applied vile names" until Bean called Bullard a "black bastard." When Bean refused to retract the statement, Bullard shot him, and Bean died soon afterward. Bullard was arrested and spent the next months in jail until January 1890. Although he pleaded self-defense, he was convicted of murder on October 16, 1889, and sentenced to be executed on January 16, 1890. But on January 14, a telegram arrived from Washington, D.C., authorizing respite to him until January 30. On Saturday, January 25, another telegram was received commuting the sentence to life in prison.

J. Warren Reed was Bullard's attorney, and he later took credit for the commutation and the pardon. Reed took, or was given, credit for many things he did not do. He claimed to have defended 160 murder cases. He did not, at least not before the U.S. District Court for the Western District of Arkansas. He claimed to have lost only two cases. He lost Bullard's case, and, as you will see later, he lost two separate murder defenses for one person. The fact of Bullard's pardon is stated in the fourth and fifth paragraphs of the commutation document:

> And whereas, the Judge who tried, and the United States Attorney who prosecuted the case, refer to said conduct of deceased as proper ground for consideration of Executive clemency:
>
> Now, therefore be it known that I, Benjamin Harrison, President of the United States of America, in consideration of the premises, divers other good and sufficient reasons me thereunto moving, do hereby commute the death sentence of the said Charles H. Bullard, to imprisonment for life at hard labor in the penitentiary at Columbus, Ohio.

Bullard's pardon, which was also issued and granted by President Harrison, states the reason for said pardon in the second paragraph:

> And whereas, application having been made for the pardon of said Charles Bullard, on the 24th day of September, 1892, based upon his present critical condition, as certified to by the prison physician, in which certificate it is stated that applicant has consumption in its second stage and will not probably live three months;

It then goes on with more whereases and therefores to grant a full and unconditional pardon.

So, it was not his defender, but his prosecutors who sent Bullard to prison rather than the gallows. Fatal disease freed him from prison.

GEORGE TOBLER

George Tobler was convicted on September 20, 1889, of the murder of Irwin Richardson in the Choctaw Nation in April 1889. He was granted respite along with Bullard to January 30, 1890, but he would not be as lucky as Bullard. His story will be told in a later chapter.

JOHN BILLY, THOMAS WILLIS, AND MADISON JAMES

John Billy, Thomas Willis, Madison James, and Stephen Graham were all named in a request for writ or warrant dated January 17, 1889. They were accused of the murder of Benjamin Blair, whose name would later be determined to be W. P. Williams, although his initials would be given by the newspapers as A. B., O. C., and possibly other variants.

It appears that the murder was a result of an all-night drinking party ending in the death of the supplier of the drink. The account of the crime is taken entirely from the proceedings before U.S. Commissioner James Brizzolara.

Stephen Graham stated that on April 12, 1888, he went to the home of Thomas Willis, the occasion being that Willis had whiskey and invited him to drink with him. John Billy and Madison James went with him, and when they arrived they found, among others, the soon-to-be-deceased Williams, whom he identified as Ben Blair. It was late evening when they arrived, and they proceeded to drink into the night. Graham got drunk and went to sleep in the yard near the fence. When he awoke, it was about daybreak. Graham went into the house to warm by the fire and saw Williams asleep on a bed and others in various states of drunkenness. About good daylight, Willis and Jackson Mushintubbee, who were very drunk, went outdoors, and Graham went too. Graham went in a different direction from the other two, and while he was relieving himself, Willis approached him and told him that there was more whiskey hidden out there and to find it and drink it. Instead Graham started home, but not before he had taken several more drinks. On the way home, he fell down and went to sleep, where his wife found him on her way to Mushintubbee's house to milk the cows. Graham went with his wife and went to sleep behind the house in the sun. While he was sleeping, Willis and Williams found him. Williams kicked him in the side, stuck his pistol in his face when he woke up, and demanded to know where his whiskey was. When Graham told him that he had no whiskey, Williams lowered his pistol and said that he wanted to go to Albion, which was about four miles away, but that he did not want to go by any road.

Graham, Tom Willis, and Williams started off on a little trail, but when they got out of sight of the house, Williams caught Graham by the coat and told Willis to go on. Williams then pulled Graham about ten steps off the trail, and they began to scuffle. Williams let go of one side of the coat and began to swing at Graham with his pistol, but Graham dodged the blows. During the scuffle, John Billy whooped, and Williams let go and ran away. When he ran, Willis told Billy and Madison James to shoot. Billy, Willis, and James ran by Graham, Billy firing his rifle as he passed. Willis, who was running behind Madison James, kept telling James to shoot. Willis then overtook James, took his rifle from him, "and took right after Dec'd and shot him down." After Willis shot Williams down with his rifle, he took the deceased's pistol and shot him six more times. Graham stood and observed the pursuit and killing, then retrieved his coat, which Williams had pulled off him in the scuffle, and went toward Mushintubbee's house. The women at the house had started toward the murder site, but Willis told them to go back, and they stopped there. Graham, after a short time, returned to the crime scene and saw that the others had stripped Williams naked and robbed him of everything he had. Willis took the pistol and ten dollars and thirty cents; Billy took the vest, pants, and drawers; James took the hat, shirt, and coat. The killers then sent Graham to get a grubbing hoe and shovel, and they dug a grave and buried the body. Later in the day Billy took the shoes to Graham's house and offered them to him, but he refused them. Tom Willis then took the shoes and wore them out. About two weeks later, Willis told Graham that there were "a good many white folks hunting cattle around there; that they had not buried him very deep and flies were all around there, that they went and burnt him up."

That was Graham's version of the events, and although most likely skewed in his favor, it was good enough that no true bill was brought against him and he was not tried for the crimes as the others were. The motive for the killing was the more than six gallons of whiskey the deceased had.

The proceedings also contain the depositions of seven other people. Jacob Benton stated that he knew all the defendants and that Thomas Willis told him that they killed a white man but he did not ask Willis any more about it. Benton said, "I bought a pistol from Willis, it was a silver mounted pistol; it was a .45 caliber pistol; bought it from Def't. Willis about July 1888; sold pistol to Pasen James Sheriff of Wade County; paid Willis $18, he did not tell me where he got pistol."

Pasen James then said, "I bought a pistol from Jacob Benton. Benton claimed to have gotten pistol from Thos. Willis. I bought pistol last February. I paid $12 for pistol. I have pistol here (here witness produced pistol) this is the pistol."

The crime was apparently not a well-kept secret. The quartet was arrested and on February 21, 1889, brought to Fort Smith by Deputy Marshal Ben Cantrell along with three others arrested for unrelated crimes.

On the back of the true bill indicting Billy, Willis, and James is this statement dated October 4, 1889:

> We the jury find the defendants John Billy, Thomas Willis and Madison James guilty of murder as charged in the 2nd count of the within indictment.
> Alford Casey, Foreman

Only two would hang, though. On Tuesday, January 14, 1890, Madison James received word that his sentence had been commuted to fifteen years in prison. This was recommended by Judge Parker and District Attorney W. H. H. Clayton, who felt that James was less culpable than Billy and Willis, who did the actual shooting.

JIMMON BURRIS AND SAM GOIN

Jimmon Burris, Sam Goin, and Jim Goin were tried in October 1889, and Burris and Sam Goin were convicted of the murder of Houston Joyce of Franklin, Texas. Joyce was traveling through Indian Territory, having left his Texas home on account of some trouble he had gotten into. Joyce stopped at the home of Jim Goin, uncle of Sam Goin, in Towson County, Choctaw Nation, for a meal and made the mistake of revealing his money when paying for the food. When he left the house, Jim Burris directed Joyce to a blind trail. After Joyce was out of sight, Jim Goin gave Burris and Sam Goin his gun and pistol and told them to pursue and kill the white man. They soon caught up with their victim in an isolated spot, killed him, stole what money and property he had, and left the body lying. Two days later, Sam Goin, possessing the intelligence of many criminals, told Solomon Bacon the whole story and told him that Joyce's horse was on the prairie and that Bacon should take the horse and post him as a stray. Bacon instead told the story to Deputy Marshal J. M. Ennis, who began to work on the case and found the scattered bones of Joyce and what remained of his clothing. With the remains, marshals found a letter addressed to J. T. Babb, Smackover, Arkansas, and presumed that the bones were the remains of Babb. In fact, the first true bill charges Burris and the Goins with the murder of "One Babb whose Christian name is to the grand jurors unknown." A second true bill states the victim was "a certain white man and not an Indian." Babb had been a member of the Arkansas Legislature and had allowed Joyce to use his name in writing to Texas. Consequently,

Joyce's letters came to him addressed to J. T. Babb. Babb's friends began an inquiry, and it was then that the identity of the deceased was discovered.

After the conviction of Burris and Sam Goin and the acquittal of Jim Goin, Sam declared that his uncle should be hanged, too, since he furnished the weapons for the murder not only of Joyce but also of another a white man.

Marshal Ennis, while working on the case of Joyce's murder, learned of another murder in which Burris and Sam Goin had participated. He had arrested Toledo Cartubee, who told Ennis the whole story, then took him to the scene of the crime and showed him where each man had stood and how they had disposed of the body and belongings. John Hyde, a white man, was traveling in the Territory unarmed, riding one horse and leading another, when he encountered Eastman Battese, Toledo Cartubee, Sam Goin, and Jim Burris. The four captured Hyde, bound his hands, and took him to Boggy River about three miles from where they had killed Joyce. They took him from his horse, informed him that his time had come, placed him in a position facing them and riddled him with buckshot and rifle fire. The killers then tied a heavy rock to Hyde's body, threw him in the river, and then did the same with his saddle. All this was explained at the scene in minute detail by Cartubee, who claimed to have taken no part in the killing. Ennis stripped off and went into the water and found the saddle, which was identified by Hyde's brothers, who had accompanied Ennis. The body was not found since the river was very high and fast at the time of the murder. This case went to the court in Paris, Texas, which was established shortly before the crime was committed. A few days before their execution, Burris and Goin confessed to the crime to a minister, their statements being consistent with Cartubee's story and the findings.

HARRIS AUSTIN

Harris Austin evaded arrest for six years, but on Thursday, April 18, 1889, Deputy Marshal Carr delivered him to the jail at Fort Smith after wounding him seriously in a shootout.

Austin's trial must have been one of the shortest murder trials of the court's duration. *The Fort Smith Elevator* reported on Friday, August 30, 1889, "Harris Austin, a full blood Chickasaw, was placed on trial Friday afternoon [August 23, 1889], charged with the murder of Thomas Elliott in Tishomingo, Chickasaw Nation, May 25, 1883. The case went to the jury Saturday evening and a verdict of guilty was returned within twenty minutes."

Elliott had been in the Territory only about two months when he was killed. On Friday, May 25, 1883, he had an argument with Jonas Pearson, half brother of Harris Austin. Pearson was drunk at the time, and Elliott accused him of stealing liquor from him. While Elliott and Pearson were arguing, Austin came up and disarmed Pearson, and the two walked a little distance away. After they had talked awhile, Austin turned and approached Elliott, who was sitting on a box in front of the store, and without warning shot him through the breast. Elliott fell from the box, and Austin shot him a second time. He then approached and, holding the pistol close to Elliott's forehead, shot him again.

Austin escaped and was on the scout for six years until Deputy Marshal Carr captured him in April 1889. Austin was known to be in the area of his home near Red River. The marshal and posse had information that he went to his home at night and left before daylight. Late one night, the posse surrounded the house. At daylight, as they had hoped, their quarry came out heading for his horse, which was grazing near the river. Carr let Austin get far enough that Carr could get between him and the house, then demanded his surrender. Austin had left his rifle at the house but carried his pistol on his belt, and with it he made a short but desperate fight. He was seriously wounded three times but recovered under the doctor's care in the jail at Fort Smith.

His trial, as described, was short, but he did not give up there without a struggle. He made two applications for witnesses. In the first he claimed that the named witnesses would testify that the deceased arrived in Tishomingo drunk, insulted the wife of another man, and said that he would kill "a damned Indian before sundown to see him kick" and was abusive and threatening to the defendant, his brother, and others. In the second, he said that the deceased was perpetrating an assault upon him. One of the witnesses whom he requested was his half brother, Jonas Pearson.

Pearson did come to attend the trial but was arrested and jailed on a charge of murder for a killing at Caddo some years before.

JEFFERSON JONES

Jefferson Jones, by his own admission, shot sixty-five-year-old Henry Wilson in the back; but if his story is to be believed, it was self-defense. However, the fact that Jones used a Winchester repeating rifle while Wilson used a single-shot cavalry weapon and was running away complicates the issue.

Henry Wilson left the home of Mary Solon near Leflore in Choctaw Nation on March 12, 1889, to go to Polk County, Arkansas, to bring back a mare for John Weeks who was farming in the area. It was known that Wilson had with him six dollars and fifty cents in silver coin, some pennies, and seven dollars and fifty cents in "greenback" and silver that Weeks had given him. How much other money he had was known only to him and his killer. He went afoot, and the trip was to take about four or five days using trails and roads through the Winding Stair Mountains in the Territory. When a week passed and Wilson did not return, his sons, Newton and George, were sent to hunt for him; they returned having failed to find him or hear of him. Wilson had planned a loose itinerary, saying that he would stay at Isaac Winton's the first night, then go as far as George Morris's the next. Inquiry showed that he had stayed with Winton but never reached Morris's or his destination in Arkansas. "The crowd," as the searchers referred to themselves, then decided to search Holson Creek, which runs out of the Winding Stair Mountains.

Sometime in the searching, the U.S. Marshal's Office was notified and Deputy Marshal Barnhill entered the search and, according to the testimony of George Wilson, was authorized to search all the homes in the area. The home of James Beams was on the trail that Isaac Winton had directed Henry Wilson to on the morning he had started the second day of his ill-fated journey. When the searchers reached the Beamses' house, they found no one at home but did find a gun in the loft. Isaac Winton testified that he had loaned Wilson a 50-caliber, single-shot cavalry gun and later identified the gun found at the Beamses' home as that gun. The posse, after finding the gun, hid around the house, and soon Beams and his wife came home. James Beams seemed to sense that all was not right and stopped outside, then he and his wife talked. She then went into the house, came out, and closed the door. The posse started to move in, and Beams ran for the woods, not stopping when halted or when shots were fired. An Indian deputy sheriff named Willis was sent to arrest Beams, and he was brought in the next day. James Beams told the posse that Jefferson Jones had left the gun at his house, and the authorities then paid Deputy Willis five dollars to bring in Jefferson Jones.

Mary Solon, who had been active as part of "the crowd," went to Leflore Station after Jefferson Jones and James Beams were arrested and questioned them while they were eating breakfast. She testified that she asked Jones in Choctaw if he had killed the old man and he answered that he had. He said that he had shown Wilson the way to the public road and that when they were near it, he (Jones) turned to go then heard a gun cock. When he looked back, Wilson shot at him. Jones said he jumped behind a small tree, and the bullet passed between his arm and body. Wilson turned and ran, and Jones shot him with his Winchester, hitting him in the left back, the bullet coming out the right breast. Wilson ran on and fell at the creek. Jones ran to his brother Jimison's house but returned to the scene of the killing the next day and took Wilson's gun and pocketbook containing his money. He told Mary Solon that he had hidden the money in a hole under the floor inside the door of his brother's house, but when they went to look, they found the hole but no money. Jimison Jones was asked about the money, and he produced from his pocket a pocketbook containing only one penny. Jimison was arrested, and Mary Solon went to Leflore Station on Saturday night to question him. Jimison told her that he knew only what his brother had told him, that he had killed a white man and had taken the money. Jefferson had told Solon that he had taken twenty-five dollars but Jimison said that there was only a five-dollar "green-back" and he had spent it at Welches. Jimison told Solon "that he had preached the gospel and didn't intend to kill anyone and to tell any lies but he was into it by reason of taking [the] pocketbook" (Hearings before the commissioner, May 20, 1889).

Jefferson Jones, after admitting to the killing, told Jerry White, an interpreter, that he would take the searchers to where he had last seen Wilson. On the way, he told a slightly different version of the events, saying that Wilson asked him to change a five-dollar bill and became angry when Jones could not do it. When they arrived at the scene, Jones showed them the creek where he said he had left Wilson lying, but the body was not there. The posse searched farther down stream and found the bones and some clothing of Henry Wilson about a hundred yards away. The jaw, one hand, and one foot were missing, as were his hat and shoes. It was two months to the day since the murder.

Jefferson Jones, Jimison Jones, and James Beams were tried jointly for murder, but on Saturday, October 12, 1889, the jury returned a verdict of guilty for Jefferson Jones only. Jimison Jones and James Beams were acquitted on the conclusion that their only involvement had been the knowledge of Jefferson's acts and possession of some of the proceeds of the crime.

By November 1889, all of those convicted of capital crimes had been tried and sentenced. On November 22, 1889, this paragraph appeared in *The Fort Smith Elevator*:

> Two of the Indians sentenced to be hung got hold of a couple of spoons with which they made knives and had them concealed in their cells where Jailor Pape found them Wednesday.

EXECUTION

Thursday, January 16, 1890, was set as the date of execution. This was the first time that an execution took place on a day other than Friday. A second execution that January would be the first time two executions were held in one month, and it would be the last time there were executions twice in one month until the last ones on July 1 and July 30, 1896.

The January 17, 1890, edition of *The Elevator* gave just a brief description of the last days of the condemned men. They had devoted their last days to religious duties assisted by Reverends Lutz and Kraus of the city and Reverend Henry Woods, a Choctaw minister. On the execution day morning, they were issued the usual suits and were visited by the ministers. At eleven o'clock, the death warrants were read. The prisoners then were handcuffed and escorted to the gallows, a guard on each side of each prisoner. On the gallows, religious exercises were "of short duration." D. L. Horner, a Choctaw, was called for and mounted the gallows, where he interpreted for each man as they said their final words. At noon, the trap was sprung, and the six men died without a struggle.

The Elevator finally got the number of executions and the number of executed correct, saying that this was the twenty-eighth occasion and seventy had been hanged. It went on to list the dates and the names of all of the executed from John Childers, August 15, 1873, to present. At other times, it had been off by as many as thirteen in the number of people hanged. In that case, in the paper's next edition, it did issue a correction, which was headlined "Thirteen Too Many."

CHAPTER 31

"MURDERED THE FIDDLER"

(The Elevator, May 3, 1889)

A Dance in Cache Bottom Terminates in
The Death of Irvin Richardson

On Monday night last, in Cache Creek bottom, about 25 miles from here, in the Choctaw Nation, a negro dance was in progress, and during the night, while the festivities were at their height, a shot startled the dancers, and their fiddler, a negro named Irvin Richardson, fell from his chair dead, a Winchester ball having passed through his body. George Tobler was the only man outside the house when the shot was fired, and as he and Richardson had quarreled about a dusky damsel Monday morning, suspicion at once fell upon him and he was arrested. It is alleged that while the dance was going on Tobler slipped out, secured a Winchester that another negro had left outside on a bed, and shot Richardson through a crack in the house, notwithstanding no one saw him fire the fatal shot. Tobler was lodged in the U.S. Jail Wednesday evening by Indian Policeman Ed Bowman.

— *The Fort Smith Elevator*, May 3, 1889

The murder occurred on Monday night, April 29, 1889. On April 30, the sheriff of Skullyville County sent a letter to Marshal John Carroll telling him of the killing and arrest, saying, "I wish you would send and get this man at once as this jail is not secure." Tobler arrived at Fort Smith the next day, May 1, 1889, and was lodged in the jail until his trial in September.

The prosecution's case was based entirely on circumstantial evidence, but it must have been very convincing. Tobler submitted two applications for witnesses, listing a total of eight who would testify variously that Richmond (the newspapers give the name as Richardson, but all existing court documents say Richmond) had been witness against two other men who had then made threats against the deceased, and that two men were seen passing the Dansby house going in the direction of the dance, and after the shooting the same two men were seen passing in the other direction. He also claimed that the witnesses had examined the tracks of horses or mules leading to the house where the killing took place and measured the distance from the house

The U.S. Federal Courthouse, on right, stands at the corner of Sixth Street and Rogers Avenue, circa 1903, with the Sebastian County Courthouse in the background, left. Note the ornate bell tower on the Sebastian County Courthouse.

to where two horses had been tied. All eight requested witnesses plus five more, thirteen in all, appeared but apparently did not testify as he had hoped or at least did not convince the jury. The back of the true bill lists the names of all thirteen witnesses and adjacent to that, this note: "We the jury find the defendant, George Tobler, guilty of murder as charged in the within indictment. J. P. Stewart, For. 9/19/89."

George Tobler was one of the nine men sentenced in October 1889 to hang on January 16, 1890, but he and Charley Bullard were respited to January 30, and on Saturday, January 25, Bullard's sentence was commuted to life in prison. On that same day, U.S. District Marshal Yoes was notified that the president "declined to further interfere" in Tobler's case. Tobler's execution was the second time an execution had been carried out on a day other than Friday and the second time an execution occurred in January 1890, making that month the first in which there had been executions twice in one month.

Tobler had declined the services of any minister, but on Sunday, January 26, he was visited by Reverend Lutz. By that time, his attitude had changed, and he asked the reverend to call again, which he thereafter did daily.

On the night before the execution, Tobler occupied the same cell as Bullard. Tobler kept up a conversation until about eleven that night and then fell asleep until about six the next morning. At eight thirty that morning, jailer Pape brought the usual suit of clothing, underclothing, and white shirt that was issued to condemned men. Tobler asked for and was given a white necktie. He then went to his cell and casually dressed while Bullard swept out the cell. About nine o'clock, Tobler was dressed and engaged in religious endeavors until ten forty-five, when the death warrant was read. He then lit a cigar and went out to meet the guard, who placed handcuffs on him, and "walked forth to die, cool, stoical and with no outward appearance of emotion. On the scaffold, while services were going on, he weakened for a moment or so, but soon braced up and when he stepped on the trap he looked as cool and defiant as usual" (*The Elevator*, January 31, 1890). He had nothing to say as final preparations were made, and at 11:05 a.m. the trap dropped, his neck was broken, and death was instantaneous. He had left a letter with Reverend Lutz proclaiming his innocence, although the day before the execution, he told Charley Bullard of dreaming of the man he had killed.

***

On the same page of *The Elevator* that describes the execution of George Tobler, another column gives a description of the capture and death of Jim Starr, husband of the late Belle Starr. Jim Starr was brought in to Fort Smith badly wounded on Tuesday, January 21, 1890. Some years before, Starr had been charged with horse stealing and had been in Fort Smith to answer that charge when he was notified of Belle's murder. He had gone home to her funeral, where he arrested and brought in her accused killer, Watson. After that, he jumped the $150 bail posted by Deputy J. H. Mershon and went on the scout. He was apprehended near Ardmore by two lawmen and was seriously wounded in the capture.

A reporter who knew Starr interviewed him in the jail hospital in the two days before his death. Starr claimed that the deputies had ambushed him and he had run only after he was wounded and that they had shot his horse three times, killing it. Starr said that he was preparing to come in voluntarily, but when asked why he jumped bail in the first place, he replied, "Oh, I don't know." The reporter interviewed Starr on Saturday and went back on Sunday when it was determined that he would not live. Jailer Pape informed Starr that he was not expected to live and asked if there was anything else he would like to tell them. Starr said he would talk only to Deputy Mershon. When informed that Mershon was in Texas and would not return before he died, Starr said that he did not have much to say to him anyway. Jim Starr, a.k.a. Jim July, died later that Sunday, January 26, 1890, and was buried in the potter's field at the city cemetery the next day.

CHAPTER 32

JOHN STANSBERRY HANGED FOR THE MURDER OF HIS WIFE

"Stoically He Meets His Fate and Without a Murmur Dies"

(The Elevator, July 11, 1890)

On Wednesday, July 9, 1890, the trap of the gallows of the U.S. District Court for the Western District of Arkansas fell for the thirtieth time, sending twenty-seven-year-old John Stansberry to his court-appointed doom. Stansberry had been arrested almost at his wife's graveside on October 14, 1889, the day after her death.

On the night of Sunday, October 13, 1889, John Stansberry rode up to the home of James F. Johnson crying out that his wife had been killed and his house robbed. In the words of Johnson Todd, who lived with the James Johnson family:

> Well, the first I knowed, he come to the place where I lived and he called out to Mr. Johnson; he called several times, and said that his wife was killed and his house robbed. Johnson and I went to his house, and his wife was killed, and her brains all out; hit with an ax, and we took his woman to Johnson's, and she died that night some time.
> —Hearings before Commissioner James Brizzolara
> October 23, 1889, ten o'clock at night

Todd went on, under questioning, to describe how Stansberry arrived, the trip to the house, entering the house, the conditions inside the house itself, and the condition of Mrs. Stansberry.

> Q. When you went in what did you find?
> A. I found a woman in bed, killed.
> Q. Was she dead?
> A. No, sir she wasn't quite dead; she had been hit with an ax.

He then answered questions as to the position of the body, where she had been struck and whether the instrument used was sharp or blunt. Todd said she had been struck with the pole of the ax (the pole being the flat or hammer face of a single-bitted ax), the pole was battered from use, and hair, blood, and brains were "sticking to it." The

194

house appeared to have been ransacked, trunks had been dumped out, clothes were strewn about, and a loaded double-barreled shotgun rested across a trunk. Mollie Stansberry was taken to James Johnson's home, where she expired around two or three o'clock Monday morning.

John Stansberry had told others during the night that on Sunday afternoon he had become "tired" (bored) and had gone for a ride on one of his mules. He had become lost during the ride and had arrived home after dark. As he approached his house, his dog ran ahead of him and barked. Sensing that something was not right, he called out to his wife and heard no answer. Entering the home, he found the situation described by Todd and went for help. He said that as he rode up to his house, he heard what he thought to be as many as three men ride away on horses. Based on Stansberry's story, James Johnson, Johnson Todd, and others went to the crime scene in daylight and looked for tracks of the fleeing parties but found only the prints of Stansberry's own horses and mules. From their testimony, it appears that they had their doubts about Stansberry's story from the beginning, and Grant Johnson, a lawman of some sort in the Territory, was summoned. He, too, investigated the scene and, not being able to substantiate Stansberry's story, arrested him at the cemetery that afternoon, immediately after Mollie Stansberry was put in the ground.

John Stansberry married Mollie Eubanks in Newton County, Missouri, in 1885. In the spring of 1889, he went to Indian Territory and became acquainted with James Johnson and others in the area. In August of the same year, he moved his wife and small daughter to the Pottawatomie Nation. In September, while his wife was visiting a neighbor, the child sustained a fatal head injury, supposedly from a fall from a bureau. After that, the Stansberrys moved to the place in the Creek Nation where Mrs. Stansberry was killed. There, Stansberry seems to have decided that he could better his situation by marrying an Indian woman, thereby gaining a right in the Territory.

According to the testimony of Rufus Dugan, on the Monday before Mollie's death, Stansberry told him that he was going to "make away with his woman and get him a right there." That night, the two men sat talking by the fire after Mollie had gone to bed. Stansberry told Dugan his plan while sitting in the same room where his wife was sleeping. The following Sunday, she was dead.

Shortly after Stansberry's arrest, Deputy Marshal Crowder Nix sent a request for writ to Marshal Yoes at Fort Smith stating that John Stansberry, a white man, killed his wife, and he named four witnesses. The request goes on to say, "We can prove by the above witnesses that he killed his wife on Sunday night, Oct. 13, 1889 fourteen miles west of Eufaula. Deed committed with an ax. No one was present but circumstance evidences is against him very strong. Please forward a writ at once."

On Tuesday, October 22, 1889, Crowder Nix arrived at Fort Smith and lodged Stansberry at "Jailor Pape's Hotel," as the newspaper sometimes referred to it.

Hearings before the commissioner began October 24 and lasted several days, taking depositions from the four witnesses Nix had named and at least four others. None of the deponents said anything favorable to Stansberry's case. They seemed to have been suspicious of him from the beginning. The fact that his year-old child had died from a head injury about a month before did not help him any. Neither did the fact that his wife was in bed in her nightclothes and there was no blood anywhere except on the pillow and in water in a wash pan. Also, a loaded shotgun that appeared ready for defense seemed inconsistent with a robbery. In addition, he claimed to have been robbed of three $100 bills, two twenties, and ten dollars in silver, but the week before, he did not have money to pay Rufus Dugan, his hired hand. James Johnson noted that he said his dog had run ahead of him and barked, but he had not mentioned his dog being with him on his "ramble." Supposedly, he had become lost, and after wandering, he had come to a road and given his mule its bridle and let it take him home. On Monday, James Johnson and others had gone to the crime scene, and Johnson had picked up a grip that was lying on the floor, and Stansberry said, "There, that's what I had my money in." The investigating party looked outside for evidence of anyone coming or going from the scene and found only the tracks of Stansberry's mules and horses. The mule he had ridden left a distinctive print, and those prints led only to the river at Stansberry's watering place and back; at no place did they cross the river as he had said he had done.

Further damaging to Stansberry was the testimony of Grant Johnson and Deputy Nix, who claimed to have overheard a conversation between Stansberry and James Johnson while Stansberry was incarcerated at Eufaula. Stansberry asked James Johnson to carry a note to his father in Newton County, Missouri, asking him to testify that he had given Stansberry $350 and owed him other considerations, the total value being $1,000. He offered to pay Johnson's expenses for the trip, and the lawmen claimed that he offered to give Johnson a gray horse he owned. Johnson testified that Stansberry did give him a note to his father but that Nix confiscated it. He denied that he was offered any reward other than his expenses. Johnson said that he told Stansberry, "John, that money story was a weak thing." Stansberry replied that he thought "the officers would get out after these fellows for two or three hundred dollars and everything would quiet down."

A true bill was filed November 14, 1889, indicting John Stansberry for the murder of his wife. On January 18, 1890, Frank Blair, attorney with the Barnes, Boudinot and Reed law firm, filed an application for witnesses in Stansberry's behalf, listing a total of thirteen, including a Mrs. Price. Price supposedly lived nearby and on the fatal day had directed two men who had asked her to prepare supper for them to the home of Mrs. Stansberry, who, she told them, would prepare a meal. Price was not found at the location given, and a later application said that she had moved to another location, and a new subpoena was issued. Price was not located at that place either. On February 18, 1890, a motion for continuance was filed, one of the reasons being that Price had not been found. But on February 27, 1890, the jury found Stansberry guilty after no more than an hour of deliberation.

On March 5, 1890, attorneys Frank P. Blair and Pres. S. Lester filed affidavits in support of a new trial. Blair stated that with the aid of prominent people in the Eufaula area he had located Mrs. Price and that she could supply information favorable to the defendant. Lester, also a member of Barnes, Boudinot and Reed and counsel in the case, stated that on a trip to Muskogee he met James Johnson and was told that W. F. Todd was a notorious liar and that he did not search as thoroughly for tracks or evidence as he had testified. On March 18, 1890, a motion for a new trial was filed but apparently to no avail, for on May 1, Stephen Wheeler signed Stansberry's death warrant, condemning him to be hanged on Wednesday, July 9, 1890.

Stansberry professed his innocence until the end. In his last days, he seemed to be unconcerned about his fate and never requested the services of any minister. He was visited by Reverend Lutz, and on his last morning on earth was visited by Reverend Dunn. On the gallows, he declined any religious services, saying that it would do no good. Seven minutes after Stansberry walked out the jail doors, the drop fell, and he was sent to his doom.

Because Stansberry maintained his innocence so stalwartly and because the evidence was circumstantial, some believed that an innocent man might have been hanged. But one month after the execution, on August 8, 1890, *The Elevator* ran this article:

The Guilt of John Stansberry

John Stansberry, the wife murderer, who was convicted and hung on circumstantial evidence, and died professing to be innocent, thus leaving a doubt of his guilt in the minds of some, told his lawyer, Col. Frank Blair, all about the murder before he went to trial, acknowledging to him that he did the killing. He said that he had been out during the afternoon and came back after dark, as he claimed in his defense; that when he returned his wife was asleep on a pallet. In the afternoon she had been talking to him about the death of their child, and he came to the conclusion that it was time to wind up the matter. Accordingly he got the ax and standing over the sleeping form of his wife dealt her the fatal blow. Blair defended the prisoner at the trial ably, and did everything possible to get a favorable verdict, but after the conviction allowed things to take their own course, knowing as he did the terrible guilt of his client. We understand that Mr. Blair related the above facts a few days ago in conversation with some gentlemen at Muskogee.

Obviously, as evidenced by the appeals and affidavits, Blair did not allow "things to take their own course" but tried diligently to get a new trial and presumably a more favorable verdict.

John Stansberry was the sixty-fourth man executed during Judge Parker's administration and the seventy-first of eighty-six who would be executed during the existence of the U.S. District Court for the Western District of Arkansas.

CHAPTER 33

BOUDINOT CRUMPTON

(a.k.a. Bood Burris)

Executed June 30, 1891

On December 22, 1889, James Lawson probed with a stick at an object at the bottom of a deep hole on the bank of the Arkansas River near the mouth of Coody Creek. He suspected that the object was a human skull and called to his brother, John, and cousin, Joe, who were hunting with him. When the remains were removed from the hole on December 24, it was determined that they were those of Samson Monroe Morgan.

Sam Morgan was last seen alive on Sunday, November 3, 1889, in the company of Boudinot Crumpton, who was also known as Bood Burris. Morgan and Crumpton had left the home of Mattie Harris on Sunday morning, stopped at Bill Harnage's place, and played cards with some men who were drinking there. Then about midday, they proceeded on with the intent to go to James Davis's to visit some girls. Both men were mounted on horses belonging to Sam Morgan and rode off appearing to be the best of friends. Late that afternoon, Crumpton returned leading the horse Morgan had ridden and having in his possession Morgan's coat and messages of how to manage Morgan's crops, horses, and finances. He explained Morgan's absence by saying that they had met a man in a buggy or hack who hired Sam to herd some ponies near the Pawnee Agency for $3.50 a day. Crumpton said that Morgan and the stranger appeared to know each other and that he assumed that they had met in Arkansas and had initiated their deal there. For some reason, Crumpton's story seems to have aroused very little suspicion at the time, even though Morgan had supposedly gone off spontaneously with a near stranger for a salary that was more than bricklayers and other craftsmen in eastern cites were paid at that time.

Boudinot Crumpton and Sam Morgan appeared to be the best of friends, even on the day of the murder. Crumpton was a Cherokee who had taken the name of his stepfather after his mother married William Burris. He had, according to trial testimony, stolen a "Dutchman's wife" and had taken her to Tahlequah in Indian Territory and abandoned her. On another occasion, he was accused of stealing someone's gun. Other than that, he appears to have been a normal citizen, working as a hired hand and occasionally getting drunk.

Samson Monroe (Sam/S. M.) Morgan, twenty-six years old, was from Georgia, where he had been committed to an insane asylum in 1883 and 1884. After his release from the institution in 1885, he moved

199

The U.S. District Court for the Western District of Arkansas, Judge Isaac C. Parker presiding in session at the new courthouse on Sixth Street and Rogers Avenue in Fort Smith between 1890 and 1896.

to the Indian Territory, where he lived with his brother, Robert, rented land, and made crops. About a week before the murder, Sam and Robert Morgan had a falling out over a horse that Sam had bought from Robert on time, so Sam moved a short distance away to board with Mrs. Harris. He had become good friends with Bood Crumpton, so much so that some neighbors said they were as close as brothers.

The Saturday before Morgan disappeared, Crumpton spent the night at Mrs. Harris's. On Sunday morning, the two friends rode off around eight or nine o'clock saying that they were going to James Davis's to visit the girls. On the way, they had stopped at other neighbors' homes and at Harnage's and played cards for a short time. Morgan then got on his horse and rode off a short distance and called back to Bood to come on if he was going with him. They rode off in the direction of the place where Morgan's body was later found, and that was the last time any of the witnesses saw him alive.

As stated at the beginning, on December 22, James Lawson and his brother and cousin discovered a body in a deep hole while out hunting. On December 24, a group of men went to the place, a hole about four feet in diameter and six feet deep, outside the perimeter of a field. Since Sam Morgan was unaccounted for and Crumpton's story was not wholly believed, the men sent for his brother, Robert Morgan. By the time he arrived, they had removed the body and begun to search for identification. The face was missing from the lower part of the forehead down except for half of the jaw and half of a mustache that was beside the head. From the description, it appears the rest of the body was fairly well intact for having lain in a hole for seven weeks. Robert identified the suit, necktie, shoes, and watch, and there were letters that helped ascertain that it was the body of S. M. Morgan.

Crumpton's story was believed only because it could not be disproved. But people were suspicious, and when Boudinot presented a letter purported to be from Morgan about a month after his disappearance, they became even more so. In the letter, Morgan inquired about his horse, his cotton crop, and Crumpton's health. On the day of his disappearance, Morgan supposedly had directed Crumpton in the disposal of the two horses, both of which he had bought on time and still owed for. In the letter, there were instructions to return the gray horse to his brother if he did not return by December 1. He said that if he did not return by Christmas, then he would not be back for three months, so Crumpton should return the other horse to its owner, Richard Colquitt, and that what he had paid on the horses would cover other debts. Bood seems to have had detailed knowledge of Morgan's affairs and remembered it all. For some reason, he took the letter to Colquitt rather than Morgan's brother, Robert. The letter was read to Colquitt by Bill Burt, who was working with Colquitt in his field at the time. The men asked Crumpton to see the envelope, but when he showed it, the address side had been torn off. Bood explained that the envelope had been torn by children.

Burt, a cousin of Morgan and the first person to read the letter, was deputized to arrest Crumpton, which he did December 27 at Garfield, Cherokee Nation, about twenty-five miles from the crime scene. After his arrest, Bood told essentially the same story but in more detail. Then he gave the name of the man in the buggy, saying it was Landrum or Langdon, and that Bill Keyes had been present when they met. In this story, Morgan, Keyes, the stranger, and a woman had gone to get whiskey while Crumpton waited in the corner of a fence. Keyes returned with the horses, coat, other belongings, and the verbal instructions that Crumpton delivered when he arrived home on Sunday afternoon.

Keyes, at trial, denied having been near where Crumpton, Morgan, and the man in the buggy were supposed to have met. He claimed he knew nothing of the events, saying that he had been picking up pecans with a man named Charley Glass. Glass substantiated Keyes's testimony but was completely confused by the defense lawyer about what had happened on that date regarding Morgan's disappearance, saying several times that that was the day the body was found. He also said that they had spent most of the day picking up pecans, but when asked how many, he replied about a quart.

Defense attorneys Wolfenberger, Neal, and especially W. M. Cravens defended Crumpton diligently, attacked witnesses aggressively, and appeared to punch holes in the prosecution's case, but in the end, it was of no avail. The prosecution called sixteen witnesses and the defense five plus the defendant. A request by defense for additional witnesses was overruled. On June 30, 1890, the jury returned a verdict of guilty. Having received a letter from a dead man, having in his possession exactly the amount and denominations of money loaned to Morgan just before his disappearance, and carrying a Colt revolver that several men identified as belonging to Sam Morgan may have been enough to convince a jury.

On August 2, 1890, Judge Parker passed sentence on Crumpton, but a bill of exception was filed, and the case was appealed to and ruled on by the U.S. Supreme Court. This appears to have been the first case from the U.S. District Court for the Western District of Arkansas to be heard by the Supreme Court. John Stansberry attempted to appeal to the Supreme Court but failed. On April 24, 1891, Judge Parker sentenced Boudinot Crumpton to hang, and on June 30, 1891, the sentence was accomplished. Crumpton maintained his innocence until the end.

CHAPTER 34

SHEPARD BUSBY HANGS FOR THE MURDER OF DEPUTY CONNELLY

On Wednesday morning, August 9, 1891, Deputy Marshal Barney Connelly rode up to the home of former Deputy Marshal Shepard Busby with the intent of serving a warrant for adultery. Within minutes, Connelly was dead with three bullet wounds and a broken neck. Exactly what happened and how were never determined, but Busby, his son, William, and the two women who lived there all told the same story from shortly after the incident until the end.

Busby had been a deputy U.S. marshal from January 1, 1890, until the spring of 1891, his service ending several months before the killing of Barney Connelly. He and Connelly did not serve at the same time and did not know each other. How Busby got to be a marshal is questionable, for he was not the most savory of characters. On file at the National Archives are documents charging him with counterfeiting, assault, and resisting arrest, apparently accrued all in one incident. The charges seem to have been dismissed, or at least he was not convicted.

Busby's telling of the story goes back several weeks before the shooting to troubles with two neighbors, S. H. Satterfield and Dr. R. M. Woods. He believed Satterfield had left a note in his yard written by Woods accusing Busby of milking Woods's cows. The note said that if it did not stop, "there will be hell to pay." Busby accused Satterfield and Woods of going to Fort Smith and telling lies to the marshals about him and trying to get out a warrant for adultery. Therefore, he felt "a mob" was out to get him and he must be on his guard at all times.

The day before the shooting, Busby went to Van Buren with Joe Boyd to get supplies and ammunition for a Winchester he had purchased from a Mr. Martin. They returned to Boyd's place late. Busby left his goods, except for the ammunition and rifle, in Boyd's wagon to be delivered the next day. He arrived home about two o'clock in the morning and went to bed about three. Later that morning, he got up and grabbed his rifle, intending to hunt squirrels. But then he remembered that Martin was coming to collect for the gun and Boyd was bringing his supplies. He said he did not feel well anyway and asked the women who lived there to prepare a pallet for him under a tree. They laid down a chair and spread a quilt over it, and Busby lay down with his head on the chair and his rifle beside him and went to sleep.

Busby, his son William, Tennessee Burns, a woman with whom Busby had two children, and fifteen-year-old Florence Jones, Busby's fiancée, were in the yard when Connelly rode up. According to Busby, Connelly called Busby by name and greeted him, at which time Busby stood, greeted Connelly, and asked his business. Connelly said he had lost a horse and asked Busby to help him look for it. Busby invited Connelly in, and Connelly dismounted, tied his horse to the fence, and climbed over. Busby said he bent to set up a chair for Connelly, at which time Connelly said, "God damn you," and threw his pistol to Busby's breast. At the same time, Connelly threw his left arm around Busby's neck, Busby grabbed the muzzle of the gun, and the gun fired, causing a small wound to Busby's hand. Busby wrenched the gun from Connelly, pushed him back, and asked who he was, what he wanted, and what he meant. Connelly advanced without speaking, and Busby fired. Connelly continued to advance, and Busby continued to fire. Busby emptied the gun before Connelly finally fell dead. While this was taking place, William, Tennessee, and Florence ran to the house, William to a corner of the home, one woman inside, and the other to the porch. When the affray was over, Busby sent William to summon neighbors to see if someone could identify the man he had just killed.

The first person Will met and told the story to was S. H. Satterfield, for he and R. M. Woods had been on a hill almost within sight of the Busby house. This brave pair was there because (their story) Connelly had enlisted them as backup in case there was trouble. However, they had gone unarmed and apparently with one horse. They were supposed to go to Connelly's aid if they heard gunshots, but when they heard the first shot, they walked a few feet in that direction and discussed it. When they heard more shots, they decided to stay where they were. Shortly after, they saw Will Busby coming across the field, and Satterfield told Woods to go ask him what had happened, but Woods told Satterfield to go because he was the one who had the horse. When they met, Busby told Satterfield the story as related in the previous paragraph. Both Busbys and both women present told the same story consistently through the depositions and the trial with only small variations depending on their positions at the time of the action.

Shepard and William Busby were charged with murder, not only because they had killed a deputy U.S. marshal, but also because his injuries were not consistent with the positions and actions described. Busby had sworn that Connelly had been facing him, advancing all the time, yet only the bullet that wounded Connelly's forearm had entered from the front. The bullets causing two other wounds had struck Connelly from opposite sides. One entered his right chest, passed through both lungs and the heart, and lodged under the skin on the left. Another entered the abdomen from the left and ranged down to the right back, lodging under the skin. When confronted by the prosecutor about the angle of the bullets and asked if Connelly ever turned, Busby said, "Well, he might have scringed." Deputy G. S. White, first officer on the scene, found black residue, which he pronounced to be a powder burn, in a spot in the house where the chinking was missing from between the logs. The defense countered that the black residue could be mold that commonly forms between the bark and wood of dead trees. The lawman contended that Will Busby had fired from inside the house.

All of the foregoing was problematic enough, but Connelly also had a broken neck, even though all witnesses swore no blows were struck. Connelly fell on the ground of his own weight, did not strike a root, rock, bucket, chair, or any other object. The injury to the neck was described in detail by the doctor who did the autopsy at Birney Funeral Home and by the doctor who autopsied again when the body was exhumed four days later. They described the type of object that would probably have caused such damage and said that Connelly was probably alive when the blow was struck. The prosecution produced a musket barrel found under a fallen limb near Busby's house, saying that it or the barrel of Busby's rifle could have caused the fracture and dislocation. The defense tried to prove that the neck could have been broken while the body was being transported to Fort Smith. The body had been loaded in a wagon on some fodder and hauled over rough roads from four or five miles beyond Dora, Arkansas, on Lee Creek to Fort Smith. On the way, the body had slid up under the driver's feet and had to be pulled back to the back of the wagon several times.

One thing that made everyone skeptical of Busby's story was his claim of taking Connelly's gun from him and pushing him back. Connelly was described as six feet tall, 175 pounds, and thirty-seven to forty years old. Busby was small, weight estimated at 130 to 150 pounds, and fifty-seven years old at the time of the killing. But Joe Boyd, when asked how he regarded Busby's strength, answered, "I thought he was about as strong a man as I ever saw for his looks; he has always been a puny man."

Through all of the 300-plus pages of trial transcript, the prosecution never tried to establish an exact scenario of the action but endeavored to discredit Busby's version. The angle of the wounds, the broken neck, and the difference in size and strength of the two men did not lend credence to the story, and the description of Connelly's acts was inconsistent with his known behavior. The theory of the prosecution was that both Shepard and William Busby had attacked Connelly, shooting and striking him. Whatever the truth, Connelly never presented his warrant, as it was still in his pocket and had been there during the shooting for it had a bullet hole in it. The jury returned a verdict on December 11, 1891, finding Shepard guilty of murder and William guilty of manslaughter. William was sentenced to ten years at Detroit House of Correction. On January 21, 1892, Shepard Busby was sentenced to hang on April 21, 1892.

Program of some of the players in this soap opera:

Shepard Busby was born in 1833 in Kentucky and served during the war in the Union Army, first in the Fifty-sixth Illinois then in the Fiftieth Missouri. He had lived the ten years previous to the killing of Connelly in Arkansas and the Indian Territory. When asked if he was currently married, he said he had been for "six or seven or eight years."

William, son of Shepard Busby, was almost twenty-three at the time of the trial.

Tennessee Burns, an orphan, went to live with Busby and his first wife in 1881 when she was twelve years old. About three years later, Mrs. Busby died. At the time of the trial, Tennessee was twenty-two and had a five-year-old and an eleven-month-old fathered by Shepard Busby, though they never married. Tennessee, or Tenny, had lived with other families and had moved back to Busby's place on March 19, 1891. She had gone to school only a couple of weeks and had never gone to church but knew what preachers were and did not regard them very highly. She knew the difference between truth and lying and that Heaven was a better place to go than Hell.

Florence Jones was fifteen when she went to live at Busby's home on March 29, 1891. A marriage license was issued January 23, 1891, for Jones and Shepard Busby in Sebastian County, Arkansas, but the certificate of marriage and certificate of record were never completed.

Louiza or Eliza Bolin, age twenty-two, was legally married to Shepard Busby for the "six or seven or eight years" he spoke of, but the two separated several times. Tenny Burns had gone to live with Busby after the last time he and Louiza separated. The marshals from Fort Smith had gone to Louiza at her parents' home to get her to swear out the warrant for Busby for adultery. In the meantime, however, she had married John Carroll without divorcing Busby. As her mother said, "They didn't have a license. They had them a little ceremony."

Deputy Marshal Asbell, the arresting officer when Busby gave himself up, was under indictment for adultery himself at the time of the trial.

Joe Boyd, friend of Shepard Busby, was Asbell's posse in the arrest. He, too, was under indictment for adultery.

EXECUTION

On Wednesday, April 27, 1892, Shepard Busby was executed, "the disagreeable job being done by Deputy U.S. Marshal G. S. White — Maledon, the old hangman declining to officiate" (*The Elevator*, April

29, 1892). Shepard Busby was fifty-eight years old at the time of his hanging, the oldest man to be hanged at the fort up until that time. He would hold that dubious honor only for two months until John Thornton's execution on June 28, 1892.

Legend has it that Maledon refused to hang Busby because both had been Union soldiers. However, G. S. White belonged to the Grand Army of the Republic, as did Busby, and White did not refuse the job. Two years later, Maledon participated in the hanging of Lewis Holder, who was also a Union soldier. Also, the October 9, 1891, edition of *The Elevator* stated that Maledon "was stricken with paralysis Monday. He was taken ill at the jail and started for home. When nearly there he was prostrated to such a degree that he fell in the street." In addition, Maledon's name appears on the list of alternate jurors in the jury pool for the November 1891 term of court, the term in which Busby was tried. Could it be that Maledon was not in good health or was not an employee of the Marshals Office at the time of the hanging, or both, and those could be the reasons for his not participating?

CHAPTER 35

"BOWING AND SMILING

John Thornton Marches Forth
To Meet His Doom"

(*The Fort Smith Elevator*, July 1, 1892)

On the evening of November 11, 1891, Simon Moynier came home
to find his bride of six days dying of a gunshot wound to the head. She
had been shot by her own father, John Thornton.

John Thornton's case is one of the most bizarre of all of the murder
cases tried by the U.S. Court at Fort Smith. He shot his own daughter in
her home for reasons that others can only guess at. He had apparently
destroyed his brain by years of alcohol abuse. His only defense was
that he was suffering delirium tremens.

Simon Moynier married twenty-year-old Laura Thornton on
Thursday, November 5, 1891, and they moved to his house at Krebs,
Indian Territory, in the Choctaw Nation. On Saturday of the same
week, the newlyweds had spent the night at the home of Laura's father,
John Thornton, at McAlester, Indian Territory. Before they left there,
Laura wrote a letter to her half brother, Charles Wilson, and Moynier
mailed the letter at McAlester. When Thornton went to Moynier's
home on November 10, he had the letter. When asked how he acquired
it, Thornton said that he had a machine in his home that would print a
letter as it was written by anyone. *The Fort Smith Elevator* reported that
in that letter, Laura told her half brother that she "had married to get
out of hell."

Thornton stayed overnight. On November 11, Moynier went to
work at the coal mine, and Thornton left to peddle jewelry around the
town. When Moynier returned from work, Thornton offered to shake
hands, but Moynier said that his hands were dirty and proceeded to
wash them. The men then shook hands and ate supper. During supper,
Moynier told Thornton how happy he was, and Thornton spoke up
and said, "Simon, your trouble is not over yet." After supper Moynier
said that he had to go to the store for some blasting powder to use the
next day. Thornton offered to go with him, but Moynier asked him to
stay with Laura, adding that he would be gone only about half an hour.
When Moynier returned from his errand, he found his wife on the floor
dying from a gunshot wound near her right eye. Laura Moynier was
barely alive and died minutes after the doctor arrived.

John Thornton had left the scene of his crime, but before leaving,
according to his testimony, he had tried to take his own life. He

claimed to have fired four shots in an effort to kill himself but failed. Stephen Fisher, a neighbor to Moynier, testified that he had heard four shots about the same time the murder was committed. Thornton's aim was much better when shooting his daughter. His one shot passed through her forearm and into her head, yet he could not manage to kill himself with the remaining shots. An article in *The Fort Smith Elevator* states that Thornton went to the drugstore in Krebs and announced that he had killed his daughter and that he would do it again under the same circumstances.

The night of the murder Deputy Marshal B. T. Shelburn was notified at McAlester that Laura Moynier had been murdered and that John Thornton was in custody. Shelburn went the next day and took charge of the prisoner. Thornton, who had been drinking the day of the crime—as he did on all the other days of his life—appeared to the deputy to still be under the influence of alcohol. When asked by Shelburn what he had been doing, Thornton replied, "I'll tell you all about it after awhile." On the way back to McAlester, Thornton told the deputy that he had killed his daughter and was not sorry for it and would do it again under similar circumstances. Quoting from Deputy Shelburn's deposition, "He first said that he killed her 'on account of a job that was put up on the day of the wedding by Shorty and his wife and the one-eyed woman on the hill.' He said, 'They are the cause of the killing.'" The next day Thornton told the same story to a reporter at South McAlester in the presence of Shelburn. He added that it was about a letter, apparently meaning the letter Laura Moynier had written to her half brother.

Thornton's trial began on Friday afternoon, March 9, 1892. The defense attorneys used insanity and alcoholism as their only defense. Judge Parker, in his charge to the jury, gave attention to the insanity plea and cited several authorities who held that a man crazed by drink could not be held accountable for actions. Apparently the argument did not carry much weight with the jury, for they delivered the guilty verdict on Tuesday, March 15, after about a half-hour deliberation.

On Saturday, April 30, 1892, Judge Parker sentenced John Thornton and two others to hang on June 28, 1892. To each man, Parker gave his usual long address, citing their crimes and ending with the admonition, "I hope you will fully realize your condition and waste no time, but use every moment in preparation for the fate which awaits you. Make your peace with God." To Thornton he dwelt particularly on the fact that he had killed the one whom he was supposed to protect. Parker went on to accuse Thornton of another crime saying, "The cause of your killing your own daughter is not absolutely known, but there is a strong, and I must say, reasonably well-grounded opinion, that you in cold blood killed this unoffending girl because you either had committed or that you attempted to commit that terrible crime which is worse than death." Parker also accused Thornton of neglect and abuse of his wives, using the plural although there is no mention of Thornton having more than one wife.

John Thornton was sixty-five years old, the oldest man to be executed at Fort Smith. He was born in Strasburg, France, and came to the United States when he was twelve and lived in Illinois until he moved to Indian Territory about twelve years before the murder. He was known to be an alcoholic, and it was said that when he could not get liquor, he would drink extracts or anything containing alcohol. He had been drinking the day he murdered his daughter, and Deputy Shelburn testified that he appeared to be under the influence of alcohol when he took custody of him the next day. His stepson, Charley Wilson, published an article in *The Choctaw Herald* saying that while Thornton lived in Rapid City, Illinois, he shot his wife, and was sentenced to the penitentiary but had been petitioned out by the Knights of Pythias. Thornton addressed a letter to the editor of *The Elevator* saying that the accusation was not true, that he was arrested for firing a pistol within the city limits and had been fined fifty dollars and costs. He produced a statement "from good and respectable men of Rock Island City and County certified to by the clerk and bearing the seal of the county court" confirming his account of the event.

Simon Moynier, called John Moynier in the newspaper, was described as a Frenchman, a hardworking coal miner employed by the Osage Coal Company. It appears that he was older than Laura Thornton, but his age was never given in available documents. He stated that he had known John Thornton since 1875.

The July 1, 1892, edition of *The Fort Smith Elevator* starts its description of the execution with these words:

> With a smile upon his face and a bouquet of flowers in his hand, John Thornton, the slayer of his only daughter, marched forth Tuesday morning to perform the last act in the drama of a life so illy lived. Nature in all its loveliness and beauty smiled upon him, and the bright, glorious sunlight of the June morning played upon the silvery hair of an old man soon to be ushered into the presence of Him who said, "Thou shall not kill!"

Thornton was said to have slept well the night before his hanging. The morning of his hanging, he rose and dressed in a new suit, as was provided all condemned men. He had his breakfast and went through his morning devotions. He had adopted the Catholic religion and be

210

lieved he would go to Heaven. He was let out of his cell and walked up and down the corridor, sometimes stopping to talk to other prisoners and admonishing them to make their peace with God and to live better lives. Father Lawrence Smythe talked with the condemned man awhile, then Thornton was read the death warrant, and the march to the gallows began, with Thornton carrying a bouquet of flowers. On the platform, Thornton bowed to the crowd and smiled. There were the usual prayers, and Thornton was asked if he had any last words. He said he wished to thank the temperance ladies who had visited him and jailer Pape and the guards for their kind treatment.

At 10:26 a.m. Deputy Marshal White pulled the lever, and John Thornton made the fatal fall. He was pronounced dead in eight and a half minutes. *The Elevator* described the scene in this way:

> The sight which greeted the eyes of the spectators as the body rebounded in the air was a ghastly one. Thornton's head was nearly torn from his body, only the tendons in the back of the neck preventing the body from falling to the ground. The blood spurted in streams all over the body, saturating the clothing of the dead man and running in pools upon the ground. A thrill of horror ran through those within the enclosure, and strong men turned sick at the sight of the hideous wound in the neck. Not only was the spinal cord severed, but all the flesh on the front part of the neck was torn away. If the rope which was tied around the crossbeam above had not slipped, the head would have been entirely severed from the body.

George Maledon, who supposedly refused to participate in the hanging of Shepherd Busby because he was a Union soldier, took part in this hanging. Thornton, Maledon, and White were all members of the Grand Army of the Republic.

CHAPTER 36

"LEWIS HOLDER
The Slayer of George M. Bickford,
Pays the Death Penalty"
(The Elevator, July 27, 1894)

Friday afternoon, January 29, 1892, A. T. Echols was on the way from Wilburton, Indian Territory, to San Bois. It being about time to camp, he walked off the road to look for water. From the top of a ridge, he looked into a hollow and saw a man lying partially on his face a short distance away. At first he thought the man was asleep, but on approaching closer and stooping down, he could see that part of his nose had been eaten away. Seeing that the man was dead, he returned to his wagon and drove on until after sundown to a good watering place. The next morning, he found the nearest house and told the occupant, John Riddle, of his find. Accompanied by six Choctaws, Echols returned to the body and removed daybooks and letters in an effort to determine the man's identity. On Monday, the body was taken to Whitefield. The documents were turned over to Deputy Marshal William Ellis.

The dead man was identified as George Bickford, who was last seen in December in the company of Lewis Holder as they went on a hunting and trapping trip into the hills where Bickford's body was found. Holder had been seen before Christmas with Bickford's wagon and mules and wearing clothes belonging to Bickford. Holder said Bickford had left him two weeks before Christmas without saying where he was going.

Given this information, Deputy Ellis arrested Holder on February 5, 1892. Holder still had the mules, wagon, a shotgun, and two trunks. He told Ellis the same story he had told others. He had given Bickford a note for $145 that he had held for fourteen years on John Stike of Newton County, Missouri, and that Stike had been dead for fourteen years. Finally, Holder told Ellis that he and Bickford had a fight and Bickford broke his little finger with a slingshot. He pushed Bickford down, and while he was on his hands and knees, he shot him. Bickford was shot at the base of his neck, and the projectile exited through his throat, taking out his larynx.

In his application for witnesses, Holder asserted that his witnesses would testify that Bickford possessed a slingshot and a small handgun. That, however, did not justify shooting a man who was on his hands and knees in the back.

Holder went on trial in the last week of August 1892. Throughout he maintained his self-defense plea, but the jury was out only a short time before returning the guilty verdict. On September 23, 1892, *The Elevator* headlined an article: "CONDEMNED TO DIE! Five Men, Convicted of Murder, Sentenced in Judge Parker's Court." All five appealed their cases to the U.S. Supreme Court, and three were granted retrials or commutations. On April 27, 1894, the newspaper announced "THE SENTENCE OF DEATH" for Frank Collins and Lewis Holder. Monday morning, April 23, 1894, Judge Parker again pronounced the sentence of death on the two men to be carried out on July 25, 1894. However, a paragraph at the end of the article under the heading, "FRANK COLLINS," says, "Judge Parker has recommended commutation of his sentence to life imprisonment; the papers are now in Washington City. Frank's sentence ought to be commuted."

The July 27, 1894, issue of *The Elevator* headed the description of the hanging, "NUMBER SEVENTY-SEVEN." Actually Holder was number seventy-five. The paper never could keep the numbers straight, once being off by thirteen in its count of executions. No wonder later writers got the numbers of condemned and executed wrong. Nevertheless, the gallows, which had sat unused for just three days short of two years and one month, was again activated.

Holder held to his self-defense argument until the last. He had requested that Judge Parker and the jury that convicted him witness his execution. His request was not fulfilled. On the gallows, he stepped to the edge of the platform and asked anyone who had a hand in his conviction to step forward. When none did, Holder said that he forgave them all but Judge Parker should resign his office and get down on his knees and beg forgiveness. The preparations were made, and jailer Baxter sprung the trap. In just two minutes, the attending physician pronounced Lewis Holder dead. The body was turned over to Birnie Brothers Funeral Home and interred in the Catholic cemetery.

CHAPTER 37

THE EXECUTION OF JOHN POINTER

On December 15, 1891, Ed Vandevere, twenty-six, and William Bolding, twenty, left the home of Vandevere's father in Wise County, Texas, near Decatur, Texas, on their journey to Eureka Springs, Arkansas. Their families never saw them alive again.

Vandevere and Bolding, along with Vandevere's brother, William, and his wife, had gone to Texas from Eureka Springs in August 1891 to pick cotton for Vandevere's father. Twelve miles out of Eureka, they were accompanied by John Pointer, whose father paid their expenses for the trip. Pointer left Arkansas riding his own horse, but sometimes rode in the wagon with Ed Vandevere as they traveled.

At Vandevere's farm, Pointer picked cotton with the Vandeveres and the Boldings for a few weeks, then left to work on a ranch for a Mr. Longley. After about four or five weeks, Pointer returned to Vandevere's, having left his horse with a lawyer in Sherman. He had gotten into some sort of trouble there, but what kind was never made clear. He had left the horse and saddle as security or bond. Prosecutor Clayton, at trial, would pursue the question of why Pointer had left his horse and saddle and with whom, but Pointer refused to reveal the details.

Pointer arrived at Vandevere's farm from Decatur, Texas, about three or four hours after Ed Vandevere and Bolding left for Arkansas. On learning of their departure, Pointer left afoot to overtake them. Pointer caught up with Vandevere and Bolding at Aurora, Texas, where they had stopped to cash a check. The trio then proceeded to Sherman, Texas, then into Indian Territory.

On December 26, 1891, Thomas Symons was rabbit hunting along a creek near Wilburton, Indian Territory, when he came upon two bodies lying in the creek bed. Symons, not knowing whether the bodies were alive or dead, went to a hay camp nearby and inquired of Harvey Flippo whether anyone was missing from his camp. Symons told Flippo that there were two men in the creek bed who were either dead or dead drunk. The men went to the site to determine which was the case. They approached from the opposite side of the creek from where Symons had first seen the bodies and in so doing found a campsite where a fire still smoldered. There was blood around the fire, on a piece of wood in the fire, and on a tree. They also found a trail of blood and drag marks leading to the high bank of the creek where the bodies had been dropped over.

Flippo and Symons went into Wilburton and sent for a law officer and a notary public. Flippo, with a group of men, returned to the murder scene. On examination, they found that the skulls of both men had been broken by multiple blows with a blunt instrument. Two of the men went to the other side of the creek and found a bloody axe inside a hollow tree. The spot where the wagon had stood and the horses had been fed was found, and the search party determined the direction the wagon had taken. The trail of people who had seen the wagon and its driver led to South McAlester.

At a stable in McAlester they located the wagon and horses and the man trying to sell them. The man was registered at the hotel as G. L. Longley of Fort Smith. With the information they had gained from witnesses along the way, the search party determined that this was the man and the wagon they were looking for. They observed him for a while and listened to his conversations with a man about selling the team and wagon. The man identified as Longley was arrested and transported to Fort Smith.

P. B. Bolding saw in a newspaper the description of two unidentified bodies found near Wilburton and went there, where he identified his son and Ed Vandevere. He then went to Fort Smith to try to identify some of the dead men's belongings. While Bolding sat in Marshal Yoes's office, George L. Longley was brought in. Bolding turned to Marshal Yoes and said, "That is John Pointer." Pointer turned to jailer Pape and said, "Who is that man? I don't know him." Bolding said, "John, you have seen me before." To which Pointer replied, "No." Marshal Yoes said, "That's enough," and Pointer was taken to his cell. Samuel Vandevere had been shown an article in *The Chicago Blade* and went to Wilburton to identify the horses and wagon, then on to Fort Smith to identify personal items of his son. Vandevere met with Marshal Yoes and was taken to the jail to meet Pointer. When Vandevere met Pointer, he asked him if he knew him, and Pointer replied, "Mr. Vandevere." Both fathers of the murdered men identified items of clothing found in the wagon and in a bag that Pointer had been carrying. He was also wearing pants belonging to William Bolding and carrying his watch.

At trial, Pointer admitted killing Bolding but claimed self-defense, saying that Bolding killed Ed Vandevere and attempted to kill him. According to Pointer, Bolding attacked Vandevere, who was crippled, in an argument over Bolding's treatment of a horse. Bolding, he said, killed Vandevere with an axe and turned on Pointer when he intervened. Pointer wrestled the axe from Bolding, who was holding the axe head. In twisting the axe away, he cut Bolding's throat. He then hit

Bolding in the head three times while Bolding continued to attack. His story was not consistent with the evidence at the scene or on the bodies. Bolding's neck wound was narrow and deep, suggesting a knife wound, and the blows to both men's heads appeared to have been directly to the top of the head. Pointer could not explain how there could have been such a violent fight for the axe in which he received not even a scratch but inflicted at least four wounds on Bolding. Pointer attributed his hiding of the bodies and axe, the burning of Vandevere's crutch and other small items, and his flight to fear and excitement. Fifteen witnesses appeared for the prosecution, but only Pointer took the stand for the defense. Testimony of those witnesses trailed the three men to the murder site and trailed Pointer to McAlester. That and evidence from the crime scene and the fact that Pointer was wearing Bolding's pants and carrying his watch were enough to convince the jury of a guilty verdict. Pointer remained nonchalant throughout the trial and showed no emotion when the verdict was read.

The motive for the killing is not quite clear. Pointer gained little of value except the horses and wagon. Contrary to what is written in *Law West of Fort Smith*, Bolding and Vandevere were not coming home flush with money after a trading expedition. They were, as stated before, coming back from picking cotton for Vandevere's father. The check they cashed at Aurora, Texas, was for thirty dollars and thirty cents, a third of which went back to the farm to be paid to another worker. Pointer said that he had fifteen dollars, and after he sold the wagon, he had $115.

Pointer, apparently, had always been a problem child, with his parents getting him out of each scrape he got into. Prosecutor Clayton tried to bring out in the trial that Pointer was wanted in Missouri for horse stealing. That, the prosecutor said, was the reason that Pointer and his father met Bolding and Vandevere twelve miles out of Eureka and why his father financed the trip. It was believed Pointer was getting out of town to avoid a Missouri warrant for his arrest.

Pointer's attorneys, Hodges and Davis, immediately filed a motion to quash the indictment, a motion for extension, and writs of error. He was sentenced on March 26, 1892, to hang on Tuesday, June 28, 1892, but his attorneys were successful in getting the case before the Supreme Court. More than two years passed before the Supreme Court affirmed the decision of the Circuit Court. On Monday, July 2, 1894, Pointer was again sentenced to hang. The date of Thursday, September 20, 1894, was set for the execution.

Through all of the proceedings, Pointer never lost his composure. On Wednesday, the day before his hanging, his father, mother, and sister visited him in the jail. His mother was so feeble that she had to be assisted when climbing the steps to the jail. Pointer held up well during the visit and at the parting. Later he seemed to be at ease and talked and joked with other prisoners and the guards.

On his final day, a different John Pointer went to the gallows. He had set his own time of execution at three thirty in the afternoon. When the time came, he asked for another half-hour but was granted only fifteen minutes. The death warrant was read, and Pointer was lead from the jail, pale and barely able to move. A short distance from the jail, he caught site of the gallows enclosure and, although he tried to make a brave appearance, he had to be supported by two guards. He started complaining that if it were not for the capsules he had taken he could walk unaided. He claimed that he had taken poison supplied to him by a trusty. At the gallows, Pointer was so weak that he had to be carried up the steps. When asked if he wished to make a statement, he made a rambling speech in which he complained about the poison then sank back on the bench, still saying that if he had not taken the poison he could bear it like a man. He recovered enough to step onto the trap where his arms and legs were pinioned. He asked that the hood be placed under the noose so that it would not tear his neck. At 4:07 p.m., the trap fell, and at 4:17, Pointer was pronounced dead. The doctors could find no evidence that he had taken any poison. John Pointer was twenty years old when he was executed. He was not quite eighteen when he committed his crime nearly three years earlier.

The Elevator erred again, assigning Pointer the same number it had assigned to Lewis Holder, saying in a subhead, "John Pointer, the Seventy-seventh Man to Die on the Garrison Gallows." He was number seventy-six; number seventy-seven would not come for another year and a half.

CHAPTER 38

THE EXECUTION
OF CRAWFORD GOLDSBY
Alias Cherokee Bill

So much has been written, partly truth, mostly fiction, about Crawford Goldsby, a.k.a. Cherokee Bill, that it is hard to tell where the truth ends and the legend begins. There are so many books and papers extant that trying to tell of his life and crimes is redundant. So this will be an effort to tell some of the less written about events, or at least to tell the story from a different perspective.

On Tuesday, March 17, 1896, *The Fort Smith Weekly Elevator* ran an extra edition announcing the hanging of Cherokee Bill, complete with picture. On the front page of the regular Friday edition, it again ran his picture with a description of the hanging

Crawford Goldsby, a.k.a. Cherokee Bill, and his mother

and his last hours. But Bill was not the first of the condemned to grace the front page. That honor went to Mary Kettenring, the third of four women sentenced to death by the U.S. District Court for the Western District of Arkansas. Kettenring had preceded Bill by about nine months in her day of infamy, but, unlike him, she would not pay the ultimate price. However, Cherokee Bill, along with the Bill Cook gang with whom he rode, probably got a bigger share of newsprint over time than Kettenring.

For most of 1894, the Cook gang, with Bill in the forefront, terrorized the citizens of the Cherokee Nation and beyond. The band, either singly or collectively, was regularly mentioned in the newspapers. Beginning with the November 2, 1894, edition of *The Fort Smith Elevator* and through December 1894 and January 1895, the gang made news almost weekly. In the November 2 edition under the heading, "After the Cooks With Rewards," the paper tells of Marshal Crump's offer of

$250 for each member of the Cook gang. The total of rewards for all the men was $3,500. The November 23 edition of *The Elevator* under the heading "Col. Bill Cook" ran an article that began "Bill Cook continues to furnish the correspondents of the metropolitan papers with daily budgets of sensational telegrams." The February 1, 1895, edition of *The Eufaula Indian Journal* published this article:

> The citizens of Lenapah, I. T. have evidently been thoroughly cowed by the outlaw Cherokee Bill. At the last meeting of the village council they passed an ordinance which grants to that worthy the privilege of coming and going there whenever he desires, and they guarantee him protection from molestation.

Lenapah citizens had had plenty to fear from Cherokee Bill and friends in the past. On November 9, 1894, Cherokee Bill and Jim French raided Shufelt's store and in the process killed E. E. Melton. Bill had seen Melton watching from behind another store window and shot Melton through the head. But the citizens had little to fear from Bill by the time the Eufaula article ran, for on the same day, February 1, 1895, *The Fort Smith Elevator* headed an article thus: "CAPTURED AT LAST," with a subhead, "Cherokee Bill, the Worst of All, Landed in Jail."

Cherokee Bill had been captured on January 29, 1895, and Bill Cook had been captured in New Mexico and arrived at the U.S. Jail at Fort Smith on January 20, 1895. But it must have been like old home week at the jail. Cook shared a cell with Henry Starr, who was indicted for murder. The Pierce brothers, also in on a murder charge, shared another cell, and other notable acquaintances were in other cells. The inhabitants of "murderers row" played cards, visited, and plotted.

On Wednesday, February 6, 1895, Cook and Cherokee Bill went on trial jointly before a standing-room-only crowd for a train robbery at Red Fork the previous July. The same afternoon, the jury was out about ten minutes before returning a verdict of guilty. They were next tried for robberies at Wetumpka and Okmulgee. In the Wetumpka robbery, they netted only thirty-five cents and the victim made it so hot for them with his Winchester that they dropped most of the merchandise they had taken. At Okmulgee they got about $350 in cash, about the same amount in checks, and a lot of merchandise. They sent the checks back after about an hour or two. This gang was adept at murder, mayhem, and terror, but not so much at stealing. Cook and Cherokee Bill faced many more robbery indictments, but most were not brought to trial. Cook was sentenced to forty-five years on the early charges, and Bill was indicted for Melton's murder, so there was no point in spending time and money trying either man on further robbery charges.

Crawford Goldsby spent his nineteenth birthday, February 8, 1895, on trial for robbery in the U.S. District Court for the Western District of Arkansas.

None of the robberies reported by the newspapers appears to have netted much cash. But, however inept they were at robbing, they were brazen; at least Goldsby was. This article appeared in *The Fort Smith Elevator* on January 4, 1895, while Bill had a reported $1,300 price on his head:

> Cherokee Bill appears to be going it alone now, and is getting unusually bold for a man with a price upon his head. A few nights ago he attended a dance at the house of ex-deputy Ike Rogers near Nowata. Tuesday morning last he killed his brother-in-law, a Negro named Brown, who lives in the vicinity of Talala. The day before he took dinner in Nowata, putting his horse in a livery stable. On Tuesday afternoon he was around Nowata some time, and just before the north bound train arrived there Tuesday night went to the depot and robbed the agent of what cash he had in the safe, about $39, after which he mounted his horse and left.

Some said he killed his brother-in-law for abusing his wife, Bill's sister. Others believed he thought Brown tried to betray him to the lawmen. Another story was that the killing resulted from an argument over hogs.

On Monday, February 25, 1895, the courtroom at Fort Smith was crowded to capacity to see Cherokee Bill tried for the murder of Ernest E. Melton. Bill's mother and sister sat in the audience near him. Judge Parker allowed the defense all the witnesses it requested, and there were many, both for the defense and for the government. Arguments in the case began Tuesday afternoon and lasted until ten o'clock that night. Parker gave his instructions to the jury Wednesday morning in what must have been a record short time for him; he took only about fifteen minutes. The jury was out a short time before returning a verdict of guilty. Bill was unemotional when the verdict was read, but his mother and sister burst into tears. Bill was reported to have said, "What's the matter with you? I'm not dead yet by a long ways." That afternoon in the jail, he played poker with Bill Cook and other like company as if nothing had happened.

On Saturday morning, April 13, 1895, Crawford Goldsby heard the sentence of death pronounced on him by Judge Parker. He had been taken to the courtroom shortly before nine o'clock, the time not being generally known to avoid the large crowd that certainly would have gathered otherwise. He was represented by J. Warren Reed, who requested a few days to complete his writ of error and to prepare for an appeal to the Supreme Court. The request was granted, and Cherokee Bill stood before Judge Parker, who began his address to the prisoner. When asked if he had anything to say as to why sentence should not now be passed, Goldsby replied, "No, sir." Judge Parker then delivered one of his long addresses ending in his usual way, saying, "Your great effort now should be to get rid of that load of guilt, so you can enter upon a new existence with your sins, wickedness and crime behind you. Do everything you can to accomplish this end, and lose not a moment's time."

He then set the execution for Tuesday, June 25, 1895, but it was not carried out on that date because J. Warren Reed had been successful in getting the case to the Supreme Court.

Lawrence Keating
Jail guard

On July 26, 1895, Cherokee Bill sealed his fate by shooting and killing guard Lawrence Keating. Obviously, this killing affected how the Supreme Court treated the appeal in the Melton murder case.

This story has been told and retold, usually with the author's own embellishments. This is the story as told by jailer R. C. Eoff and other witnesses in the trial transcript:

On the evening of July 26, 1895, jailer Eoff was locking the prisoners in their cells for the night. Guard Lawrence Keating accompanied Eoff, walking outside the metal grating that separated the cells from the corridor that ran around the building. There was a lever and locking system that locked and unlocked all the cells on one side at once. The jailer then locked each cell individually. Keating moved with Eoff as he went from cell to cell. At the cell occupied by Dennis Davis and Andrew Jackson, Eoff found that something had been put into the lock that kept it from locking. Eoff made a comment to Keating that there was something wrong, and at that time, Cherokee Bill charged from the next cell. Bill stuck a pistol through the grating and ordered Keating to throw up his hands and give up his gun. Keating at the time was stand-

221

ing with his right hand on the grating and his left on his hip. When Keating did not respond to Bill's command, Bill shot him at point-blank range, the bullet passing through Keating's cartridge belt and into his belly.

George Lawson
Deputy Marshal

It appears that Cherokee Bill's legendary marksmanship is just that, a legend. He hit Keating with the first shot and then fired three more at a distance of not more than six feet, for that is the width of the corridor. All three missed by a wide margin. Bill then fired two shots at the retreating Eoff and missed with those also. In the following gun battle, he never fired an effective shot.

The cell occupied by Cherokee Bill and Israel Carr was on the west side of the first floor. Eoff ran to the east side with Bill pursuing and firing. Eoff found refuge behind a partition where he was partially protected from further shooting. George Pierce was also in Bill's cell, although he belonged in a cell with his brother, John. Pierce somehow had obtained a heavy table leg with which he intended to attack the turnkey, Eoff.

Deputy Marshal George Lawson, Tommy Parker, and William McConnell were sitting outside the jail when they heard the shots. The three men rushed in, McConnell in the lead and Lawson following. Lawson took Parker's pistol, and Parker ran to the guard's area and grabbed a pistol and a shotgun. When McConnell entered the corridor, he met Keating, who had just fallen from the effects of his wound. McConnell spoke to Keating, and Keating made an unintelligible response. McConnell, sensing that Keating was dying, took his gun and ran on. McConnell and Lawson immediately began firing in Cherokee Bill's direction. Will Lawson then showed up with a pistol. By then George Lawson had emptied the gun he had and asked Will for his, but Will told his father he could not use two guns at once, then George left to get another gun. Heck Bruner and others showed up, and Tommy Parker returned with his pistol and shotgun. From the testimony of witnesses, it appears that the shotgun was never fired.

The other prisoners had taken cover in their cells, and soon Henry Starr called out to the guards that he would get Bill's gun if they would not shoot him. The guards answered back that they were making no compromises. The guards were in a mood to make an end of Crawford Goldsby then and there. Finally the guards relented and allowed Starr to get the gun. The weapon was described by one of the guards in testimony as a Colt double-action, .38-caliber, and they thought it had ivory grips. For some reason, that weapon was never entered into evidence at the trial, and the disposition of it is still a mystery.

The guards were in a high state of emotion after the gun was surrendered, and some wanted to kill Goldsby while they had the opportunity. But cooler heads prevailed, and Heck Bruner and George Stockton went into the cell and shackled and searched Bill. In his pocket, they found a tobacco sack of .38-caliber ammunition. Fort Smith Chief of Police Henry Surratt, having heard the shots, arrived on the scene and went to the cell. He asked Bill why he shot Keating, and Bill relied, "Because he wouldn't throw up." Jailer J. D. Berry arrived and asked the same question and got the same response.

The number of shots fired during the affray was a small matter of dispute among the guards who were witnesses. One said that not more than twenty rounds were fired; another said possibly as many as thirty. But they agreed it had not been more than thirty. Two witnesses were asked about smoke in the building when they entered. Both said they could smell and see smoke but not to the extent that it obscured their vision.

The shots must have been heard all over town. One deputy sheriff was at Fourth Street and Garrison Avenue when he heard the shooting. Chief of Police Surratt must have been in the vicinity of the present-day Isaac Parker Federal Building, judging by his testimony at the trial. By the time the shooting was over and all the prisoners confined, a large crowd of all ages and sexes had gathered. Some of the citizens were armed and in a lynching mood, but jailer Berry was successful in dispersing the crowd without incident. However, extra guards were called in and were on duty all night. Cherokee Bill was locked in a cell alone, where he stayed for the rest of his incarceration.

The staff at the jail had been aware that something was going on for two or more weeks. Among other indications, a .45-caliber Colt had been found two weeks before in a bucket of wet clothes in a bathtub in the back of the jail. After the shooting was over, a .45 bullet was found under Bill's pillow. Also, a letter had been intercepted that told of a plan to kill a guard. The letter was, according to testimony of an illiterate inmate, Ben Duff, dictated by him and written by Cherokee Bill. Duff had wanted to instruct Kirk Barnes, on the outside, about the branding of some cattle. He claimed not to know what was written because he was so illiterate he could not even read his own name when it was written. They had intended to smuggle the letter out either by a trusty or a prisoner who was being released. There was some controversy at the trial over whether to introduce the letter in evidence because that required it to be read aloud and it contained "a lot of blackguard stuff." Finally, the parts referring to killing a guard were read, and the letter was given to the jurors to read individually.

On Thursday, August 8, 1895, at two fifteen in the afternoon, the case of the U.S. v. Crawford Goldsby began. From the beginning, it was a battle of wills between Judge Parker and J. Warren Reed. Reed challenged everything. He complained of jury prejudice. He challenged the jurisdiction of the court, claiming that the jail, where the crime occurred, was in the city of Fort Smith and not within the jurisdiction of the Western District of Arkansas. He questioned guards and prisoner witnesses at length about the number of shots fired and by whom and the amount of smoke in the building. He questioned prisoners about how fast Keating was running as he passed their cells. He questioned a number of people about the three shots that hit the wall opposite Bill's cell and the angle at which they struck. He never voiced it specifically, but his intent was to show that a guard, not Bill, had fired the fatal shot. Reed questioned prisoners who were confined with Bill about his mental state prior to the shooting. Judge Parker blocked Reed at every turn though, telling him that he was just preparing his case to be heard by the Supreme Court, saying these were just "outside capital" and "make-weight" issues. In the end, Reed's efforts were for naught. The jury was out thirteen minutes and returned with a verdict of guilty.

That was the second of two—and only two—thirteens associated with Cherokee Bill. The first was that he went to trial thirteen days after the murder of Keating. The gallows has twelve steps, and real nooses usually have no more than nine turns; any more than that is wasted rope. He was the seventieth man executed during Judge Isaac Parker's administration and the seventy-seventh executed in Fort Smith. Mythology has changed all of the aforementioned numbers, including the months Goldsby spent in jail, to thirteen.

On Monday, August 10, 1895, Crawford Goldsby was sentenced to hang on Thursday, September 10, 1895. But by September 10, Reed had succeeded through technicalities in getting the case appealed to the Supreme Court. When the day arrived, people who had not heard of the delay had traveled long distances to see the killer swing. Reporters estimated the crowd to be 500 to 600 people. The crowd assembled in the jail yard and stayed most of the day in spite of being told by jailer J. D. Berry that there would be no hanging. Someone at the jail decided to disperse the crowd by turning Berry's pet bear loose, which accomplished little except to knock down one boy and "scare him out of a year's growth." The bear was tied up, and the crowd reassembled. Later a trusty was dressed in a long coat and wide-brimmed hat and was led to the gallows enclosure. The crowd rushed for the gallows and, finding themselves shut out, began to climb the walls. Finally realizing that there would be no hanging, they went home.

> [W]hen it is decided that Cherokee Bill must hang
> the ELEVATOR will announce the fact. Until that time
> none need apply. Marshal Crump assures us that when
> the interceding time arrives the execution will be done
> in public, and due notice will be given of the fact.
> — *The Elevator*, September 13, 1895

In the last week of August 1895, between sentencing and the assigned hanging date, September 10, Henry Starr, George and John Pierce, Ed and John Shelly, James Casherego alias George Wilson, Sherman Vann, and Lou Shelly, wife of Ed Shelly, were indicted after a grand jury investigation implicated them in the jail break plot. Vann and Shelly were suspected of bringing the guns for the attempted break.

On Monday, December 2, 1895, Judge Parker received a telegram from Washington saying that the Supreme Court upheld the decision of the district court in the case of Crawford Goldsby, accused of killing Ernest E. Melton. On Monday, January 13, 1896, Judge Parker received the formal official notice of the decision of the Supreme Court. The next day, Crawford Goldsby appeared in court to receive the third sentence passed on him. Again the room was packed, but Bill, by "His appearance and manner showed that he did not care a tinker's denunciation whether he was hanged or not" (*The Elevator*, January 17, 1896). Judge Parker sentenced Cherokee Bill to be hanged on Tuesday, March 17, 1896, for the November 1894 murder of Ernest E. Melton. Reed immediately applied to President Grover Cleveland for a stay of execution. No one expected a stay to be granted, and they were not disappointed.

Marshal Crump's promise to the crowd on September 10 to have a public execution was overruled by the attorney general at the urging of the local school board and prominent citizens. With no law governing such a matter, it was entirely within the discretion of the attorney general.

The night before his hanging, Bill was reported to have gone to bed about nine o'clock. He rose around six the next morning, and as usual, showed no concern for what was about to happen. He ate a breakfast sent from the hotel by his mother. He declined the suit provided to all condemned men, saying that the clothes he had on were good enough. About 9:20, his mother and the old "Aunty" who raised him were allowed into his cell, and a little later Father Pius of the German Catholic Church was admitted. About eleven o'clock, Bill had a short conversation with Marshal Crump, who announced that the execution would be postponed until Bill's sister arrived. She was expected on the one o'clock train but it appears that she did not arrive on time.

U.S. Marshal George J. Crump, shown with his staff.

After his visitors left, Bill remarked to a guard, "Well, I am ready to go now most any time." At two o'clock, a pathway was cleared, and Crawford Goldsby started his last walk. His mother and "Aunty" were on each side of him and Father Pius behind. Once outside, Bill said, "This is about as good a day to die as any." At the south end of the jail, he looked over the crowd and said, "It looks like a regiment of soldiers."

After mounting the gallows, Bill, looking around and seeing his mother, said, "Mother, you ought not to be up here." She replied, "I can go wherever you go." Marshal Crump directed Bill to the bench on the platform, but he replied, "No, I don't want to sit down." The death warrant was read, and Bill was asked if he had anything to say. He said, "Not without he (meaning Father Pius) wants to say a prayer." After the prayer, Bill stepped forward to the trap. Deputy George Lawson and others bound his arms and legs as Bill spoke to acquaintances in the crowd. Just before the hood was put in place, Bill said, "Goodbye to all you chums down that way." Just then a man in the crowd snapped a picture with a Kodak and quickly pulled it back. The trap fell, and twelve minutes later Crawford Goldsby, alias Cherokee Bill, was pronounced dead. The body was taken to Birney Funeral Home, then to the Missouri Pacific Depot and sent to Fort Gibson, Indian Territory. (All quotes are from *The Elevator*, March 20, 1896)

Cherokee Bill has been quoted as saying in various ways that he came to die, not to talk. If all of the newspapers that covered his execution could be assembled, it would probably be found that he was quoted differently in each one. *The Muskogee Phoenix* made him sound like a Shakespearian actor, quoting him as saying: "I came not here to talk, but to die. Proceed with the killing business."

Cherokee Bill also was reported to have said that his execution would be easier to accept if Ike Rogers were dead. Rogers was an ex-deputy marshal and, Bill thought, a friend, but it was Rogers and Clint Scales who captured Bill at Rogers's home. Three years after Cherokee Bill was hanged, his brother, Clarence Goldsby, then twenty-one, shot Rogers down at a train station.

Miscellany: The prisoner named Andrew J. Jackson, who testified at the trial, was an eighty-four-year-old black man indicted for horse stealing. He was in the cell next to Cherokee Bill on the "murderers row." There is no way to ascertain it, but he is probably the oldest person ever incarcerated at the U.S. jail at Fort Smith. His story of how he acquired his name, if true, is that his mother was captured by Andrew Jackson at the battle of Horseshoe, Alabama. He was born and raised in Jackson's house one mile east of Nashville, Tennessee. (From his testimony at the Keating murder trial.)

CHAPTER 39

"WEBBER ISAACS, MOLLIE KING, BERRY FOREMAN AND GEORGE AND JOHN PIERCE

To Be Hung April 30"

(*The Elevator*, March 6, 1896)

It was an assortment of scoundrels that faced Judge Parker on Wednesday morning, March 4, 1896, when for the fourth time in his career and the second time in less than nine months, he sentenced a woman to hang.

MOLLIE KING

Mollie King and Berry Foreman were neighbors, but apparently much more than neighbors. Mollie and her husband, Ed King, had been estranged, off and on, for three or four years. Foreman, who lived nearby with his sister, Mariah Lewis, also lived part time with Mollie. On Sunday, August 4, 1895, Mollie tried to get Ed to come home with her. During her pleading, Ed told her that he was not going home, that he had nearly been killed over her before. He was apparently talking about the knife wound in his back he had received in a fight with Foreman three or four weeks before. That afternoon, Mollie stopped by the blacksmith shop of Charles Hill where Ed King worked and asked where Ed was. She told Hill that she was tired of Ed's foolishness and that if he did not stop it she would "fix him" or have it done. Eventually Mollie found Ed and convinced him to go home with her.

Later that day, George King, Ed's brother who lived near Ed and Mollie's home, heard shots and hollering. He went to Ed's house and found only two small children there who knew nothing of the whereabouts of their father or mother. But on the porch, he found Ed's coat and hat. George King and others searched through the night and finally found Ed's grave. The next morning, George returned to Ed and Mollie's house, and the hat and coat were gone. They were found wrapped in a shawl and hidden in a trunk.

In daylight, the searchers found blood where the murder took place and drag marks and tracks leading to where Ed was buried. The body had scrape injuries and rope burns on the ankles from the dragging. Tracks were also found leading to where a mule was penned, the mule that was used to drag Ed King to his grave. On the basis of evidence found and past history, Mollie King and Berry Foreman were arrested, and a warrant for Alex Martin was issued. Martin had assisted in the murder but was never found.

Mollie and Foreman were tried jointly, convicted and sentenced, but the Supreme Court reversed the Circuit Court ruling, and the case was retried. Trials and appeals carried the case into 1898, when Mollie was convicted of murder and Foreman found not guilty. The jury's verdict has the handwritten word "without" inserted in the blank before "capital punishment." She was sentenced to prison "for the rest of her natural life" at hard labor. The Final Mittimus, dated Saturday, January 15, 1898, committed her to Ohio State Prison in Columbus.

WEBBER ISAACS

M. P. Cushing made his fatal mistake one day in late August 1894 when he hired Jack Chewie to guide and assist him in peddling his wares. Webber Isaacs, who assisted Chewie in killing and robbing Cushing, made his fatal mistake the day when he told John Stop about his crime and offered him five dollars not to tell anyone. And that was not the end of it; he also told Frank Roe and offered him five dollars.

Frank Bolin was another person to whom Isaacs told his story. The following are from Bolin's deposition, as recorded Saturday, October 20, 1894, in the hearings before Commissioner James Brizzolara:

> Q. What did he tell you?
> A. That him and Jack Chewie killed a peddler. He says, "Me and Jack Chewie killed a white peddler the other day." He says: "Jack Chewie shot him first." Right at the start the peddler went to Webber's house and Jack Chewie was there and the peddler hired Jack Chewie to go around with him and help him peddle. Jack Chewie hired to him and took him over the hill, after going over the hill they strike the bottom, in an old field, and Jack told Webb to catch up with him, is what Webb says. Webb caught up with him, Webb says he nods at Jack, Jack pulls out his pistol and shot the peddler, and when Jack shoots the peddler the horse got scared and struck a lope; about that time Webb shot at him again, and Jack shot the horse down again. That is what Webb says.

After killing Cushing and his horse, they cut the reins from the horse and used them to drag Cushing to a spot where they piled brush on him and used coal oil to burn him. They placed Cushing face down, and the fire did not consume the body, so when it was found, the face was recognizable and his papers in his pockets were not burned.

Webber Isaacs and his brother, Jim, were arrested, but Chewie escaped. By the time Webber was convicted on February 8, 1895, Jim Isaacs had died, and Chewie was still on the loose. But justice has its ways. On March 27, 1896, just a little more than one month before Webber was hanged, Deputy George Lawson and posse shot Chewie when he chose to draw rather than surrender. Chewie was about twenty and Isaacs twenty-three years old.

Webber Isaacs and Cherokee Bill both received their death sentences on Saturday, April 13, 1895. Both were to die on Tuesday, June 25, 1895; both would make numerous appeals and be resentenced and push their final day further into the future.

GEORGE AND JOHN PIERCE

The Pierce brothers' crime sounds like a sequel to John Pointer's crime in December 1892. Pointer bludgeoned his traveling companions, one of whom was named Ed Vandevere, in their camp and threw the bodies over a high creek bank. The posse followed his wagon tracks to McAlester, Indian Territory, where he was arrested.

On Monday, January 14, 1895, George and John Pierce and William Vandevere passed the house of A. A. Brown. Vandevere rode a

John and George Pierce

gray mare and led a colt while the Pierces rode in a wagon. They made camp a short distance from Brown's home. Early Tuesday, Brown heard the report of a gun. About half an hour later, the Pierces passed by, one in the wagon, the other on a gray mare. They had been down by a creek and could not get across and stopped to ask Brown how to get to Whiskey Creek. After breakfast, Brown went by the campsite. As he approached the spot, his team became skittish. Brown thought something was wrong, so he went to get a neighbor, B. F. West, and they and others went to investigate. At the site, they found "considerable blood" and followed its trail to a creek bank. Below the bank, they found Vandevere dead, his head wrapped in a blanket. He appeared to have been shot in the forehead and hit with a hammer. The posse followed the tracks of the wagon, and since the trio had been seen by a number of people the day before, they had a good idea for whom they were looking. The Pierces were arrested in Tahlequah, Indian Territory, the week of their crime and were taken to Fort Smith.

Once in jail at Fort Smith, the Pierces got a fairly speedy trial and conviction. They arrived in the last week of January 1895 and were tried and convicted on March 1. Two months later, they were sentenced to hang on the first day of August 1895. But incarceration did not stop their criminal activity, especially George's.

On July 26, George took part in the plot in which Cherokee Bill killed Larry Keating by somehow acquiring a sturdy table leg with which he intended to do in turnkey Eoff. In the meantime, his lawyer was appealing his case so that in March 1896, he and John were still in jail. On March 13, 1896, *The Elevator* reported: "When George Pierce was taken to court last week to receive his sentence, it was discovered that he had dug a hole nearly through the wall of his cell. When taken back he was placed in new quarters. He was at first inclined to demur at the removal, but seeing that kicking would avail nothing, yielded, though rather ungracefully." Two weeks later it was discovered that George had broken his shackles. Jailer J. D. Berry ordered Pierce to move to the cell formerly occupied by Cherokee Bill, who had been occupying a casket since March 17. Pierce refused. Berry had the prisoners rung into their cells and entered Pierce's cell to persuade him to go. When that did not work, Will Lawson and George Franklin entered and "after a short struggle" moved him to his new cell.

On April 30, 1896, George and John Pierce and Webber Isaacs were executed quietly and without much fanfare. Marshal Crump had become tired of the crowds at the hangings. After Cherokee Bill's hanging, Crump said he would limit the spectators to the events in the future. At the hanging of the Pierces and Isaacs, only newspapermen, law officers, and doctors were allowed. Among the doctors present were several who were attending a meeting of the Medical Association.

During the final week, the brothers' father, two sisters, and John Pierce's son came to visit them. On Tuesday, before their execution, the brothers were baptized by Father Lawrence Smythe of St. Mary's and Isaacs was baptized by Father Pius of the German Catholic Church.

It was reported that the three men bore up well during the procedure. Isaacs showed the effects of the jail and the consumption he had suffered from for some time. It was consumption that had taken his brother, Jim, sparing him from the gallows. Webber Isaacs was twenty-three years old, John Pierce was twenty-nine and George twenty-eight.

The total number of men executed since August 15, 1873, now stood at an even eighty.

CHAPTER 40

THE BUCK GANG
Ten-Day Terrors

The Western Union Telegraph Company:

RECEIVED at: 7:10 p.m.   Aug. 9, 1895
Dated: Muskogee, I. T.
To: Crump Marshal
  Have in charge Sam Sampson, Meoma, Bud Lucky, Rufus Buck. They have committed 4 rapes and killed two men. Issue writs. Subpoenas in rape case Rosetta Hasson, Henry Hasson, Dick Rhine. Answer, expecting mob.
        S. B. Irvine, Deputy

Deputy Irvine understated his desire to get rid of the gang before the citizenry of Okmulgee and the Creek Nation applied its own form of justice. He listed only six of the crimes these degenerates were known to have committed in ten days. He has one discrepancy in his text. The Bud Lucky he refers to is really Lucky Davis, the only non-Indian of the gang. Bud Lucky was already incarcerated and had no connection with the Buck Gang. Meoma is Maoma July.

The first recorded crime of the gang was committed on July 30, 1895, when Rufus Buck, Lewis Davis, and Lucky Davis murdered Deputy Marshal John Garrett. They had gone to Okmulgee with the intention of robbing Parkinson's store to get ammunition. As they approached the back door of the store, they encountered Deputy Garrett coming out of the door on his way home. It was between eight and nine o'clock at night. It was raining, and both Garrett and Davis were wearing slickers. All three outlaws appear to have been carrying rifles. When Garrett turned, Lucky Davis pulled his rifle from under his slicker and fired. They must have been the original "Gang who couldn't shoot straight." Lucky fired one shot, which he claimed was the fatal shot. Buck fired twice and Lewis Davis three times. Out of the six shots, one hit Garrett in the left breast, one inflicted a minor wound on his ankle, and one hit the store. Garrett ran into the store and collapsed. He was taken to another building on a cot and died at 3:20 the next morning.

After the Garrett killing, Buck, Sam Sampson, Maoma July, and Lewis and Lucky Davis went on a terror spree. Four of the gang en-

Rufus Buck Gang, 1895
The story of the Buck Gang is one in which "The Hell on the Border" writers may have had first-hand information and gotten the story right. Samuel W. Harmon, who with J. Warren Reed co-authored the book, and George Maledon were in the jury pool for that term of court, although not necessarily on these juries. Any or all of them could have talked to the gang members and observed the trial. From left are Maoma July, Sam Sampson, Rufus Buck, Lucky Davis, and Lewis Davis.

countered Mrs. Wilson, who was moving with two wagons and the help of her fourteen-year-old son and another man to another farm. They made the two men go on in one wagon and made Mrs. Wilson get down, and each of them raped her. On August 1, all five men went to the Hasson home where they held Henry Hasson at gunpoint while his wife, Rosetta, prepared a meal for them. Afterward, they tied up and raped Rosetta. They then made Henry Hasson fight with another man who was present while they shot near their feet.

On Berryhill Creek near Okmulgee, the gang met a man named Shafey and robbed him of his horse, saddle, bridle, watch, and cash. They then took a vote on whether to kill Shafey. He was spared by a vote of four to one. Sam Huston was not so lucky. On August 4, he was shot and killed. They robbed a man named Stockman and took his boots, then shot at him but only grazed his ear. At the same time, they shot and severely wounded a black boy who was present. They stole a horse near Duck Creek where the owner put up a fight. They shot up his house, but he was uninjured.

The day after robbing the Norberg store and the Orcutt store near McDermott, the gang was dividing up its loot when a posse of deputy marshals and Creek Lighthorse came upon them. All except Lucky Davis were captured after a gunfight. Lucky was wounded slightly but escaped into the woods. Davis went to the home of a man named Richardson, who notified the authorities. The next morning, they were nearby when Davis went out to wash. Davis set his rifle aside when he began to wash. Richardson grabbed it, then the marshals appeared and made the arrest. Lucky Davis arrived at the jail on September 3.

The telegram from Deputy Irvine says that the gang had committed four rapes; *The Fort Smith Elevator* reported that two of the women died of their injuries.

The court dealt with the Buck gang almost as fast as their outlaw career had been. All but Davis were captured on August 8, 1895. The request for writ was received at 7:10 p.m. August 9; the writ was issued on August 10. By August 12, hearings before the commissioner were being held. Lucky Davis's arrival on September 3 made the group complete. The trial of all five of the gang for the rape of Rosetta Hasson was completed and verdict delivered on the morning of September 23, 1895. On the afternoon of the same day, the trial of Buck and Lewis and Lucky Davis for the murder of John Garrett began, and the guilty verdict was delivered on September 24, 1895.

The usual round of appeals was made, and the case went to the Supreme Court, which upheld the circuit court's decision. Appeal for clemency was made to President Grover Cleveland, and on June 26, 1896, *The Elevator* announced: "Marshal Crump is in receipt of a communication from Attorney-General Harrison stating that President Cleveland had refused to interfere in behalf of Maoma July and Sam Sampson, members of the Buck gang, who are under the sentence of death; consequently they must suffer the extreme penalty of law."

For several days before their execution date, July 1, 1896, Father Pius of the German Catholic Church instructed the members of the gang. On Tuesday, June 30, he baptized then. That night they spent in devotional exercises and prayed and sang until about three o'clock in the morning. Tuesday morning's activities must have presented a curious sight in the jail. *The Elevator* reported that the prisoners on the lower tier, "murderers row," joined the gang in singing hymns and that the upper-tier prisoners joined in.

On Tuesday, there was a difference of opinion among the condemned men. It was decided that the hour for the execution would be at one o'clock Wednesday afternoon, but Lucky Davis wanted to be hanged at ten in the morning. He wanted it over with in time to get his body on the Cannon Ball at eleven thirty for his homeward journey. Buck objected, saying that if they were hanged in the morning, his body would wait several hours before he could start home. Lucky then suggested he be hanged by himself, but Marshal Crump objected to that and set the hour at one o'clock in the afternoon on Wednesday, July 1, 1896.

At 1:07 p.m. Wednesday, the prisoners started their last walk. Buck, July, and Lucky Davis wore large boutonnieres on their black suits. They were followed to the gallows by the sisters of Sam Sampson and Lucky Davis. The hanging, by order of Marshal Crump, was a private affair—only physicians and reporters admitted. The sisters of Sampson and Davis entered the gallows area and stayed during the prayers and until the black caps were put on, then exited until after the trap fell. The bodies were taken to the Birney undertaking establishment and shipped to their homes.

The crime for which the five were hanged was the rape of Rosetta Hasson. It is believed to be the only occasion when five men were sentenced and executed by one court for rape. These five men were the only ones of the eighty-six executed at Fort Smith for rape. *The Elevator* mistakenly stated, "The case of murder, with which they were charged, never came to trial, neither were any of the other offenses charged against them." It is true that not all of the killings or other crimes were prosecuted, but the killing of Deputy Garrett was. *The Elevator* reported on it, and the trial transcript still exists.

CHAPTER 41

THE LAST MAN TO GO

James Calvin Casherego, Alias George W. Wilson

> Oh, what a tangled web we weave when first we
> practice to deceive.
>
> — Sir Walter Scott

James C. Casherego, tried and executed under the alias George W. Wilson, seems to have been weaving his web for years; but in the end, he became entangled in it. He must have used the alias of George Wilson for some time and been known to family and acquaintances by that name, for that is how he signed his letters to them until his identity was revealed about three months before his death.

James Calvin Casherego
a.k.a. George W. Wilson

Casherego was executed for the murder of Zachariah Thatch, his traveling companion. Early on Sunday, May 26, 1895, Stroder See saw buzzards circling over Rock Creek near Keokuk Falls in the Creek Nation. Thinking they might have been circling a cow or other animal, he went to investigate and found the decaying body of a man in the creek bed. See immediately went to John Butler, who sent for J. C. King. A crowd gathered at the scene and began to investigate a campsite that Thatch and the man they knew as Wilson were known to have used. There they found burned fabric, buttons, and spent cartridges in the ashes of a fire. Nearby they found evidence of blood and pieces of quilt with bloodstains. Although the body was badly decomposed and appeared to have been dead from ten days to two weeks, it was presumed to be Zach Thatch. Wilson must have been presumed guilty by association, even though he never left the general vicinity. About May 13, he had moved from the camp on the creek to near Willie Chisholm's barn.

None of the group that first investigated the campsite was a law officer, either of the U.S. Marshal's Office or tribal police. But J. C. King went to where Wilson was living in his wagon and arrested him. He made no resistance, even though King would not tell him why he was under arrest. Wilson was taken to the body, where, according to John Butler's testimony, he said, "This is undoubtedly the body of my uncle, but how he come here, I know as little as the rest of you and am just as anxious to know who done this." He added, "All I ask is a fair trial." On the witness stand, Casherego denied saying any of those things. J. Bargo, who saw the body, said that it was so decayed he could not have recognized his own father in that condition.

Casherego/Wilson had joined up with Thatch west of Springdale, Arkansas, in April 1895 when he was taken to him by Thomas Presley. Thatch was preparing to go into the Territory and had sent Presley to find someone to travel with him. Casherego and Thatch had met each other before, about 1891, when they both worked for John Porter near Okmulgee, Indian Territory. At some time during their 1891 acquaintance, Casherego loaned Thatch money, which Thatch repaid before they left Arkansas on the trip that would be Thatch's last.

The two men left on April 12, 1895, in Thatch's wagon with six horses belonging to Thatch. Casherego owned nothing and was afoot when he joined up with Thatch. They left with the covered wagon apparently loaded to capacity with Thatch's belongings and traveled into Indian Territory. Thatch's intent was to try to buy some land or town lots. By early May, their travels had taken them to the Keokuk area, where they camped on Rock Creek for a few days to doctor a foundered horse. Several people testified that they had seen and spoken to both men while they were there and had observed the sick horse.

Shortly after they had camped by the creek, Thatch was seen no more, and Casherego moved the wagon up near Willie Chisholm's barn and camped there until the body was found and he was arrested. When arrested, he was in possession of all of Thatch's belongings except one horse. He claimed that Thatch had left May 13 riding the other horse to go to the opening of the Kickapoo lands to acquire a claim. Casherego had bought—and traded for—all of Thatch's property except one horse. In support of that claim was the fact that he had branded all of the horses except that one.

Casherego's undoing came in the fact that he also had Thatch's trunk, tools, quilts, and a straw tick bed. The quilts had blood on them, and the bed had a pillowcase sewed on one side and a flour sack sewed on the other. When the patches were removed from the bed, bloodstains were found and the straw inside was found to be bloody. Casherego claimed that the blood on the quilts had come from a prairie chicken he had killed and from bleeding the sick horse. To his credit, two people did testify to seeing a dead prairie chicken in the camp and seeing the men bleeding the horse. The bed was another thing, though. Casherego said he traded a bridle to someone who was traveling through for the bed and that it had the patches on it when he got it.

At trial, Susan Hale, Thatch's sister, testified that she had spun the thread that had made the tick when she was a child. Minerva Rose, another sister, and Thomas Presley identified the tick and said that it had been in the family for twenty-four years. W. H. Thatch, a brother, identified the wagon, horses, trunk, quilts, shoes, a .32 Winchester, and the bed. W. H. Thatch and Susan Hale also identified the pillowcase that covered the bloodstain. Casherego stuck to his story, which was much more elaborate than simply trading a bridle for the bed. He told of a long conversation, discussing trading horses and repairing the bridle, and stated that if that man could be found, he would confirm the story.

Casherego had many witnesses who could not be found. In a letter to a relative or acquaintance before the trial, he said he had twenty-seven witnesses and that he "would come clean." When it came time for the trial, though, he had only ten witnesses, and one of those said he never knew Casherego and did not remember any of the things he claimed. A. J. Jennings and F. F. Jennings did testify that they had seen Thatch in El Reno in June when T. C. Lemasters and Thatch had come into A. J. Jennings's office to have a contract drawn up. Lemasters confirmed that he and Thatch had talked of trading a horse and cash for a claim in the Kickapoo opening.

Thomas and Mark Whinnery were quite another story. The prosecution read letters from Casherego to each of those men asking them to testify in his behalf. In both letters, Casherego laid out the events as he wanted the men to recall them, starting several sentences with, "You remember." If they had read and remembered all that was stated in the letters, they might have made credible witnesses. However, only Mark Whinnery appeared in court, and he testified he had never met Casherego and remembered none of the events in the letter to him. In the letters, Casherego mentioned Frank Carver and said to Mark, "Frank Carver said to tell you to send him a piece of money."

Frank Carver was a gambler and a drunk from Muskogee who was in jail at the same time as Casherego. Carver was convicted of murdering Annie Maledon, daughter of George Maledon. Carver, a married man, was living with Annie Maledon in Muskogee without benefit of clergy. He shot her in the back in a fit of drunken jealousy. Annie had "left her home and entered a fast life."

The prosecutor questioned Casherego at length about where he was born and where he had lived. For some reason, he seemed to pursue this vigorously. Casherego said he was born in Obion County, Tennessee (his death certificate says Faulkner County, Arkansas), and that he had moved with his mother and stepfather to Springdale, Arkansas, when he was small and went from there to live near Conway, Arkansas. He said that when he was older, he worked as a sewing machine salesman and collector for the sewing machine companies and traveled several Arkansas counties and into Indian Territory and that he could not remember where he was at a specific time. The prosecutor made a great effort to trap Casherego into a statement, but Casherego stuck to his story on this subject and all others and would not be dissuaded.

The trial started on December 15, 1895, and the guilty verdict was returned on December 19, 1895. The case was appealed to the Supreme Court.

Casherego wrote several letters to family and acquaintances while in jail, always professing his innocence and signing them G. W. Wilson. But on April 21, 1896, he wrote to his Uncle Sam, "Lewis Moore came in jail to see me yesterday. He said Uncle Wat told him to come in and see me. DeJarnatt ought not told him nothing. No one but my lawyer did not know but what my name was Wilson." In that letter he still believes that his case will be reversed by the Supreme Court and says, "I will come clean if I get all my witnesses."

Between April 21 and April 30, Casherego received a great disappointment. On April 30, he wrote his uncle, "My case has been affirmed by the Supreme Court. This being a total surprise to me and all the officials." He still professed his innocence and that he could have proved it if all his witnesses had been summoned. "My lawyer is going to send depositions to Grover Cleveland." Further on in that same letter, he told his uncle, "I want you to send me some money at once, for if I can not get justice done in a lawful way I can only look out for myself. If I can get some money I can do what I done at W" (ink appears to be deliberately smeared).

That letter was signed G. W. Wilson and apparently carried out of the jail by a friend, not by the regular mails. The next day, July 1, Casherego again wrote to the same uncle complaining that he had sent two letters and heard nothing. In the July 1 letter, he said that he was sentenced to hang July 30. Casherego continued to write letters until near the end of July, and at the end, he got quite poetic and melancholy.

At noon on July 30, 1896, the gallows trap fell under George W. Wilson, and James Calvin Casherego went to his death. He was attended by Father Lawrence Smythe and was buried under his real name at Conway, Arkansas.

Death certificate for George Wilson, a.k.a. James Casherego

James Casherego, alias George Wilson, was the eighty-sixth and last man to hang at Fort Smith. The Buck gang had been executed on July 1. This was only the second time in the twenty-three year history of hangings at Fort Smith that there had been two hangings in one month. The first seven months of 1896 saw more hangings than any full year of the twenty-three years.

All of the foregoing information in this article is from court documents and Casherego's own letters.

EPILOGUE

THE END OF AN ERA

When the era of the "Hanging Judge" and hangings at Fort Smith came to an end, it came with a crash. For years there had been pressure to establish courts in the Indian Territories. During 1895 and 1896, the newspapers had been full of articles regarding the local court and courts in the Indian Territories. In May 1896, Congress passed a bill that would end the authority of the U.S. District Court for the Western District of Arkansas as it had been since 1871. On July 30, 1896, the last execution at Fort Smith was performed. On September 1, 1896, the congressional bill of May 1896 took effect and ended the function of the

Judge Isaac C. Parker

court as it had been for twenty-five years. On November 17, 1896, Judge Isaac C. Parker died after a five-month illness, and the era was past.

A congressional act on February 26, 1897, transferred a large part of the garrison property to the city of Fort Smith. George Maledon appealed to the city council to purchase the trap doors of the gallows for his traveling show. The response to Maledon's request was not recorded. The citizens of Fort Smith had seen enough of executions, and in the summer of 1897, the mayor ordered that the gallows be dismantled and burned. Afterward, the garrison wall was torn down and streets extended through the area. The court continued to try cases that were pending when the congressional act of May 1896 took effect in September 1896 until that slate was cleaned. The newspapers commented weekly on the dwindling jail population and lack of activity in the court. The U.S. District Court for the Western District of Arkansas still exists today but with a very different function.

241

The old U.S. jail in Fort Smith, Arkansas, today.

To their credit, Samuel W. Harmon and J. Warren Reed realized that they had witnessed the passing of something unique and proceeded to write their book, *Hell on the Border*. Unfortunately, they chose to lie.

The Fort Smith Elevator had begun to create the myth of Maledon in the 1880s, and Harmon and Reed completed the job. *The Elevator*, in the end, attempted to deflate the Maledon myth. On February 22, 1895, they wrote:

> Mr. Maledon has had nothing to do with the execution of any federal convicts or anyone else, for more than four years, having declined to act in that capacity since he retired as jail guard. He is now keeping a modest little store on Catholic Avenue and is seldom, if ever, seen about the court house or jail.

On September 24, 1897, their article was more pointed.

> George Maledon, the gentleman who officiated for so many years as hangman of the federal court at this place, has been airing himself through the St. Louis press and putting up some wonderful tales — at least his tales are wonderful if he puts them up. He says he Is still hangman at Fort Smith, whereas he has not offi-

242

ciated in the capacity of hangman for at least five years. He dropped that position while Col. Yoes was Marshal. He did not hang the number of men he claims to have hanged. He did not hang Cherokee Bill, and the number of men executed on the gallows here is nothing like so great as he represents. Besides he was not the first executioner of the court here. The first six or eight men who stepped off the gallows here were hung by Charley Messler, a saloon keeper, well remembered by all of the old attaches of the court. Messler executed John Childers, Tuni and Young Wolf and several others. Afterwards Charles Burns, who was jailor for several years, dropped a number. Maledon figured to some extent at several of the early hangings, but only by tying the wrists and feet of the condemned and putting the black caps on their heads. If the records were looked up closely it would be discovered that only about half the men hanged in the old yard met death at his hand.

But the myth lived on.

Reed created his own image of the skillful and intrepid barrister, attacking Judge Parker and claiming to have defended more than 160 murder cases and lost only two. To do that, he would have had to have defended virtually everyone charged with murder between 1889, when he came to Fort Smith, and 1896. He lost two separate murder cases with Cherokee Bill alone.

Samuel W. Harmon lived near Fayetteville in Washington County and probably, as he stated, served on several juries. So far his name has been found on only two petit jury pools, but since jurors served for the three months of a court term, each juror served on several juries during that time. Harmon's name appears in the November 1889 term of court petit jury list, and in 1896, both he and George Maledon were in the petit jury pool during the term of court when the Rufus Buck gang was tried.

The era ended but the fascination with it may never end.

REFERENCES

CHAPTER 1: National Archives Records; *The Weekly Herald* and *The New Era* of Fort Smith, Arkansas; with help from Eric Leonard, U.S. Parks Department Ranger, and Joyce (Childers) Bear

CHAPTER 2: *The Fort Smith Weekly Herald, The Fort Smith New Era, The Cherokee Advocate*, National Archives

CHAPTER 3: *The New Era* of Fort Smith, Arkansas; court documents from National Archives, Fort Worth, Texas

CHAPTER 4: *The New Era* and *The Weekly Herald* of Fort Smith, Arkansas; National Archives records

CHAPTER 5: National Archives, *The Fort Smith Independent, The Fort Smith Weekly Herald, The Fort Smith New Era*, with the help of Eric Leonard, U.S. Parks Department ranger

CHAPTER 6: National Archives, *The Fort Smith Independent, The Fort Smith Weekly Herald, The Fort Smith New Era*, with the help of Eric Leonard, U.S. Parks Department Ranger

CHAPTER 7: *The Fort Smith New Era, The Fort Smith Weekly Herald*, National Archives Records

CHAPTER 8: National Archives; *The New Era* and *The Weekly Herald* of Fort Smith, Arkansas

CHAPTER 9: National Archives; *The New Era* and *The Weekly Herald* of Fort Smith, Arkansas; with help from Eric Leonard, Park Ranger, Fort Smith National Historic Site

CHAPTER 10: National Archives; *The New Era* and *The Weekly Herald* of Fort Smith, Arkansas

CHAPTER 11: *The Fort Smith Elevator, The Fort Smith New Era, The Wheeler's Independent* of Fort Smith

CHAPTER 12: National Archives, *The Fort Smith New Era, The Fort Smith Weekly Elevator, The Fort Smith Weekly Herald, The Wheeler's Independent* of Fort Smith

CHAPTER 13: *The New Era, The Wheeler's Independent, The Fort Smith Elevator, The Weekly Herald*, National Archives

CHAPTER 14: *The Journal* of Kansas City, Missouri; *The Elevator, The Wheeler's Independent*, and *The New Era* of Fort Smith, Arkansas; National Archives records

CHAPTER 15: National Archives; *The Elevator, The Independent*, and *The New Era* of Fort Smith, Arkansas

CHAPTER 16: National Archives; *The New Era* and *The Elevator*, Fort Smith, Arkansas

CHAPTER 17: *The Fort Smith New Era, The Fort Smith Elevator*, National Archives

CHAPTER 18: *The Fort Smith New Era, The Fort Smith Elevator*, National Archives

CHAPTER 19: National Archives; *The Fort Smith Elevator; Oklahombres*, Vol. VII, No. 1, 1996.

CHAPTER 20: *The Fort Smith Elevator*, National Archives

CHAPTER 21: *The Fort Smith Weekly Elevator*, National Archives

CHAPTER 22: National Archives, *The Fort Smith Weekly Elevator*

CHAPTER 23: *The Fort Smith Elevator*, National Archives

CHAPTER 24: *The Fort Smith Weekly Elevator*, National Archives

CHAPTER 25: *The Fort Smith Weekly Elevator;* National Archives; *Handbook of Federal Indian Law, Readings in Oklahoma History*, Aldrich and Peterson

CHAPTER 26: National Archives; trial transcripts and depositions; *The Fort Smith Weekly Elevator*

CHAPTER 27: National Archives; depositions, petitions and telegrams; *The Fort Smith Weekly Elevator*

CHAPTER 28: *The Fort Smith Weekly Elevator*, National Archives

CHAPTER 29: *The Fort Smith Weekly Elevator*, National Archives

CHAPTER 30: National Archives, Office of U.S. Pardon Attorney, *The Fort Smith Elevator*

CHAPTER 31: National Archives, *The Fort Smith Elevator*

CHAPTER 32: National Archives, *The Fort Smith Weekly Elevator*

CHAPTER 33: National Archives; depositions, court transcript and death warrant; *The Fort Smith Elevator*

CHAPTER 34: National Archives; trial transcripts and depositions; *Fort Smith Weekly Elevator*

CHAPTER 35: National Archives; Depositions and other papers; *The Fort Smith Elevator*

CHAPTER 36: National Archives; Proceedings before the commissioner; *The Fort Smith Elevator*

CHAPTER 37: National Archives; depositions, trial transcript, writs and other documents; *The Fort Smith Elevator*

CHAPTER 38: National Archives; Trial transcript of Keating murder trial; *The Fort Smith Weekly Elevator; The Real Cherokee Bill: Oklahoma Outlaw*, Art Burton

CHAPTER 39: National Archives; depositions, appeals, mittimus; *The Fort Smith Weekly Elevator*

CHAPTER 40: National Archives; transcripts, warrants, subpoenas, telegrams; *The Fort Smith Elevator*

CHAPTER 41: National Archives; Trial transcript; Letters of James C. Casherego; Death certificate of George Wilson-Casherego; *The Fort Smith Elevator.*

INDEX

253